MW00804110

EROS AND EVIL

THE

SEXUAL PSYCHOPATHOLOGY OF WITCHCRAFT

BY *R. E. L. Masters*

The Julian Press, Inc., Publishers : New York : 1962

© Copyright 1962 by R. E. L. Masters
Library of Congress Catalog Card Number 62–19302
Published by The Julian Press, Inc.
80 East 11th Street, New York 3

Manufactured in the United States of America
by H. Wolff, New York
Designed by Robin Fox

TO

MY FRIEND, JACK KINDRED

(*Raconteur and Bon Vivant*)

Contents

Hymn to Pan

Thrill with lissom lust of the light,
O man! My man!
Come careering out of the night
Of Pan! Io Pan!
Io Pan! Io Pan! Come over the sea
From Sicily and from Arcady!
Roaming as Bacchus, with fauns and pards
And nymphs and satyrs for thy guards,
On a milk-white ass, come over the sea
To me, to me,
Come with Apollo in bridal dress
(Shepherdess and pythoness)
Come with Artemis, silken shod,
And wash thy white thigh, beautiful God,
In the moon of the woods, on the marble mount,
The dimpled dawn of the amber fount!
Dip the purple of passionate prayer
In the crimson shrine, the scarlet snare,
The soul that startles in eyes of blue
To watch thy wantonness weeping through
The tangled grove, the gnarléd bole
Of the living tree that is spirit and soul
And body and brain—come over the sea,
(Io Pan! Io Pan!)
Devil or god, to me, to me,
My man! my man!
Come with trumpets sounding shrill
Over the hill!
Come with drums low muttering
From the spring!
Come with flute and come with pipe!
Am I not ripe?
I, who wait and writhe and wrestle
With air that hath no boughs to nestle
My body, weary of empty clasp,
Strong as a lion and sharp as an asp—
Come, O Come!

I am numb
With the lonely lust of devildom.
Thrust the sword through the galling fetter,
All-devourer, all-begetter;
Give me the sign of the Open Eye,
And the token erect of thorny thigh,
And the word of madness and mystery,
O Pan! Io Pan!
Io Pan! Io Pan Pan! Pan Pan! Pan,
I am a man:
Do as thou wilt, as a great god can,
O Pan! Io Pan!
Io Pan! Io Pan Pan! I am awake
In the grip of the snake.
The eagle slashes with beak and claw;
The gods withdraw:
The great beasts come, Io Pan! I am borne
To death on the horn
Of the Unicorn.
I am Pan! Io Pan! Io Pan Pan! Pan!
I am thy mate, I am thy man,
Goat of thy flock, I am gold, I am god,
Flesh to thy bone, flower to thy rod.
With hoofs of steel I race on the rocks
Through solstice stubborn to equinox.
And I rave; and I rape and I rip and I rend
Everlasting, world without end,
Mannikin, maiden, maenad, man,
In the might of Pan.
Io Pan! Io Pan Pan! Pan! Io Pan!

ALEISTER CROWLEY

Introduction

This book is divided into two main parts. The first explores the sexual relations of humans with demons (*incubi* and *succubi*) as reported in the writings of witch-era scholars and those concerned with the apprehension and punishment of witches. Considered too are the works of earlier authors who laid the foundation for the theoretical and practical development of the witch persecution as it evolved in the fifteenth, sixteenth, seventeenth, and eighteenth centuries.

The second part briefly inquires into the nature and meaning of the strange phenomena presented in detail in the first. The sexual pathology of witchcraft is examined in the light of medical and psychological and other knowledge of the present day. The examination is necessarily speculative in the main. Obviously, we will never know what actually took place in the minds of the men and women of those not very remote days. What is *not* speculative is the knowledge that what occurred then was evil, or diabolic, if you will: a ferocious blood-letting that passed, and a sexual trauma that still endures. The Devil was in fact abroad during those terrible centuries; but His proper garb was clerical.

The main period of what has come to be known as the Witch Mania or Witch Delusion lasted from roughly the middle of the fifteenth to the middle of the eighteenth century. However, consideration of data should not be rigidly limited to that interval. The first witch to be executed for copulating with a demon was put to death in 1275, one year after the death of Saint Thomas Aquinas, a Doctor of the Church, whose contribution to the witch-incubus belief was considerable. Moreover, witches were executed in the last half of the eighteenth century in Bavaria, in Spain, in Switzerland and in Poland. (Unofficial executions of witches—lynchings—were continuing up into the nineteenth century: in Germany, 1836; in France, 1850; in England, 1863. From 1860 to 1877 an epidemic of witchcraft raged in Latin America and many alleged witches were burned. A witch was consigned to the flames in Peru as recently as 1888; and in Milan a witch was mobbed and almost lynched in 1891.)

In the year 900 A.D., the Church had denied the possibility of sexual intercourse between humans and supernatural beings —although many early Christian writers, even including Saint Augustine, had declared such intercourse to be a fact. The tide seems to have turned again in the thirteenth century, under the impact of the writings of Aquinas and Gervasius of Tilbury, and the belief that humans copulated with demons began to exert a fatal fascination upon the minds of theologians. But trials for the offense did not begin in earnest until the fifteenth century. (Hansen, however, says that Christian belief in *incubi* began somewhere around the year 1100, and that previous to the twelfth century the demons said to have intercourse with humans were only beings derived from mythology and poetry, and were not taken seriously by theologians. George Lyman Kittredge, another important witchcraft scholar, writes in his *Witchcraft in Old and New England:* "By the year 1100—to take a safe date—the Incubus Dogma was solidly established as an article of learned faith throughout Western Europe.")

Reginald Scot (*The Discoverie of Witchcraft*) took note of the shift of theological dogma that gained general acceptance after 1400. According to this revised position, the Church had been correct in its early teaching that incubi and succubi exist and have intercourse with humans. However, the demons of the early Christian period *forced* their attentions upon humans —in other words, committed rapes. But after 1400, the intercourse of demons with humans took a new and sinister turn.

Witches appeared in great numbers, and for the first time the intercourse with demons was *voluntary* on the part of the humans engaging in that gravest of sins. (Soldan, in his *Geschichte der Hexenprozesse,* suggests that the idea of humans voluntarily engaging in coition with demons was brought back to Europe by the Crusaders, who had learned about Oriental beliefs on the subject.)

Lastly, as to the chronology of the witch-incubus belief, I will quote the psychoanalyst Ernest Jones (*On the Nightmare*), who observed: "The belief in *lustful indulgence* between Witch and Devil is again a relatively late constituent of the Witch delusion. The idea of such intercourse between human and supernatural beings was of course always present among the people . . . but it was for long strenuously denied by the Church, e.g., in 900 by Burkhard. Until the twelfth century it was quite distinct from sorcery, and became connected with it only through the linking of the Sabbath idea with heresy, about 1250."

There is of course no way to determine just when it was that men first began to believe in supernatural beings and the sexual relations of humans with them. We are certain only that such beliefs are prehistoric, their origins lost in depths of time that no degree of scholarship suffices to fathom. The gods of the oldest known religions copulated with mortals. A prehistoric bowl records the existence of belief in a vampire-succubus. The earliest literatures of many peoples are acquainted with such beings.

In ancient Egypt it was believed that there existed demons who were sexually attracted to human females—a belief Plutarch, taking note of its existence among the Egyptians, sought to refute. Beauty incites lust in the interest of propagating the species, he said, while demons, being of fixed number and having no need to propagate, would therefore not respond to feminine charms.

Demonic possession—later to drive the nuns of the witch era to erotic frenzies—was also known in ancient Egypt. One of the most famous cases of possession was that of the Mesopotamian beauty Bent-ent-resht, sister-in-law of the Egyptian king Rameses II. His father-in-law, the Prince of Bekhten, sought Rameses' aid when Bent-ent-resht became possessed by a demon, and Rameses sent the statue of the god Khonsu Nefer-hetep, along with five boats of lesser gods, to Mesopotamia to terminate the possession. Arriving, the god Khonsu was at once taken to the princess, magical ceremonies were conducted, and the demon was successfully exorcised.

Alphonseus Joseph-Mary Montague Summers, in general one of the most excellent of authorities on matters of witchcraft and demonology, declares that once the ceremonies had been performed the demon "incontinently departed." Such, however, was not precisely the case—as Summers assuredly well knew.

The statement is a kind of half-truth, since it would be accurate to say that the demon incontinently departed the mind and body of Princess Bent-ent-resht. But once that had occurred, the demon acknowledged his submissiveness only to Khonsu and called for a feast to be staged in his (the demon's) honor. It was only after a great celebration that the demon departed from Bekhten.

As the egyptologist Sir Wallis Budge (*Egyptian Magic*) validly remarks, "The demon who possessed the princess recognized in Khonsu a being who was mightier than himself, and, like a vanquished King, he wished to make the best terms he could with his conqueror, and to be on good terms with him." This is a far cry from the relationship of a demon to a Christian exorcist—the Christian (especially Catholic) style being to hold the demon to be an altogether damnable and depraved spirit, and to have no friendly commerce with him of any kind. One surmises that it was Summers' wish to suppress this difference of status, suggesting that Egyptian religion held the evil spirits in loathing equally as great as did the Christian. I will mention at least one other instance in which Summers is guilty of suppressing and distorting evidence, although I could cite many.

It is a matter of fact that pre-Christian demons were often considered to be neither necessarily good nor evil. The word *demon* means merely "replete with wisdom." If an individual demon was good, the word for him was *eudemon;* if evil, *cacodemon.*

That the gods and goddesses of the Greeks and the Romans had sexual relationships with mortals is known to everyone. Semi-divine beings, such as Satyrs and Centaurs, also copulated with humans in the Greek and Roman mythology. Many early representations of devils were no more than Christianized Satyrs, or Pans. The derivation is discernible even up to the present time.

It is an axiom of demonology that the gods of the old religion become the devils of the new. Christianity, gaining ascendancy, consigned to the roles of devils not only the gods of all the pagan religions, but also the whole host of supernatural beings with which the world had been populated by legend, myth, and the beliefs of the people. Paul, Justin Martyr, and the Church Fathers declared as one that all non-Christian gods were devils.

Demons not only fornicated with men and women, they possessed humans and caused them to engage in all manner of venereal excesses. By urgings from without, too, they led mortals into carnal sin. Daniel Defoe, in his *Political History of the Devil,* expresses long-standing and general belief when he credits the Devil with inspiring three of the major erotic events of the Old Testament: the incest of Lot with his daughters; the homosexual incest of Noah with his son Ham (or grandson Canaan); and Eve's corruption of Adam, acquainting him with his nakedness and inducing in him a sense of shame and of sinfulness.

Demons no less than gods reflect in the behavior assigned to them the desires and phantasies of their human creators. The Greek gods were lascivious but essentially healthy. The demons of the Hebrews (in general) experienced a natural sexual desire and indulged it. But as the Christian demonology evolved, it reflected the morbidity of the Christian, and in particular the Catholic, view of human sexuality. Demons did not seek sexual intercourse with humans in order to gratify erotic appetites. Rather, their aim was to corrupt and degrade men and women and lead them into eternal damnation by way of irremediable sin. The intercourse with the Christian demons was painful and sometimes repulsive, and the perversions were extreme—corpses and human waste products playing a prominent role in the sexual aspects of witchcraft.

Various terms were applied to the intercourse of supernatural with human beings. Some authorities classed it as sodomy, and others (Aquinas, Cajetanus and Bonacina, for example) as bestiality. John Caramuel, in his *Fundamental Theology,* proposed the term *demoniality,* which was later taken over and given a rather special application by Ludovico Maria Sinistrari of Ameno, a professor of theology at Pavia.

Nietzsche has written that Christianity poisoned Eros. It is probably the conviction of most students of human sexuality in the West that Nietzsche spoke the truth. We are accustomed to charge Saint Paul in particular with having administered the fatal draught. It may well be that he is the arch-villain, but the potion he provided was slow in taking maximum effect. It was not until the fifteenth century that man truly began to writhe in full agony as a consequence of the poison. Then that terrible neurotogenic brew ravaged mankind for three centuries before the effects began, all too slowly, to diminish. We are poisoned still; but science and other branches of truth-seeking are providing at long last the only effective antidote—knowledge.

Christianity, Catholicism especially, equated sex with evil. Even within marriage sexual pleasure was to be held to the unavoidable minimum. The sexual organs and the sexual act of coition were for procreation only. To use them as instruments of voluptuous delight was to court the awful wrath of a vengeful God.

Women were regarded by the ideologists of the Church as more lustful, more inclined to depravity than men. Because of this belief, female witches greatly outnumbered male ones: by ten-to-one, by one-hundred-to-one, by ten-thousand-to-one; it depended upon the authority.

The inquisitors Kramer and Sprenger, authors of the *Malleus Maleficarum* (first edition c. 1486), most influential of all books on witchcraft and responsible for the deaths of thousands of persons, expressed the prevailing view of the nature of women:

"Now the wickedness of women is spoken of in *Ecclesiasticus XXV:* There is no head above the head of a serpent: and there is no wrath above the wrath of a woman. I had rather dwell with a lion and a dragon than to keep house with a wicked woman. And among much which in that place precedes and follows about a wicked woman, he concludes: All wickedness is but little to the wickedness of a woman. Wherefore Saint John Chrysostom says on the text, It is not good to marry (*St. Matthew XIX*): What else is woman but a foe to friendship, an unescapable punishment, a necessary evil, a natural temptation, a desirable calamity, a domestic danger, a delectable detriment, an evil of nature, painted with fair colors! Therefore if it be a sin to divorce her when she ought to be kept, it is indeed a necessary torture; for either we commit adultery by divorcing her, or we must endure daily strife. Cicero in his second book of *The Rhetorics* says: The many lusts of men lead them into one sin, but the one lust of women leads them into all sins; for the root of all woman's vices is avarice. And Seneca says in his *Tragedies:* A woman either loves or hates; there is no third grade. And the tears of a woman are a deception, for they may spring from true grief, or they may be a snare. When a woman thinks alone, she thinks evil."

After grudgingly allowing for the possibility of a good woman, the authors add: "Wherefore in many vituperations that we read against women, the word woman is used to mean lust of the flesh. As it is said: I have a woman more bitter than death, and a good woman subject to carnal lust."

All this was used to explain why it is that women are more prone to witchcraft than males. Woman's frailty, both of body and intellect, are important factors, Kramer and Sprenger said, but the main explanation for her frequent alliance with the evil forces lies in the fact that "she is more carnal than a man, as is clear from her many carnal abominations. And it should be noted that there was a defect in the formation of the first woman, since she was formed from a bent rib, that is, a rib of the breast, which is bent as it were in a contrary direction to a man. And since through this defect she is an imperfect animal, she always deceives. . . . To conclude. All witchcraft comes from carnal lust, which is in women insatiable. See *Proverbs XXX:* There are three things that are never satisfied, yea, a fourth thing which says not, It is enough; that is, the mouth of the womb. Wherefore for the sake of fulfilling their lusts they consort even with devils."

The hatred of the flesh which by the time of the witch mania had assumed near-psychotic proportions did not come from the founder of the Christian religion, and was alien to him. A rigidly antisexual Christianity could be justified only by perverting the teachings and example of Christ. Marcus Bach (*Strange Sects and Curious Cults*) notes that the Church Fathers much preferred Christ's teaching, namely, "He who looketh upon a woman with lust hath committed adultery with her already in his heart" to his other (and seemingly much more liberal) one, "that there is nothing unclean of itself, but to him who esteemeth anything to be unclean, to him it is unclean." The religionists then proceeded to transform (harshen and mutilate) the image of Christ:

There ". . . emerged the image of an intolerant Christ, a Prophet who, born without sin, condemned in others a passion he had never felt. And with this unyielding approach began the first real estrangement between the institutionalized Christ and mortal men. No longer was Jesus recognized as a man of peculiar tenderness, of sensitive understanding, and of divine capacity for love and tolerance. Gone was the gentle Galilean who, hating sin, had dined with sinners, had forgiven a prostitute, and had pardoned a woman taken in adultery. He had now become instead a judge to be feared and a moralist to be avoided, a preacher who uncompromisingly proclaimed, 'If thine eye offend thee by bringing lust into your heart, pluck it out!' "

Predictably, those who hated the flesh became obsessed by the flesh. Inquisitors and others who dealt with witches doted upon every erotic detail of the confessions and testimony, encouraged the morbid and the sensational, examined naked witches for the Devil's Mark (shaving their bodies the better to find it), and in all displayed such shameless avidity in matters erotic as to provoke public criticism.

The Devil's Mark, which often resembled the foot of a hare or of a toad, was believed placed by Him on the flesh of each witch so that the witch could not later attempt to deny that a pact had been made. It was often concealed in the female genitals and in the rectum, and was anesthetic. To make certain that some blemish was in fact the Devil's Mark, long pins would be inserted into the flesh of the witch. One may well imagine that sadists were attracted to the work of driving pins into the breasts and genitalia and other sensitive body parts of witches.

In some places it was the practice for the judges themselves to shave and singe all of the hair from the bodies of persons accused of witchcraft, and then to probe vagina and rectum for concealed amulets and drugs as well as for the Devil's Mark. No doubt the search was regarded as much too important to be entrusted to others. But the judges so obviously relished the assignment that objections arose, probably from women. The task was turned over to guards and executioners and others, who not only performed their work with great brutality, but who often raped any woman or child who took their fancy. Still later, the job of searching the witches was turned over to women especially trained for it, and who were brutal enough, but it was not believed that they took sexual pleasure in their efforts.

Witches were so seldom acquitted, or given less than the

death penalty, that those who abused them had little cause to fear subsequent retribution. Confessions were certain to be obtained, and if repudiated, to be obtained a second or a third time—the tortures inflicted by good Christians equaling any to which the martyrs of the Church had been subjected by the Romans—and in any case the entire legal procedure was a travesty. Friedrich von Spee, in the early seventeenth century, wrote bitterly of the injustice of the proceedings, especially denouncing the fact that defense attorneys either were not allowed or could not be obtained by an accused. No lawyer would defend a witch, he pointed out, because by so doing the attorney himself became suspect of being a witch or else was denounced as a patron of witches. Few even dared to voice such criticism as Spee's.

(Today a somewhat similar situation all too widely prevails. Our more literate and humane attorneys and legislators recognize the desperate need for sex reform legislation and for abolishing obsolete and unrealistic laws. But very few dare to introduce such legislation or to work in its behalf lest they be accused of seeking to "legitimize vice." Those who defend the much-abused civil rights of such persons as homosexuals are likely to find themselves accused of that deviation—just as those who defended witches were accused of themselves practicing witchcraft.)

The judge and witch-burner De Lancre placed the trials beyond all criticism. In one of his several books on witchcraft he set forth the sockdolager that if anyone said the confessions of witches were merely the result of torture, or based on illusions, then that person would be guilty of accusing the Church of criminal error in executing witches. To thus impute criminal error to the Church would be not only a misstatement of fact but also a grievous sin—and a sin likely, as some discovered, to have serious and even fatal consequences for the skeptic.

Who actually were the witches and what was witchcraft? One theory has it that the accused were prostitutes and women of loose morals, persons dabbling in the occult arts, persons who had made themselves obnoxious in various ways, etc. The basic phenomena were all invented by the witch-burners, with the victims—who were eager to oblige and so avoid further torture—elaborating upon the stereotypes and fantastically fleshing the grim skeleton. But this, I think, is an extremist view and one which the facts do not support. The same may be said of the belief—in fact, a shaky and hollow hypothesis—that the witches were members of a surviving pagan cult or religion. This last-mentioned theory, usually associated with the British anthropologist Margaret Murray, although she did not originate it, has attracted a wide and influential following. I will not pass up an opportunity to say that it is very strange that the views of Dr. Murray, repudiated by almost every significant contemporary scholar in the field, continue to prevail so far as the *Encyclopaedia Britannica* is concerned. H. C. Lea's findings, and those of George Lincoln Burr, contradict Murray's fanciful maunderings; Montague Summers directly challenged her theory and proved it wanting; Ernest Jones stated his opposition. So did H. T. F. Rhodes, in a recent and scholarly work on the satanic mass. So untenable is the Murray position that it is a marvel she should have even a single disciple among those who have studied witchcraft and demonology with any degree of care.

We have considerable information about, and the names of, a goodly number of even quite obscure cults and sects of the witch period and much earlier. If there was a religion of the witches that continued the worship of the Horned God or whatever, dating back to paganism and with many thousands of members, why is there any question as to its name and the very fact of its existence? The answer undoubtedly is that there was no such surviving pagan cult to which more than a few of those persons called witches belonged. In the beginning, witches must have been members of a variety of heretical sects, all lumped together by the Church as devil-worshipers. Later, of course, when the madness was raging in full frenzy, accusations of witchcraft were levelled without any factual basis of any kind: Against those who were old and ugly, or young and beautiful, those whose property or position was coveted, and especially those whose names some witch happened to think of as she was being pressed to incriminate others while her nipples were being pulled off with hot pincers or her vagina poked with a glowing and razor-edged sword. There must also have been large numbers of the mentally ill who responded to the expectations of the witch-hunters by supposing themselves to copulate with demons.

It was said that the witches gathered on mountaintops, in deserted churches, at crossroads and elsewhere to worship the Devil. Their meetings were usually called *Sabbats* (or *Sabbaths*—and *Synagogues*, by the anti-Semitic). Some writers distinguish between *Esbats*, small meetings of individual covens held at frequent intervals, and Sabbats, held less often and where whole "congregations" were present. At these meetings, it was said, there occurred eating, drinking, dancing, and probably promiscuous intercourse, or orgies. To that plausible list the demonologists added human sacrifice and cannibalism, especially the slaughter and eating of infants, a great variety of perverted and scatologic practices, and copulations with devils. Almost identical descriptions had been given centuries earlier of the meetings of the Manichaeans and other heretics. It is probable that meetings of some groups of persons declared witches by the Church did in fact take place, and it would not be surprising if sexual orgies were staged. As I will show later, such behavior would not have been unusual at the time.

Some held that witchcraft was not only a plot to overthrow Christianity and the Church, but also a political conspiracy to launch popular revolutions, assassinate monarchs, and engage in other terrorist activities. A number of specific plots were attributed to witches—in part, it would seem, in the interest of persuading secular authorities to join with the Church in the suppression of the heretics.

Many of the charges most often made against witches are set

forth in the *Bull of Innocent VIII,* issued at Rome in December of 1484, which unleashed the inquisitors Sprenger and Kramer and empowered them to put down all "heretical pravities." The document had far-reaching effects and is one of the most important in the history of witchcraft. I will quote a portion of it:

"It has indeed lately come to Our ears, not without afflicting Us with bitter sorrow, that in some parts of Northern Germany, as well as in the provinces, townships, territories, districts and dioceses of Mainz, Cologne, Trèves, Salzburg, and Bremen, many persons of both sexes, unmindful of their own salvation and straying from the Catholic Faith, have abandoned themselves to devils, incubi and succubi, and by their incantations, spells, conjurations, and other accursed charms and crafts, enormities and horrid offenses, have slain infants yet in the mother's womb, as also the offspring of cattle, have blasted the produce of the earth, the grapes of the vine, the fruits of trees, nay, men and women, beasts of burden, herd-beasts, as well as animals of other kinds, vineyards, orchards, meadows, pastureland, corn, wheat, and all other cereals; these wretches furthermore afflict and torment men and women, beasts of burden, herd-beasts, as well as animals of other kinds, with terrible and piteous pains and sore diseases, both internal and external; they hinder men from performing the sexual act and women from conceiving, whence husbands cannot know their wives nor wives receive their husbands; over and above this, they blasphemously renounce that Faith which is theirs by the Sacrament of Baptism, and at the instigation of the Enemy of Mankind they do not shrink from committing and perpetrating the foulest abominations and filthiest excesses to the deadly peril of their own souls, whereby they outrage the Divine Majesty and are a cause of scandal and danger to very many." (This *Bull* is given in its entirety by Summers in his edition of the *Malleus Maleficarum.*)

It seems to have been the case that the extreme licentiousness of the times, in combination with the antisexual doctrines of the Church and the near-panic brought about by very widespread torture and execution of alleged witches, resulted in epidemic mental illness, especially hysteria. Possession and obsession, demonomania and demonophobia, spontaneous trances and hallucinations were all commonplace. Potent deranging drugs and alcoholic beverages were freely used, often worsening the mental disturbances.

Demons copulated with men and women in phantasies, in nightmares and other dreams, and in hallucinations. The guilt resulting was severely destructive and sometimes deadly. The intercourse was usually reported to be extremely painful—testimony to anguish and anxiety, with dread of terrible punishment both in this world and throughout eternity. The Church did not succeed in suppressing sexual acts, which flourished and even multiplied in both fancy and fact; but it succeeded in creating guilt and terror so intense that the authority of the Church, which alone could grant absolution, survived well beyond the time when otherwise it would have sunk into decline.

It is true that Protestants, too, burned witches. However, they did not contribute much of importance to the theory and trappings of witchcraft, merely taking over in the main the ideas and practices of the Inquisition. Almost the entire blame for the hideous nightmare that was the witch mania, and the greatest part of the blame for poisoning the sexual life of the West, rests squarely upon the Roman Catholic Church. About this, and about the psychosexual and other medical aspects of witchcraft I will have considerably more to say in the last sections of this book.

I have quoted liberally in these pages from the writings of the demonologists, the inquisitors, and the other witchcraft authorities—so that the reader may discern for himself the morbidity and deluded character of their beliefs. Some of the stories they tell seem today to be quaint and amusing, and to be told with good humor. But let it always be kept in mind that the narrators were completely and grimly in earnest, and that they were dealing with matters of life and death. When one recalls the tens of thousands of executions, the tortures so devilish one wonders that the human mind could conceive them, then the seemingly light vein of the stories related by the witch-burners makes them all the more grisly and detestable.

This book is not, it should be understood, a history of witchcraft. For the most part, it deals only with those sexual phenomena of witchcraft involved in the intercourse of witches (and others) with demons. Those who would *fully* acquaint themselves even with the sexual phenomena will be obliged to study witchcraft and demonology in their other aspects. Sufficient references are included in this book to serve as a guide to such a study.

I am painfully aware of many limitations. For example, it was with the greatest reluctance that I abandoned my initial plan to analyze the incubi-succubi phenomena by nations, by regions, and by intervals of time, but I have been able to find no way to handle the data in terms of such breakdowns without extending this work to an impossibly unwieldy and probably tedious length.

There are important, and some might say compelling, reasons for a geographic breakdown. Testimony reveals highly significant psychological differences between the experiences of witches in various regions—for example, witches in one area of Italy found great pleasure in the coition with demons while witches of a region of Germany found the intercourse agonizingly painful. And to give but one more example, there is a great difference between the experiences of those living in mountainous regions and those living in the flatlands. Temporal differences are no less significant and I can only hope that my work is not too seriously damaged by these and other well-recognized and lamented limitations.

I have attempted in this Introduction to ease the task of understanding for the reader who is less than completely informed about witchcraft. To the reader who is not well equipped in the area of sexual pathology, I recommend my book *Forbidden Sexual Behavior and Morality,* which will shed much light on the content of the present volume.

And how nicely can doggish lust beg for a piece of spirit, when a piece of flesh is denied it!

NIETZSCHE

1. *Origins of incubi and succubi*

The origin of demons was for many centuries a critical and perplexing problem for theologians. That God might have created them directly was an unpalatable doctrine, though one occasionally presented. However, granting the malefic character of demons, it seemed that to accept God as their creator would be to accept also the belief that evil might flow directly from God, among whose attributes was that of Perfect Goodness. This being the case, and such a contradiction not to be endured, it seemed better to suppose that the demons were creatures endowed by their Creator with free will, and who freely chose evil (as human beings are wont to do).

Hebrew thinkers, rising to the challenge, produced any number of theories, many of them still extant in apocryphal, rabbinical, and other literature. One of these theories was that the demons were fallen angels. As Lea[1] has noted, this explanation, though only one of many advanced by Hebrew demonologists, was taken over by most Christian dogmatists as the sole possible solution of the problem of the existence of devils, so that they proceeded to erect their entire demonology upon that foundation.[2]

In a widely accepted Hebrew version of the Fall, it was held that the angels or Sons of God (presumably the angels were all male) looked upon the Daughters of Men (human females) and "lusted after them." The angels then descended to earth, copulated with the human females, and the children so conceived were giants three thousand ells in height. These angels, led by Semjaza (or Azazel), were then punished by God for their transgression. The angels were usually held to be corporeal, having the forms both of men and of beasts, though some said that they became corporeal as a result of remaining upon the earth for seven days, and then were doomed to remain in that degenerate condition. Theorists who were agreed on this point fell into dispute as to whether the fallen angels themselves became demons or whether it was the offspring of their unions with the daughters of men who became demons. (Since the angels seem to have been vigorously heterosexual, it may be that to consider the offspring as demons solves at least one problem—that of the bisexuality of demons, who may be alternately and indifferently incubi and succubi.)

The character and status of the angels who fell provided subject matter for much further disputation. Some speculated that angels tempted to fleshly indulgence were inferior ones, while another and higher class of angels was exempt from any such frailty. It is suggested by later writers on the subject that the inferior angels are to be equated with the *Jinn* of the Muslims—demons notoriously lustful after humans.

Jewish angelologists who distinguished various classes of angels held that angels of the highest (chaste, or asexual) order were readily recognizable by the fact that they were created circumcised. Lower orders of angels—those who copulated with women—were not circumcised. (Apparently, the belief was already prevalent, if this was not the origin of it, that the circumcised are less lustful than those whose foreskins remain unmutilated. Many today are of the same opinion, or hold related beliefs.)

It should also be noted that the giants, children of fallen angels and mortal females, are said to have lain with women in their turn—which, owing to anatomical discrepancies, must have posed certain problems. However that may be, they are said to have reproduced; and the giants are believed to have taught their wives sorcery and incantations, so that the wives of the giants are sometimes regarded as the first witches.

One rabbinical version had it that God foresaw that Satan would procreate with His wife Lilith, and so castrated Him. Thus the children of Satan, who would have been demons, were not born. However, God (by this same argument) apparently did not foresee that demons would be born anyhow by the wicked deeds of men. Every time a man does an evil deed, it was thought, a demon is born.

According to other Hebrew interpreters of the Old Testament, Adam and Eve were separated for approximately one hundred years, following the birth of Abel and before the birth of Seth. During this rather lengthy separation both Adam and Eve had sexual relations with spirits. The offspring of these respective adulterous liaisons were the incubi and succubi.

In a more specific version, Adam's wife during this period was said to have been the succubus Lilith. Others, however, held that Lilith was Adam's first wife, and that she left him either because they had quarreled over who was to have the greater authority, or because she was seduced by the Devil and ran away with Him.

That incubi and succubi came into being as the result of Adam's intercourse with Lilith was also a theory subject to a variety of interpretations. By one of these, Lilith is the personification of the "morbid imagination." Thus, Adam's seed, released by masturbation or phantasy activity or as the result of a nocturnal pollution, would not have impregnated an actual being but would have been spilled upon the ground, so that the incubi and succubi would have developed out of the spilled seed and would have had no mother except for Adam's phantasied sex partner.

A contemporary occultist theory is rather close to the one just mentioned. Some occultists believe that the human imagination, when excited by lust and lewd phantasies, secretes a non-corporeal sperm. Incubi and succubi are said to be born -as a result of such ejaculations of the imagination.[3]

Christians, seeking data on the fall of the angels and the origins of devils, received from an Albigensian heretic an account that was to have some influence upon later theologians. Satan, the Albigensian revealed, was attempting to recruit angels to His own ranks and tempted them with word pictures of the daughters of men and the ecstasies of the sexual embrace. When they failed to respond to His descriptions, He made a hole in the wall of heaven and brought a woman and placed her just outside of the hole. The angels, seeing her, were awakened to lust and swarmed out through the hole. Finally God, seeing what was happening, and perceiving that the entire population of heaven might be lost if he failed to act, plugged the gap in his wall, locking out all of those angels who had already departed. These became and remained the followers of Satan.[4]

It has often been remarked that the Christian heaven is one of the least attractive because of the absence of carnal delights. Mohammed promised true believers an afterlife blessed by sexual raptures with both tender soft-skinned boys and houris with dark flashing eyes. There would be seventy-two houris for every man, and it was only necessary to wish to make them virgins again. The Lithuanians, like the Arabs, inclined to a heaven where tangible pleasures would be available. The old Lithuanian paradise for fallen warriors held out the promise of beautiful women, good and abundant food and drink, perfect health and freedom from all cares, while appetites and the capacity for their gratification were to be increased by one hundredfold. And there is the report of a skeptic who, being granted the merest glimpse of the Manichaean heaven, fell into an orgasm that lasted for three hours. Other religions and supernaturalist movements have offered similar post-terrestrial rewards—even including the belief that heaven is an orgasm, infinitely extended.

(Saint John Chrysostom[5] was moved to wonder why men would follow Satan who sends them to hell, rather than Christ who promises heaven; and Lea remarked of this that it was indeed "a puzzle in the divine economy." It seems clear, however, that the hell envisioned by Satanists is not the one described by Christians, where blood boils in the veins of the damned and torment is unending, but a hell more along the lines of the Lithuanian heaven, where pleasures are intensified and the capacity to experience them vastly increased. A few demonologists have expressed a similar opinion.)

With regard to the story told by the Albigensian, the belief that angels could be seduced by women shows how ravening the sexual desires of males (including angels) were thought to be; and how irresistibly tempting in a carnal way women were considered to be. The angels could not withstand their lustful allure (how much less mere mortals?), and the sexual contact with them was so contaminating and evil as to turn angels into demons, or to produce demon offspring, while bogging men deep in the quagmires of sin. Such stories also establish the belief in the awful evil power of sexual intercourse.

Turning now to the views of Christian, mostly Catholic, thinkers, it was declared by Justin Martyr[6] in the second century that angels copulated with women and demons were born into the world. These demons then introduced evil into the minds of men—not only lust, but also murder, war, and the whole gamut of the vices. The early Christians decided, and the idea was to remain prevalent, that the ranks of the demons included all of the gods of antiquity, especially those of the Romans and the Greeks.[7] (That angels capable of sexual intercourse with mortals are relatives of the gods of mythology seems clear enough.)

Early in the fifth century, Sulpicius Severus[8] agreed that the angels fell as the result of their erotic attraction to mortal females. However, apparently wishing to remove some of the tarnish from angelic reputations, he distinguished himself by asserting that it was only to virgins the angels were attracted. But even a virgin was capable, it seems, of corrupting an angel; and as a result of the unions and their offspring, mankind, no less than the angels, fell into evil.

Clement of Alexandria,[9] Commodianus,[10] and Tertullian,[11] all in the third century, held that the angels fell because they lusted after women and copulated with them, becoming so corrupted by the contact that they were unable to return to heaven. Clement said that the angels forsook the eternal beauty of God for the beauty that fades. Tertullian remarked that the offspring of the unions of angels with women were demons, but Commodianus declared that they were giants who could not be admitted into heaven, wandered aimlessly over the face of the earth, and were worshiped as gods by the pagans.

Lactantius, who died near the middle of the fourth century and was known as the "Christian Cicero," said that the angels who mated with women were originally sent to earth by God to protect the women from the Devil, who was tempting them. But the women seduced their guardian angels, who then went over to Satan's legions. The offspring of the angel-human intercourse were evil-working spirits.

The thought that the angels would mate with human females was denounced, however, by Saint Philastrius, who called it a heresy and declared the idea to be nothing more than a shabby derivation from the legends of the doings of the pagan gods.[12]

Other theologians, pondering the story of the fall of the angels, preoccupied themselves with recondite technicalities—the velocity at which the fallen angels fell being a topic for heated debate in subtle and ingenious disputation.

As the Dark and Middle Ages waned, many of the theories lingered on, but there continued to be modifications, and sometimes new ideas. Theophrastus Bombastus von Hohenheim, better known as Paracelsus,[13] held in the early sixteenth century that incubi and succubi (succubas, he said, considering demons to have sex) are formed of the semen of those "who commit the unnatural sin of Onan"—by which he seems to have meant masturbation, not *coitus interruptus*. The lustful demons came to men and women by night and caused the dreams popularly known as nightmares. Paracelsus believed that the demons are basically to be understood as the spawn of "intense and lewd imagination of men and women," which causes them to masturbate.

Some thought the incubi and succubi were mere imports. The view later expressed by Soldan that the Crusaders may have acquired from Orientals the idea of humans copulating with supernatural beings of the incubus variety had a small following. The famous magistrate Pierre de Lancre,[14] author of *Tableau de l'Inconstance des mauvais Anges* (1613), thought that at least some demons came to Europe from the Orient, but he did not think them imaginary. France had been invaded, he said, by devils from Japan and the East Indies, evicted from their homelands by the pious labors of Christian missionaries. These immigrant devils had been seen flying through the skies toward France in great and menacing hordes.

Still others suggested that the odor ("stench") of sexual intercourse spawns demons; while some held that they are the products of nocturnal (dream) copulations and pollutions, whether those of males or of females. But by most demonologists such beliefs were regarded as at best mere superstitions; at worst, damnable and dangerous heresies.

Eighteenth- and nineteenth-century and some earlier medical explanations of the incubus experience were various and conflicting. According to different authorities the phenomena derived from a superabundance of semen in the testicles; from a disease of the semen; from a morbid imagination; from malfunctions of the uterus; from hysteria. Incubi and succubi were described as amorous illusions; as hallucinations; as the result of religious and moral derangements; as the rotten fruits of *hyperesthesia psychica sexualis;* as symptoms of insanity.

A modern writer, Hoefler (*Medizinischer Daemonismus*, in *Zentralblatt für Anthropologie*, 1900), inclined to the view that the belief in demons originated in nightmares, and that the belief in incubi originated in erotic dreams. Ernest Jones reposed some faith in this theory,[15] adding that nightmares are erotic anxiety dreams stemming from repressed incestuous conflicts.

The relationship between nightmare and witchcraft had been noted long before Hoefler. Nider[16] in the fifteenth century and Del Rio[17] in the sixteenth, along with others, remarked that witchcraft was at its most prevalent in mountainous regions where nightmares are also very common. However, witchcraft authorities of the fifteenth and sixteenth centuries were not likely to believe that incubi and succubi were no more than phantasies derived from dream experiences. They said that the poverty and lack of education found among mountain people accounted for their interest in witchcraft; and that the many natural calamities to which they fell prey, encouraging acceptance of belief in causation of the catastrophes by evil spirits, also inclined them to devil-worship (in hope of propitiating the demons and so avoiding their mischief-making).

The above by no means exhausts the theories of the origins of incubi and succubi, but is hopefully considered sufficient to provide a foundation upon which the investigation may proceed.

2. The anatomy of the devil

Theological, juridical, and other writers on demonology and witchcraft commonly spoke of "the Devil," both when they were referring to *the* Devil—often called Satan— and when they were referring to the general run of devils, or demons. Since Satan Himself was rather rarely involved in the intercourse with witches, delegating such dealings to demons (and in some cases to sorcerers in devilish disguise), it may be assumed that in most cases where "the Devil" is mentioned, the reference is in fact to *a* devil rather than to *the* Devil. I will not attempt in this book to establish in each case where "the Devil" is mentioned whether *the* Devil or *a* devil is meant.

In case there should happen to be even a single reader who is not aware of the fact, I will also pause to note that if one is to use the term *incubus* in its strictest theological sense, then the usage must be limited to demons *in human form*. When the same demons assume, say, animal form, even if for sexual connection with humans, then they are no longer incubi (and the same is true for succubi). However, the term *incubus* is almost always used more loosely, referring to any demon who has sexual intercourse with humans, and ignoring the form he may assume. Following the practice of the more unscrupulous demonologists, I will use the word in this looser sense.[1]

That much said, I will proceed to the accounts of the Devil, or of devils, supposedly gleaned from first-hand and intimate experience of that Gentleman, or those gentlemen. Succubi, or devils in female form, or in forms suitable for intercourse with human males, will also be discussed. But as the reader is aware, devils, even when in female form, are most often considered to be male, or else to have no sex at all.

It is interesting, though doubtless to be expected, that the earliest Christian accounts of the Devil either endow Him with an imposing and even majestic form of His own, or else have Him appearing in the form of some other divine, semi-divine, or otherwise supernatural being of high rank. It was the later demonologists who reduced devils to the degenerate status, including form, characteristic of them in their association with witches.

In the fourth century (and occasionally up through at least the twelfth century) the Devil often appeared in the form of one or another of the classical gods. Thus, He is said to have appeared to Saint Martin sometimes as Jupiter (Zeus) and sometimes as Aphrodite (Venus) or Minerva (Athene). It might be recalled that to lie with a god or a goddess was often to become impotent and prematurely aged, and it may be that the belief that intercourse with a demon or a witch sometimes had a similar effect is related to the appearances of demons as gods and goddesses. Or perhaps the later belief is merely a plagiarism from the earlier one.

That the Devil very often appeared in the likeness of Pan, or of a Satyr, is well known, and even today such representations of devils are rather common. This form, with the goat-like lower body, horns, tail, and cloven hoofs, maintained its vogue during the period of the witch epidemic also, though it may have been somewhat less common than at an earlier date. In most of these Pan-ic appearances He is represented as wearing a beard—a red one sometimes, after Thor—and He stinks, as do by ill repute both goats and devils. Often He is described as limping—a symbol of impotence, according to some writers —and He is frequently black in color. He was early depicted as having a torch under his tail, though most witches testified that He had a second face on His bottom. Sometimes the tail was a second phallus.

On a few occasions the Devil appeared as a giant—for example, to Saint Brigitta and to Saint Anthony,[2] who described Him as "a monstrous giant whose head reached to the clouds." At other times He showed Himself in the form of a fiery dragon (to Saint Anthony and Saint Coleta), and also as a snake. When He did not assume the form of a snake His arms might still be serpentine; His penis was also often described as being snakelike in movement as well as in configuration.

The well-known exorcist Brognoli warned that incubi and succubi may even be so shameless and bold as to appear in the guise of Angels of Light, thus hoping to persuade deluded mortals that the hellish copulations have the approval of God. But more often, said Brognoli, the demon would appear in the form of a small, black, shaggy man with a huge phallus. Then, coition with him was very painful, and his semen as icy as his embrace.

In early Christian days, as mentioned, the Devil was frequently a beautiful, handsome, or otherwise imposing figure, possessing a remarkable majesty and dignity, and sometimes closely resembling Christ. There were also occasions, some said, when He appeared in the exact form of Christ.

One occasion when the Devil appeared in the form of Christ was to Brother Rufinus, a theologian and author of the fourth century. But that holy man, suspicious or at least wishing to take all possible precautions, requested the Savior to open his mouth so that Rufinus could put some dung in it. Presumably, the true Christ would have acceded to this request, though it is an uncommon one to put to a stranger, but the Devil would not. And in His rage He disappeared into solid rock, so creating the famous fissure in Monte Alverno.

That the Devil appeared in the *exact* form of Christ was held to be not completely true. As demonologists were forever pointing out, God in his mercy would not permit the Devil to perfectly imitate any being. Thus, in the Christ form as in others, the resemblance was always in some way imperfect. There would be a deformity, such as a tail, and it was up to the individual to make certain that he or she was not deceived by an impostor. That the average believer might be hesitant to order Christ or even an Angel of Light to disrobe, so that some imperfection might be searched for, seems not to have troubled demonologists.

While it was not too rare for the Devil to appear in the likeness of Christ, it was an almost unique event that He should take that particular symbolic form of Christ known as the Lamb of God, or *Agnus Dei*. Yet so is He said to have made Himself known to the witch Agnes Wobster, in 1597. The Devil also, though rarely, aped the Holy Ghost, manifesting as the Divine Dove.

(Montague Summers, loath to believe that even the Devil would, or could, presume to such impieties, maintained that the Devil did not appear as the snow-white *Agnus Dei*, but as a black lamb, hideous and malformed; while He came as no snowy dove, but as a darkling and wretched caricature of that manifestation of the Holy Spirit. However, Summers' main basis for these dogmatic declarations seems to have been wishful thinking.)[3]

A few authorities asserted that the Devil not only appeared in the form of Christ, but that He had twelve apostles and a *Bible*—a copy of which is said to repose even today in the Stockholm Royal Library—and that His designation as the "Ape of God" refers to these and similar impostures and accoutrements.

Also in the pre-witchcraft era, demons democratically appeared as working-men, as blacksmiths, as cobblers, as tanners, as headless Negroes, etc.—all for purposes of copulation. A favorite costume, doubtless because of its seductive effect on silly young girls and dullard domestics, was a military uniform. Usually that of an officer, it was chosen with a view to foppish elegance. Bright red, with epaulets of gleaming gold and a cap with a plume or some similar ornament was not uncommon. Thus eye-catchingly attired, a demon would sometimes arrive mounted on a magnificent black stallion.

It should be remarked here that the demon's initial seduction is frequently accomplished in a pleasing form—that of a handsome youth or beauteous maiden. Later, however, he copulates with the witch in all manner of bestial and other horrible shapes. The reason is obvious: In the beginning, the witch might be frightened or revolted; but later, the demon asserts his ascendancy and by the terrors and horrendous impudicities to which he subjects her he further confirms the witch in her conviction of her irrevocable damnation.

During the period of the witch epidemic the demon appeared most often of all as a "black man." In fact, some writers held that he never assumed any other human (male) form, although such a claim is contradicted by a wealth of testimony. (No one has bothered to wonder, so far as I know, why succubi did not equally often appear as *black women*.)

One of the earliest Christian reports I have found of a demon or devil appearing as a "black man" is that of Cassian in the early fifth century who relates that the demon Zabulus, in the form of a "hideous Ethiop," appeared to Abbot John of Lycus. An even earlier account was that of Rufinus, who said that the desert anchorite Saint Macarius the Younger saw little demons "like foul Ethiops" flying around a gathering of monks. One of the more detestable tricks of these demons was to substitute little lumps of coal for the host at Holy Communion.[4] (It may be that the Devil so often appeared as a black man because the negro savages known to the Christians were infidels and devil-worshipers, noted also for their indiscriminate fornications, and so admirably suited to the adaptation. It may also be that a significant part of the racial hostility of modern times derives from this earlier religious antipathy.)

However, detestation of the behavior of savages by no means suffices to explain the whole of the phenomenon of the black man, which derives also from such ancient and mystical notions as the blackness of the void and the eternal conflict between the forces of darkness and the forces of light—in turn derived, perhaps, from the authentic terrors of the primeval night.

One has to keep in mind, for example, that not only did the Devil appear as a black man, and as some black beast, but sacrifices and gifts to Him were often required to be black. As Nicolas Remy,[5] an important demonologist of the sixteenth century, observed: "No doubt the reason is, as Pythagoras writes, that this colour has some kinship with evil; and it is appropriate that what is dedicated and sacrificed to the author and instigator of all evil should be black in colour." [6]

Henri Boguet,[7] an eminent jurist, also dealt with the problem, saying: "But whenever he (the Devil) assumes the form of a man, he is, however, always black, as all witches bear witness. And for my part I hold that there are two principal reasons for this: first, that he who is the Father and Ruler of darkness may not be able to disguise himself so well that he may not always be known for what he is; secondly, as a proof that his study is only to do evil; for evil, as Pythagoras said, is symbolized by black. This is what Tamburlaine the Great had in mind when, while he was besieging a town, he set up black tents on the third day as a sign that he would put all the inhabitants to the fire and the sword if they did not surrender. And long before him, the Greeks regarded it as a bad omen if, in drawing lots, one of the lots were black." [8]

The instances in which the demon appeared as a black man are very numerous and I will cite only one of them here. A demon in the form of an Ethiop presented himself to young Magdalena Cruz of Cordova, and when at the age of twelve she became his mistress, he promised to make her the head of her religious order. He is said to have kept his word, since she in fact became head of her order in Spain, as well as abbess of her convent. But she eventually repented, managed to break her pact, and was forgiven (a rarity) by the Church.

It may be of some interest to remark that Negroes of Haiti, Cuba, and Brazil, perhaps by way of retaliation, often portray the Devil as a "white man." Martin Fierro has taken note of this in a poem: "The White paints the devil black/The Black paints him white." A similar controversy has had to do with Christ and with the Christian God, the Negroes sometimes claiming that he is black. (A few years ago, Juliette Greco popularized a song titled *"Dieu est negre."*)[9] Black Christs are employed by modern Satanists also, but in this case the blackening of the figure is intended as sacrilege and is based upon the traditional view of black as the color of evil.

Interest in the anatomy of the incubus was especially centered upon his penis, or penes, since he not infrequently had several. Descriptions both of its size and its substance varied considerably.

Some witches reported that the penis of the demon was situated at his rear; others, that he had one penis fore and another one aft. Prierias[10] (*De Strigimagis*) announced in 1521 that the incubus employs in his fornications a penis forked like the tongue of a serpent. This permitted him to copulate and engage in pederasty simultaneously; and, as if that were not enough, he was sometimes credited with possessing a three-pronged penis, rather like a trident, so that he might require of a witch that she engage in not only coitus and sodomy, but also fellatio, all at once. Antiquaries will recognize here the diphallus and triphallus which used to be associated with Dionysus (Bacchus). The question is raised, too, of the relationship to the trident or "pitchfork" the Devil is even today represented as carrying.

The penes of demons were most often described as being made of horn, or of half flesh and half iron. Some said that they were covered with scales and that these, once penetration had been effected, might open out like barbs, so that each withdrawal movement was excruciatingly painful. It was reported in this connection that witches often screamed and groaned during intercourse with incubi, and that they bled copiously during the act or after it was completed. The penis was reported variously to be sinuous, supple and serpentine, and hard and unbending as metal or stone.

Estimates of the size of the Devil's organ varied greatly. A witch of Labourd said that her demon's member was as long and as thick as an arm, and most beautifully proportioned; but a witch of Franche-Comté described the penis of her incubus as being no longer and no greater in circumference than a finger. This led the demonologist De Lancre to remark, with a quip that guaranteed him immortality, that Satan served the witches of Labourd much better than He did those of Franche-Comté. One Claudia Fellet provided the additional datum that demons have no testicles.

Like the Hindu god Siva, whose penis is always erect, and who is honored as the first deity to be stricken with satyriasis (a condition much reverenced and sought after by some Indian holy men), Satan is occasionally described as omni-potent, either in the sense of being forever erect, or in the (more favorable) sense of being capable of having one orgasm and erection after another. (On the other hand, some demons seem to have had potency problems, so that witches complained that their incubi either could not obtain erections or else ejaculated prematurely.)

Dr. Johann Meyfarth, a seventeenth-century Lutheran professor at Erfurt, declared that according to the celebrated Thummius, demons have no penes at all. However, Meyfarth conceded, an illusory intercourse may take place. As evidence that the fornications were mere illusion he cited the fact that virgins claiming to have copulated with demons were found to have their hymens still intact. Some authorities, granting that the demon is without an instrument adequate to coition, held that he conducted the preliminary courtship in person and then, at the crucial moment, skilfully substituted a sorcerer who then consummated the intercourse. This was not, however, one of the more widely accepted theories.

Intercourse with incubi was almost always described as a painful experience, although there were exceptions. While I will deal with the meaning of this pain element elsewhere, I will here give a few examples of testimony concerning it.

Thivienne Paget, for example, likened the pains accompanying intercourse with her demon to those of child-bearing. Most witches described the demon's member as icy cold, while male witches said the same of the vaginas of their succubi. Francoise Secretain, however, said that while the instrument of the demon was in her she felt as if her whole belly were on fire. Sylvanie de la Plaine, as if attempting to reconcile these conflicting reports, testified that it was like ice when it entered, but like fire when it came out.

Remy, in his *Demonolatry*, cited many witches who testified to the painfulness of the intercourse:

"But all they who have spoken to us of their copulations with Demons agree in saying that nothing colder or more unpleasant could be imagined or described. At Dalheim, Pétrone of Armentières declared that as soon as he embraced his Abrahel all his limbs at once grew stiff. Hennezel at Vergaville, July 1586, said that it was as if he had entered an ice-bound cavity, and that he left his Schwarzburg with the matter unaccomplished. (Abrahel and Schwarzburg were the names of their succubas.) And all female witches maintain the so-called genital organs of their Demons are so huge and excessively rigid that they cannot be admitted without the greatest pain. Alexée Drigie (at Haraucourt, November 10, 1586) reported that her Demon's penis, even when only half in erection, was as long as kitchen utensils, which she pointed to as she spoke; and that there were neither testicles nor scrotum attached to it. Claudia Fellet (at Mazières, November 2, 1584) said that she had often felt it like a spindle swollen to an immense size so that it could not be contained by even the most capacious woman without pain. This agrees with the complaint of Nicole Morèle (at Serre, January 19, 1587) that, after such miserable copulation, she always had to go straight to bed as if she had been tired out by some long and violent agitation. Didatia of Miremont (at Preny, July 31, 1588) also said that, although she had many years experience of men, she was always so stretched by the huge swollen member of her Demon that the sheets were drenched with blood. And nearly all witches protest that it is wholly against their will that they are embraced by Demons, but that it is useless for them to resist." [11]

Several comments are needed on the above. The size of the demon's member was often small, as already mentioned. It did not always lack accompanying testicles.[12] The intercourse was not always cold, though it usually was. Neither was it always painful. The witches did not all protest that the intercourse was against their will. They described their experiences, one supposes, in terms of the expectations of their judges and torturers, somewhat as analysands of today produce dreams and "memories" in terms of the theories of their analysts. It is not very difficult to understand, by the way, why the penis of the demon should have been phantasied as very large; why it should have been phantasied as excessively small poses a real problem.

The attribution to demons of great virility has been mentioned, but the subject should not be abandoned without taking note of a theory advanced to explain it. Churchmen, noting that women sometimes claimed to have copulated with their demon lovers more than half a hundred times in a single night, felt obliged to render the incubi less potent (lest all women be seduced to witchcraft). They argued, therefore, that only one or two of the half a hundred copulations were actual, the others illusions, intended by the incubi to deceive the women and impress them with the incomparable virility of demons. This is not, it must be said, a very satisfactory theory. After all, an illusory copulation that seems real provides satisfactions no less great than an actual ("in the flesh") one. However, the interpretation may have had some slight success in deterring the inexperienced.

The coldness of the bodies of demons, and especially the coldness of their sexual parts, was emphasized again and again. Ponsète of Essey, for example, convicted of witchcraft in 1583, testified that when she laid her hand upon the bosom of her incubus she felt it to be cold and hard as stone.

Summers, in his notes to Boguet's *Discours des Sorciers* (*Examen of Witches*), cites a number of instances of witch testimony concerning the icy sensation experienced in contact with the flesh of incubi and succubi:

"A Belgian witch, Digna Robert, in 1565, said that the devil 'était froid dans tous ses membres.' At the North Berwick Sabbat in 1590, 'he caused all the company to com and kiss his ers quhilk they said was cauld lyk yce.' In 1661 a Forfar witch 'Katheren Porter confesseth that the divill tooke hir by the hand, that his hand was cold.' In 1662 Isabel Rutherford confessed 'that ye was at ane meeting at Turfhills, where Sathan took you by the hand and said "welcome, Isabel," and said that his hand was cold.' In 1697 Thomas Lindsay, a boy, gave witness that 'Jean Fulton his Grand-Mother awaked him one Night out of his Bed, and caused him to take a Black Grimm Gentleman (as she called him) by the Hand; which he felt to be cold.' " [18]

Summers, like a good many other writers, thinks that the reports of the coldness of the Devil's penis, and of His semen, should be understood as pointing to the use, sometimes, of artificial penes (hollow, and down which were poured cold liquids). However, this would not explain the testimony just cited as to the coldness of the hands, chest, and other parts far removed from the genital region. Summers comments:

"The coldness of the Devil and the repeated assertion at the trials that his semen was nipping and gelid would seem to point to the use upon occasion of an artificial penis. In many of the cases of debauchery at Sabbats so freely and fully confessed by witches, their partners were undoubtedly the males who were present; the Grand Master, Officer, or President of the Assembly, exercising the right to select first for his own pleasures such women as he chose. Yet when we sift the evidence, detailed and exact, of the trials, we find there foul and hideous mysteries of lust which neither human intercourse nor the employ of a mechanical property can explain. . . . Mother Bush of Barton in 1649 said that the Devil who visited her as a young black man 'was colder than man, and heavier, and could not performe nature as man.' In 1662 Isobel Gowdie and Janet Breadheid of Auldearne described the Devil as 'a meikle, blak, roch man, werie cold; and I fand his nature als cold within me as spring-well water.' 'He is abler for us that way than any man can be,' said Isobel, 'onlie he was heavie lyk a malt-sek; a hudg nature, verie cold, as yce.' " [14]

Demons often seduced women by appearing to them in the forms of their husbands or lovers. When a demon wished to seduce a child, he might appear to the child in the likeness of the parent of the opposite sex. Since he frequently chose to approach women in their beds, while they were half asleep, it was not difficult for him, in the guise of husband or lover, to accomplish the deception and achieve his ends. Only after he had acquired power over the woman by virtue of his copulation with her would he reveal his true identity. Then the woman might be persuaded that she had already committed a mortal sin, laid herself open to inquisitorial punishment, and must now put her whole trust and reliance in her only remaining ally—the Devil.

The woman who desired some particular man and was unable to have him was easy prey for the incubus, who would offer to have connection with her in the likeness of the man she desired. One supposes that had there been film heroes at the time, incubi would have done a thriving business as replicas of "stars" lusted after by female admirers.

On occasion, the Devil assumed the form of a ball of thread to copulate with witches, usually old women, and it may be that this particular item was in common use as a masturbatory instrument and so entered the realm of incubus phantasies.

Of demons assuming the forms of beasts to copulate with witches I will have something to say elsewhere. One instance, however, I would like to mention presently. The Devil, evidently given to much variety in His fornications, and (unlike the Christian God) not lacking a sense of humor, sometimes changed form in mid-coition. Thus, the indictment against one

Margaret Hamilton read that "Yow had carnall cowpulatiown with the devil in the lykness of ane man, bot he removed from yow in the lykness of ane black dowg."

Witches condemned at Avignon in the late sixteenth century were charged with frequenting the Sabbats at an unseasonable hour, there by the light of a hellish bonfire to fall upon their knees and kiss the most noisome, nasty and stinking anus of the Devil. (They also committed on those occasions the execrable act of sodomy, fornicated with incubi and succubi, and otherwise damnably disported themselves despite the icy coldness of the venery.)

While the Devil might sometimes have an anus of the usual (human) sort, which the witches kissed, more often He had a face on His bottom, or at least a mouth. In any case, De Lancre was told by witches he examined that "I'd rather kiss Satan's arse than my husband's lips." It might be remarked that wives of all times and places have been known to give tongue to similar sentiments, which present-day cynics and materialists hold to be mere figures of speech.

It was frequently reported that the Devil has a hollow back. Anna Miller confessed that the Devil had "forced himself into her as often as he desired but he was hostile and of cold nature and his back was as hollow as a melter (a wooden pitcher)."

It is noteworthy that almost never does Satan appear in the form of a fat man, although some fat and some pot-bellied demons are reported. But of few, save for Behemoth, elephantine Demon of the Delights of the Belly, could the witches voice that complaint stated in classical form by an anonymous Assyrian slave girl: "I want a lover whose penis is not in his belly, but in mine."

Of the senses of demons, Saint Augustine held that they are more acute than those of men; also, that demons are able to move more swiftly, and that their longer experience gives them the advantage over men of being able to forecast future events. How demons were able to speak troubled many writers, and some held that they accomplished it by manipulating the winds. Ambrogio de Vignati (*Tractatus de Haereticis*) insisted that demons neither have nor may assume corporeal bodies. Everything is illusion. The demon seems to talk, but he can have no real voice and so it is something else that one hears. He appears to eat, but this too is false. And he can have no sexual intercourse with mortals, although he seems to have such intercourse.[15]

All of the deficiencies (as men saw them) of demons were marks of the imperfection which must always characterize beings of that kind; and if a demon should assume a seemingly flawless form, then he still was unable to deceive all of the human senses at once—the reason why he seemed cold, why his voice might sound like "air through a hole," and so on. But more often there was a visual imperfection as well—for the protection of the faithful.

Remy took note of this in a statement which must have seemed to his colleagues a bit over-optimistic and exaggerated: "And herein is most wonderfully manifested the loving-kindness of God towards wretched mortals; for Demons can never so completely ape the human shape but that the deception is apparent to even the most stupid. Either their countenance is of a hideous foulness; or their hands and feet are distorted and hooked with claws like those of obscene vultures; or else they are conspicuous by reason of some evident mark which betrays the savageness of their natures." [16] Hundreds of persons accused of intercourse with demons testified otherwise about the obviousness of the imperfection, but Remy, who was familiar with the fact, chose to ignore their testimony.

The whole of witchcraft is permeated with bisexual phantasies. The demons may assume either male or female forms; sex changes of humans are often noted; there are sex-reversing drugs; and devils are frequently represented as hermaphrodites, with both male and female sex characteristics or organs, or with female bodies, save for the penis.

Demons functioning as succubi usually appeared in attractive female forms—possibly because the human males could

not have responded to them and so accomplished coition otherwise. (However, men sometimes were obliged to perform cunnilingus on their succubi, tonguing at gaping and clammy
apertures from which exuded dung, urine and other awful
juices and stenches.) It was generally agreed that demons appeared much less often as succubi than as incubi, but this was
probably owing only to the fact that there were far more female than male witches, and not to any prejudice against the
female role on the part of the demon.

The Christian hermits of the desert had been very often
tormented by demons appearing to them as seductive females
and seeking to lead them into sin. The holy men were usually
staunch in their resistance, and did not succumb. But Rufinus
told of an exception: A hermit who had begun to take pride in
his piety was approached by a demon in the form of a beautiful woman who told him she was lost in the desert and ur-
gently needed a night's lodging. He took her in, and she caused
him to succumb to her charms. But when he attempted actually to penetrate her, she vanished with a mocking laugh,
leaving in her wake a crowd of demons who "assailed him for
his lust." This hermit, it was said, then abandoned his religious
life, returned to the world, fell into vice and depravity, and was
lost to the Evil One.[17]

Boguet says: "Sometimes the Evil One takes the form of a
woman, as we are taught in the stories of the lives of S. Anthony and S. Jerome, among others: and the two demons which
appeared to Dion were in the form of women, as also seems to
have been that which Curtius Rufus saw as he was walking late
one day along a gallery. In Boethius also we have the story of
a very beautiful young man who was burdened with a Succubus devil with a very fair face. What we know of Succubi is
proof enough that the Devil often assumes the form of a woman,
and that he chiefly does so at the Sabbat, as is evidenced by
the words of Thivienne, of Jacquema Paget, and of several
other witches."[18]

Succubi of the early Christian period did not appear only to pious hermits. It was reported in the fourth century that a demon in the form of a raddled but beguiling bawd approached a monastery blacksmith, who wrathfully branded her on the face with an iron. Thereafter, God rewarding him for his virtue, the blacksmith could handle hot iron without injury.

In the Middle Ages, Pope Sylvester II, who ruled briefly (999-1003), was noted as a magician and occultist. His real name was Gerbert, he hailed from Aurillac, and he was said to have had as his life-long mistress a demon called Meridiana who gave him both wealth and carnal pleasures, and who was understanding enough to forgive him his infidelity with an old sweetheart who returned and seduced the Pope by getting him drunk. Shortly before his death Sylvester repented (like many another old ex-roué who hopes for the best of both worlds), and was buried in the Lateran where his tomb sweats just before some prominent person dies. If a pope is about to die, this perspiration becomes a stream that runs down onto the ground and makes a sizable puddle.[19]

Eparchius, Bishop of Tuvergne, decided to pay a visit to his church late one night and found there an abominable conclave of demons engaged in defiling an altar. Satan, dressed in women's clothing and sitting in the bishop's chair, was presiding over the celebration. Eparchius, outraged, made the error of denouncing Satan as an "infamous whore," whereupon the Devil promised to give the bishop all the whores he might want and then some, seeing that the bishop was so concerned with whorishness. It is related that "poor Eparchius felt the torments of the fleshly appetites each night until his death."

A favorite trick of demons was to substitute themselves for one of the human participants in a lovers' rendezvous. Thus, one Johann, scholasticus of the abbey at Prüm, arranged with a certain woman to come to his bed. But the Devil learned of the arrangement, caused the woman to fall into a slumber, and assumed her form. Then He kept the appointment and after a night of ardent love-making revealed His true identity to Johann. However, the intrepid scholasticus, far from being horrified or otherwise impressed, merely laughed irreverently in the Devil's face.

Pico della Mirandola,[20] in an early sixteenth-century work, tells of an unusual Sabbat presided over by a female devil called *la Signora*. Sexual intercourse at her Sabbat—women with incubi, men with succubi—offered raptures infinitely superior to any enjoyed in the mundane coitions of men with women. *La Signora* was said to be extremely beautiful and to bear a notable resemblance to the Mother of God.[21]

It is remarkable in the many stories of the relations of men and women with demons how often men were able to resist, in contrast to women who customarily found the incubi irresistible. This did not, of course, imply that succubi were less seductive than incubi, and in fact the reverse seems to have been the case. The stories rested upon the belief that women, ragingly lustful and naturally inclined to vice, would always put up defenses more feeble than those offered by males. I will close out this account of the anatomy and forms assumed by devils by recounting an (incomplete) encounter of a male with a brace of succubi. It is taken from Richard Bovet's *Pandaemonium* (London, 1684),[22] and was titled by him "An Account of one stripped of all his clothes after he was in Bed, and almost worried to death by Spirits."

"I had occasion to make mention of a Nobleman's House in the West of *England*, and to give two Relations of what passed there of my own knowledge: I shall now add another, known to the Lady, and all the Family; which is thus.

"One night, as we were at Supper, one of the Ladies Footmen complained he was pained in his Head, whereupon he had orders to go to Bed, which he did some hours before the rest of the Family. His Lodging was by the side of a fair Gallery, where there were several *Alcoves*, with Beds, for the Servants, and they were planted near Sir F's Lodging. When the Lady was disposed to go to her Chamber, the other Company waited on her up the Stairs (most of us lodging the same way) we passed into the aforesaid Gallery, and when we came over against the Alcove, where the Page was, we found the door of it open, and out of it issued a steam, which by the light of the Candles appeared like a thick Fog: which occasioned some of us to look into the Room, where we saw the poor young Man lying speechless on the Bed, his Eyes were staring very wide, and fixed on one side of the Room, his Hands were clutched, his Hair erected, and his whole body in so violent a sweat, as if he had been in the *Bagnio* (bath, not brothel); all the Clothes of the Bed were flung, some in one part of the Room, and some in another, his very shirt was drawn off his Body, and cast into one side of the Room; and it was near half an hour before he could recollect himself, and gather breath, so as to speak to us: At length, having taken somewhat to recall his Spirits, he gave us this surprising account of what had past from the time he went to the Bed, which we guess'd to be about three Hours. He told us that he lay about half an hour, endeavouring to compose himself to sleep, but could not, because of the pain in his Head, that about that time there came into the Room to him two in the appearance of very beautiful young Women, whose presence enlightened the place, as if it had been day, though there was no Candle near it. That they endeavoured to come into the Bed to him, being one on the one side, the other on the other side thereof, which he resisted with all the power he could, striking at them several times with his Fists, but could hit nothing but empty shadows; yet were they so strong, that they drew all the Bed-clothes off him, though he endeavoured with all his force to hold them, that after they had stripped him of his shirt; and he had contested so long with them, that he concluded within himself he should die under their violencies, during all that time he had no power to speak, or call for aid; but was at last reduced to that condition wherein we found him. Some were ordered to continue that night; and the next day he was bleeded, having been much bruised in the Conflict; however he had no sickness after it, nor did I hear that ever after he had any disturbance from them." [23]

3. *Problems of demonic substance*

The question of whether incubi and succubi have material bodies, and if they do not, how they still manage to have sexual intercourse with humans, was a much debated one. The answers most often advanced were these: Demons do have physical bodies of their own which they use (and which may be shaped as desired); they create temporary bodies for themselves out of condensed water or gases; they animate corpses; they make use of the bodies of persons who are drunk, drugged, entranced, or bewitched; they have no bodies, but are able to create an illusion in which it seems to the human partner that they are corporeal.

Saint Augustine, coming dauntlessly to grips with this problem, declared that incubi and succubi possess only "phantasmal," not real, bodies. (Later, however, he seems to have changed his mind and to have joined many of his contemporaries in believing that demons do have material bodies.)

Saint Thomas Aquinas (*On Power*) discussed the sexual relations of humans with demons and claimed to have personal knowledge of such cases. According to Aquinas, the bodies of incubi and succubi are sometimes phantasmal, as Augustine said; but it is also the case that demons may borrow the bodies of living men and women.

Nicolaus of Jauer, a professor of theology in the late fourteenth and early fifteenth centuries, held that demons have no bodies of their own, but are able to "assume" bodies. (Following Augustine, Nicolaus said that demons do not really change men and women into animals, but appear to do this since they are able to create illusions.)

Saint Basil[1] and others argued that the bodies of demons, which they use for carnal intercourse with humans, are formed from a concretion of condensed vapors. The English philosopher Henry More endeavored to give this fourth-century notion a seventeenth-century scientific basis, and sought also to explain why the flesh of demons was so frosty to the touch. It was only natural, More said, that the body of the demon should be cold. He manufactures it of coagulated water, and so it is like snow or ice. That is why the penis of the demon feels to the witch as if it were an icicle.

However, the coldness of the incubus, and the icy feeling that persisted in the human vagina after intercourse with him, was taken by others as evidential of the fact that the copulation was with a cadaver, temporarily animated by the demon for the purpose.

Most of those who believed that demons made temporary use of cadavers, held that only fresh (uncorrupted) bodies could be thus animated. There is a similar belief with regard to vampires—that once a cadaver has begun to decay, there is no longer any danger that it will become the material abode of a vampire.

Since a rotting corpse would have little appeal to those the demons wished to seduce, the restriction may seem a trivial one. But there were those who were firm in their insistence that demons do use decaying bodies—the proof for this being the stenches for which all witches are notorious, and which are the result of lying in the putrescent embraces of cadavers.

That the idea of necrophilia was connected with the belief that demons used dead bodies for their copulations with humans seems evident from remarks made by Jerome Cardan,[2] a physician, mathematician, and philosopher of the sixteenth century, who held that to so lie with a corpse, falsely animated, would be an "atrocious torture."

Demons, even if regarded as corporeal, were generally conceded the power to be visible or invisible as they preferred. The authors of the *Malleus Maleficarum*[3] affirmed that a demon may copulate with humans while invisible, "but he prefers to perform this visibly as a Succubus and an Incubus, that by such filthiness he may infect body and soul of all humanity, that is, of both woman and man, there being, as it were, actual bodily contact." [4]

Cardan told a story suggesting that demons retain their natural forms while copulating with humans, but cause the humans to perceive them in some other form.

A beautiful young woman turned up pregnant, Cardan related, and confessed to her parents that she had for a lover a handsome youth who would mysteriously appear in her room, go to bed with her, and then vanish. The parents decided to spy on their daughter, and when one day they heard suspicious sounds in her room they broke down the door, finding her in the embrace of a hideous monster. The Gospel of Saint John was read to the demon whereupon he departed, crashing through the ceiling and setting fire to all the furniture as he went. The girl later gave birth to a monstrous infant, which was destroyed by burning. The girl never saw her demon lover as her parents had seen him, but only as a handsome youth, presumably because he had cast some spell over her, or hypnotized her, to make her see only the kind of lover who would most appeal to her sense of beauty and most arouse her desires.

That demons might obtain control of the bodies of living persons and use them to carry out their missions as incubi and succubi was occasionally proposed; and the theory often advanced was that the demon might borrow or steal the body of one hypnotized, or in mediumistic trance. Summers suggests that the bodies of demons may be made of that ectoplasm known in connection with seance materializations. If the dead are able to materialize, he inquires, then why not demons? Especially, he said, is this likely to occur when the discarnate evil intelligence is aided and urged "by the longing thoughts and concentrated will power of those who eagerly seek them." Continuing along this line of exploration, he notes that ectoplasm is described as being to the touch a cold and viscous mass, reminiscent of the body of a reptile.[5]

To conclude this brief section, I will relate a story, perhaps not irrelevant, that was told to me by a person in close touch with the event and persons described. The incident is alleged to have occurred not in the 1590's, but in the 1950's. While I will leave it to the reader to draw his own conclusions about the tale, I will add that I do not doubt its authenticity on the psychological level. Anyone who has investigated the world of occultism will recognize that the occurrence was not an extraordinary one in terms of that world. Western psychologists neglect occultism—psychology's Bohemia—at considerable expense to themselves. Occultists, by way of their own highly developed techniques, are able to induce *and banish* mental phenomena otherwise found only among the gravely (mentally) ill. Such control over little understood phenomena is surely well worth investigating, but investigation is deterred by the shady reputation of occultism, the secrecy and chronic duplicity of occultists, and by other factors. But to get to the story.

A young woman of twenty-five went to see a female medium of rather sinister repute. This medium, in her late thirties, had taken some care to develop a personal legend of association with voodoo practitioners, black magicians, narcotics addicts, criminals, etc. Her face was ghastly pallid (with the aid of cosmetics), and her lips a crimson slash across the gaunt high-cheekboned countenance. She resembled, by intent, a vampire.

The young woman, in part seeking a morbid thrill, but also drawn to the medium for reasons consciously more profound, attended several group seances and then arranged for a private sitting. The medium agreed, but stipulated that her client would have to promise to meet all conditions.

The first of these conditions, as it turned out, was that both should be naked for the sitting. They then sat down in upholstered chairs in a gloomy parlor, facing one another across a space of a few feet. The silence, both before and after the medium entered her trance, was unnerving, and the young woman fidgeted in her chair, half wishing she had not come, but unwilling to leave.

After about half an hour, as she reckoned it, and when she was becoming rather drowsy, the client saw issuing from between the medium's legs, chalk white against what seemed an abnormally large mass of wiry black pubic hair, a vapor that grew rapidly more solid, elongating and taking on a sinuous serpentine form. Fascinated, and more than a little horrified, the young woman watched as this presumed ectoplasmic mass, clearly phallic, approached her. Then, "like an automaton," she spread her thighs and the thing penetrated her own vagina, linking it to the medium's, whence the phallus emanated.

It was, she said, icy cold, and felt somewhat like an icicle, though not quite so hard and glassy and more supple. She recalls experiencing an overwhelming sense of dread, and yet a kind of "unholy pleasure," after which, as best she could tell, she fainted. When she awakened, the medium, still naked, was bending over her; and then the woman attempted to force the nipple of a flabby breast between her lips.

Somehow the young woman managed to fend off her assailant (as she thought of the medium), recover her clothing, and take flight. Her sensations of course recall those of witches in intercourse with their incubi.

4. *The semen and the demon*

For the most part, demonologists were agreed that human females may sometimes conceive as a result of their erotic intercourse with demons. The authorities disagreed, however, on a considerable range of details. They debated such matters as whether the woman is fertilized with the demon's own sperm or with semen injected by the demon but obtained from a human; how demons might be able to transport and inject semen obtained from human males; and who should be considered the father of a child conceived by intercourse with a demon employing human sperm for the insemination.

While it was occasionally argued that demons are fertile, it was much more often held that they are sterile. The most often voiced theory was that a demon would act as a succubus to a male in order to obtain semen; and after that as an incubus to a female, into whose womb the semen was introduced.

But demons might obtain semen in a variety of other ways. Sometimes they would recover semen spilled by masturbators, or in nocturnal pollutions (which the demons caused for that purpose), or in *coitus interruptus* (copulation where the penis is withdrawn and ejaculation occurs outside the vagina). Or semen might be obtained by milking the penes of recently deceased males. The ejaculations of hanged men were yet another source. There then arose questions as to how the corporeal semen might, by incorporeal demons, be transported from one place to another; and how it might be kept warm and fertile or otherwise prevented from spoiling.

Albertus Magnus, *Doctor universalis* and teacher of Aquinas, was one of those who believed that demons act first as succubi, procuring semen from the man, and then as incubi, injecting the semen into the woman. He rejected the argument that the semen becomes infertile in transport, noting that demons are notoriously skillful in preventing the natural dissolution to which material things are subject.

Saint Thomas also thought that demons acted alternately as incubi and succubi, but Ulrich Molitor,[1] fifteenth-century savant and author of *De Lamiis et Phitonicis Mulieribus*, denied that fertilization could be so accomplished, asserting that the semen would certainly spoil along the way (although some said the trip required but an instant, and that the semen was injected into females without any time-wasting preliminaries).

The authors of the *Malleus Maleficarum* thought that the same demon might act as incubus and succubus, or that an incubus demon might receive semen obtained by a (co-operative) succubus. They rejected the idea that cooling or evaporation would endanger the fertility of the sperm, pointing to the great speed with which demons are able to move from place to place. They also considered certain objections raised against the ability of demons to transport matter:

"Also there is the argument that objects that the motion of the whole and of the part is the same thing, just as Aristotle in his *4th Physics* instances the case of the whole earth and a clod of soil; and that therefore if the devils could move a part of the earth, they could also move the whole earth. But this is not valid, as is clear to anyone who examines the distinction. But to collect the semen of things and apply it to certain effects does not exceed their natural power, with the permission of God, as is self-evident."[2]

Prudent demonologists advised burying the dead without delay. This precaution was essential so that incubi would not so readily be able to milk the carcasses of their semen and make illicit use of it. Also, semen from a cadaver carelessly left lying on top of the ground might blow through the air and impregnate some innocent maiden—somewhat after the manner of the pollination of flowers. And if corpses were rudely tossed into the sea, their semen might fertilize fishes, with dreadful sea monsters being born as a consequence of the negligence.[3]

Saint Peter of Palude, a fourteenth-century Thomistic theologian, and Martin of Arles,[4] sixteenth-century writer on demonology, both held that demons fertilize witches with sperm obtained from dead bodies. Remy, however, called this idea of those two learned gentlemen into question, subjected it to rigorous logical analysis, and at length ruled it "as ridiculous as the proverbial dead Donkey's fart." (The dead donkey's fart was indeed proverbial. Many writers spoke of it, and Rabelais, not one to be content with but a single explosion, spoke of "a salvo of farts from the rump of a dead donkey.")

Remy gave a number of arguments against impregnation of women by demons. First of all, he said, it is well known that a member of one species cannot reproduce as a consequence of intercourse with a member of another species. Secondly, that which is devoid of animal life cannot impart animal life to another: "For the process of procreation is governed by the laws of nature, according to which no semen can be fertile unless it comes from a living man."[5] That a demon, acting as a succubus, can obtain semen from a man is unlikely, since the vagina of the succubus is icy cold, and cannot titillate the nervous system sufficiently to cause ejaculation. And even if this occurred, and if the demon hastened to a woman, acting as her incubus, even so it is notorious that the ejaculate of the incubus is cold, and therefore probably infertile.

Remy also spoke elsewhere of this widely reported coldness of the ejaculate of demons. It is a fact, he said, "that all witches who make a Demon free of their bodies (and this they all do when they enter his service, and it is as if it were the first pledge of their pact with him) are completely in agreement in saying that, if the Demon emits any semen, it is so cold that they recoil with horror on receiving it. In Psellus, *De Daemonibus*, Marcus makes a similar statement: 'If they ejaculate any semen it is, like the body from which it comes, so lacking in warmth that nothing can be more unfit or unsuitable for procreation.' " [6]

The coldness of the demon's member and of his semen was noted also by the Moslems. Compare with the testimony of European witches, as set down by the demonologists, this passage from Allen Edwardes' *The Jewel in the Lotus:*

"Among females, voracious incubi made for heated conversation in the bath-house. Some professed disappointment, others complained of utter exhaustion. Not a few complained that the black *jinn*-semen caused an icy feeling in the womb. A young lady coyly but fretfully inquired if she could possibly become impregnated by spirits. M'lady was relieved to learn that *jinn* propagated their own kind, by stealing the seed (*nutfeh*) of living men, and that the cold fluid which entered her matrix was a sterile substance." [7]

(Note, also, the familiar preoccupation with the semen, and the familiar explanations: that it is sterile, and that it is taken by the demons from human males; also, the complaints about the intercourse—besides the coldness of it, the exhaustion following—complaints nonetheless supported, as was so often the case with witches, by no great inclination to put an end once and for all to the experience. It seems likely that whether Christian or Moslem, we are dealing with related or identical experiences.)

Under what conditions may a man be both a virgin and a father? One turns for the answer to this riddle to Aquinas, who explained that demons might gather up semen spilled in nocturnal pollutions and use it to impregnate a woman. Then the man whose seed had been so used would be the father of the child, even though he might never have engaged in any act of sexual intercourse. (Aquinas advanced this view in his *Quaestiones Quodlibetales,* thus rejecting the assertions of those who held that nocturnal emissions could not be so used by demons —being protected by the benevolence of God from such pernicious employment.)

Many occultists still hold the belief that semen ejaculated in "wet dreams" is exempt from utilization by evil spirits. The semen emitted during such dreams, they say, may not, like the physical ejaculate produced by masturbation, or the imaginary semen secreted by the imagination, be used for the purpose of hatching out monsters. This is held to be true for the reason that such ejaculations occur "without an effort of the imagination." In other words, the emission is involuntary, the individual is blameless, and the product may not be misused.

Demons by no means always sought to fertilize their human sex partners. It was often declared that an incubus could impregnate a witch only if she agreed to the insemination. And, of course, some witches, because of age or other causes of barrenness, could not conceive. In such cases, the incubi did not try. This was because, some authors said, demons abhor superfluity. Thus, when copulating with young and fertile witches agreeable to insemination, the demons might go through the transaction of first acting as succubi to obtain the semen, and then injecting it into the witch. But when copulating with prepubertal girls, or with withered and sterile crones, the incubi would not bother to obtain any semen, since that would have been a waste both of energy and of sperm.

One of the few later (seventeenth century) authorities to hold that incubus demons are corporeal and have semen of their own was the Reverend Father Sinistrari of Ameno.[8] "It may be objected," he wrote in his *Demoniality*, "that the sperm of Demons, which must, by nature, be most fluid, could not mix with the human sperm (*sic*), which is thick, and that, consequently, no generation would ensue.

"I reply that . . . the generative power lies in the spirit that comes from the generator at the same time as the spumy and viscous matter; it follows that, although most liquid, the sperm of the Demon, being nevertheless material, can very well mix with the material spirit of the human sperm, and bring about generation."[9]

Sinistrari denied the validity of the traditional belief that demons acted first as succubi, then as incubi. A woman could not be fertilized as the result of such a process, he declared, because "It is . . . not possible that the Demon should preserve in a fit state for generation the sperm he has received; for it were necessary that whatever vessel he endeavoured to keep it in should be equally warm with the human genital organs, the warmth of which is nowhere to be met with but in those organs themselves." [10]

(Had Sinistrari lived in our age of sperm banks, he might perhaps have argued that demons quick-freeze the sperm, then thaw them out when ready for use.)

Sinistrari also adduced a rather typical theologian's argument to prove that an incubus using semen from a human male could not use it to fertilize a woman. The male from whom such semen was taken could not be the father of the child conceived, he pointed out, because it is not by his agency that the sperm reached the womb; and the demon could not be the father, since "the sperm does not issue from his own substance. Consequentially, a child would be born without a father, which is absurd." [11]

Still, he could not reject the "proved" fact that conceptions do result from the intercourse of demons with humans. That was why he necessarily arrived at the conclusion ("subject to correction by our Holy Mother Church") that the "Incubus Demon, when having intercourse with women, bigets (*sic*) the human fetus from his own sperm." [12]

(Sinistrari, one should not be so derelict as to omit pointing out, was a formidable sexologist. Happily, his little book *Peccatum Mutum*[13] has lately become available in this country. In it he deals with such rarely discussed matters as how vicious matrons who have the clitoris large corrupt young boys by buggering them.)[14]

In closing this chapter, I will note that witches sometimes attributed a superabundance of ejaculate to their demon lovers. This is a stock in trade of pornographic literature, and many readers will have noted in the witch testimony a substantial number of other details such as are found among the traditional pornographic stereotypes. One witch mentioned what must be called a super-superabundance. Her incubus, she reported, discharged an amount of semen equal in quantity to the normal output of one thousand human males.

5. *Offspring of demoniality*

For those who believed, as did the masses of the people, though perhaps not the majority of jurists and theologians, that sexual unions of humans with demons might produce offspring, there were many complex theological and scientific problems to be resolved. Certainly not the least of these was whether children born of such unions had souls.

Aristotle had declared that the soul is not contained in the semen, and must therefore be presumed to come from without —i.e., from God. Iamblichus (*De Mysteriis Aegyptiorum*) said that according to the theology of the Egyptians and the Assyrians, the material body of man resulted from the act of coition, but the "character" came from the higher and universal Cause. Seneca held that "If you consider the true origin of mind, it does not grow from the gross earthly body, but descends from that Heavenly Spirit."

Nor was it unanimously believed that the soul enters the "body" at the instant of conception as many occultists hold today—the idea being that copulation creates a psychic vortex into which souls waiting to incarnate are sucked down, entering into and becoming a part of the fertilized ovum.[1] Saint Augustine, for example, instructed that God creates the soul, endows it with reason, and implants it in the body of the foetus at the time when the limbs begin to take shape—approximately forty-five days after conception.

Since a very early stage in the history of mankind's sojourn upon the earth men had believed that there were creatures in the world born of the unions of women with demons, or of the unions of women (and men) with other sorts of supernatural beings. Hebrew thinkers explained the Great Flood on the basis that it was intended by God to sweep the earth clean of the fallen angels and the giants they had spawned in their iniquitous intercourse with the daughters of men. In fact, demons were wantonly seducing even the sons and daughters of Noah himself, so that he felt obliged to caution his children to shun all commerce with them. At this point God sent the Flood, but insofar as he intended to eliminate demons, the Deluge was a washout in more ways than one. Some of the incubi and succubi survived it, and no sooner had the waters subsided and the creatures from the Ark set foot upon the earth than lascivious demons were once again coupling lewdly with the children of Noah and leading them down the scarlet path to perdition.[2]

During the Middle Ages and for some time thereafter, Christians were haunted and terribly tormented by the belief that the coming of the Anti-Christ, Who would destroy the whole world, was imminent. And the Anti-Christ, it was frequently said, would be born as the result of a union of a woman with a demon. Among the prominent and widely heeded pundits who subscribed to this theory were Bellarmin, Suarez, and Maluenda, as well as many others.[3] (It would seem that one would have to believe that unions of demons with women may be fruitful in order to believe that the Anti-Christ might be so conceived; but theologians, by a process of reasoning that would be curious if practiced by some other profession, argued that the fact that the Anti-Christ would be so conceived proved the fruitfulness of such unions.)

The belief in the coming of the Anti-Christ had been taken over by Christianity from Hebrew eschatologists, and during the Dark Ages its vogue had waxed and waned sporadically. But once the idea gained obsessive proportions, in the Middle Ages and thereafter, it is difficult to imagine the terror the prospect inspired in the people. Some attribute the ferocity of the witch trials to the fear that a witch, united with an incubus, would bring forth the Anti-Christ.

During the fourteenth and fifteenth centuries especially, evangelists preyed upon the anxieties of the people and fanned their fear to fever pitch. Finally, early in the sixteenth century, the situation had advanced so near to general panic that the Fifth Lateran Council issued a ban on all preaching to the effect that the coming of the Anti-Christ was imminent.[4]

Some individuals were said—usually by their enemies—to *be* the Anti-Christ, born of a union between a woman and an incubus. Some Catholics, for example, said this of Martin Luther; while Luther's followers, not to be outdone, held that the Anti-Christ was embodied in each successive Pope.

It was seriously reported of any number of famous men that their fathers had been demons. Sinistrari, whose list is neither original nor unusually lengthy, names as offspring of demons the following persons (along with the authorities making the charge):

Romulus and Remus, founders of Rome, according to Livy and Plutarch; Servius-Tullius, the sixth king of Rome, according to Dionysius of Halicarnassus and Pliny the Elder; Plato the Philosopher, according to Diogenes Laertius and Saint Hieronymus; Alexander the Great, according to Plutarch and Quintus-Curtius; Seleucus, king of Syria, according to Justinus and Appianus; Scipio Africanus the Elder, according to Livy; the emperor Caesar Augustus, according to Suetonius; Aristomenes the Messenian, an illustrious Greek commander, according to Strabo and Pausanias; as also Merlin or Melchin the Englishman, born from an incubus and a nun, the daughter of Charlemagne; and, lastly, as shown by the writings of Cochloeus quoted by Maluenda, that damned Heresiarch ycleped, Martin Luther.[5]

Sinistrari does not exhaust the list of those to whom such origin was popularly attributed. Another quite famous offspring of a demon sire was Belkis, Queen of Sheba, who was additionally distinguished by being the possessor of a luxuriant shag of silky black pubic hair that ranged upward to her navel and extended downward to her knees. All of the people of the island of Cyprus were said to descend from demon fathers, as were the Huns. Some of the individuals sired by demons were born, it was said, as a result of the Devil's effort to bring the Anti-Christ into the world. Merlin and Robert der Teufel were two such attempts, and Nero, Mohammed, Luther, and several of the popes were others. Some of the allegations will bear a bit of expansion.

The Huns, for example, were said to have descended from demons after Filmer, King of the Goths, became angry at the camp prostitutes who had attached themselves to his army and drove them off into the woods. There, lacking human lovers (and being insatiably lustful, as prostitutes are always thought to be by the ignorant), they mated with devils and their offspring were the Huns.

Both divine parentage and birth by immaculate conception were sometimes attributed to Plato. The philosopher was born, it was said, of a virgin; while it was held that his father was the god Apollo.

The assertion that one of Plato's parents was a demon comes to us from Diogenes Laertius, the biographical doxographer who is the source of much of the existing knowledge of pre-Socratic philosophy. His version of Plato's birth was of course the one preferred by demonologists. (In any case, and as mentioned, Christians held that all of the old Greek and Roman gods were only demons.)

An account of Martin Luther's origin relates that the Devil took the form of a traveling salesman (jewel merchant) to seduce the daughter of Luther's grandfather, a gentleman generous enough to have provided the incognito Evil One with lodging for the night. (It seems that traveling salesman stories were as much in vogue in the sixteenth century as they are now.)

Another curious little tale describes the conception of Merlin

the magician. The Devil came to the house of Merlin's grand-
mother, who was the wife of a rich Briton, and murdered her
husband. He then easily enough seduced two of the daughters
of the house, but the third daughter resisted His importunate
advances. Still lustful, and disinclined to engage in further
contest with the reluctant virgin, the Devil caused an enchanted
slumber to fall upon her; after that, He assaulted her while she
slept. The girl became pregnant as a consequence of the rape
and would have borne the Anti-Christ; but Merlin was baptized at birth and the Devil's fiendish plot was foiled.

Molitor, however, denied that Merlin was the son of an incubus (or of the Devil), although he conceded that Merlin's
own mother believed such to be the case. But Merlin's mother,
Molitor declared, was deceived by her incubus, who made her
think she was pregnant by causing her to fill with flatulence.
Then, when the time for childbirth arrived, the demon de-
flated her and placed a stolen infant in her bed, so that she
honestly believed herself to have borne it.

Such false pregnancies, no more than gas bloating the belly,
were not infrequently visited upon women by demons who for
one reason or another wished to deceive their human paramours. In the *Malleus Maleficarum* one reads that "At times
also women think they have been made pregnant by an Incubus, and their bellies grow to an enormous size; but when the
time of parturition comes, their swelling is relieved by no more
than the expulsion of a great quantity of wind. For by taking
ants' eggs in drink, or the seeds of spurge or of the black pine,
an incredible amount of wind and flatulence is generated in the
human stomach. And it is very easy for the Devil to cause these
and even greater disorders in the stomach." [6]

It would surely be inexcusable not to recall here that in
1545 at Esslingen a young woman named Margaret experienced a most remarkable and distressing pregnancy following
intercourse with her demon lover. So immense did her belly
become that it was with difficulty visitors to her bedside were
able to find her face and her feet. From within her stomach,

cacophonous, and against all nature, a veritable chorus of animal cries were heard—cocks crowing and hens cackling, the meowing of cats and the bowwowing of dogs, the baaing of sheep and the whinnying of horses, etc. By some accounts of the event this was all a fraud. It is claimed that she was afterward discovered to be wearing a skin stretched tight over hoops, and so to have deceived a host of eminent physicians and learned ecclesiastics who came from around the countryside to have a look at her. Inside of the fraudulent contraption, it is said, was the body of a young woman most delectably formed. Others, however, say that her pregnancy was entirely authentic and that she bore all manner of strange, loathly, and bestial creatures.[7]

Angela de Labarethe (or Angèle de la Bathe), a 56-year-old noblewoman of Toulouse, stands out among witches bearing offspring of incubi for the reason that she was the first woman to be executed by the Inquisition (in 1275) for copulating with a demon. The monstrous child she bore had the head of a wolf and a tail like that of a serpent. She added to the enormity of her crimes by feeding the foul infant—who required such a diet—the flesh of babies, whom she kidnaped and ruthlessly slew.

Some children born of unions with demons might at first blink appear to be quite normal. But they could always be detected. Johann Wier,[8] a sixteenth-century physician who once saved a virgin from being carried off by the Devil, declared that the children born of such damnable conjunctions are puny in appearance, but when weighed prove to be heavier than other children. They die earlier, seldom surviving beyond the seventh year, and meantime display many disagreeable traits of character—laughing mockingly at household misfortunes, keeping everyone awake all night with their bawling, and demanding more milk than any three wet nurses might reasonably be expected to provide (although failing to grow fat as a result of their gluttony).

On the other hand, it was reported that offspring of demoniality sometimes grew at an unusual and even astounding rate, as was the case with such a child born to a Herefordshire woman in 1249. At the age of six months the babe was as tall as a grown man and had a full set of teeth. It may be that a foetus of extraordinary dimensions was carried by a woman of Kingsley who died in 1337, having been tricked into intimacy by a cunning and duplicitous demon. She perished, God be praised, before conceiving, and it required the best efforts of eight stout men to remove her swollen cadaver to its final resting place.

Authorities held that those offspring of unions with demons who survived early childhood often possessed such characteristics as extreme hardiness and boldness, pride and wickedness. They were also likely to be exceptionally tall, which the physician Vallesius[9] attributed to the fact that when demons wish to procreate children they go as succubi to the most robust men, selecting from among such virile and large-limbed stock those whose semen is particularly abundant, thick, warm, and rich in spirits.

It was also believed that some of the infants seemingly born of demon-human intercourse were not "real," or not authentically human. They were "effigies," or "fantastic," used by the Devil to deceive women and to make them think they had given birth. Such fantastic infants usually disappeared in a few hours or days or weeks, so that their mothers thought that the Devil had spirited them away. However, some few remained with their mothers for several years, and a woman could not really be certain (if she had lain with a demon) whether her child was authentic or merely an effigy. (No more, it may be said, could a husband know what it was that lay at his side in the bed by night. That seeming flesh might be but an effigy of his wife who could be miles away engaging in the adulterous fornications and even more sinister debaucheries of the Sabbat.)

Many instances were cited of women giving birth to Elves after intercourse with demons. The Elf-children assisted the witches with their evil deeds, delighting to inflict harm on all mankind. Elves were usually, though not always, born in lots of two, or as twins. At one period it was believed that Elves were the only possible offspring of unions with demons.

Relating a few more beliefs about conceptions resulting from demoniality will have to suffice, although the subject is far from exhausted. One of these was that children born of such intercourse are very often stillborn. Another belief was that by special copulative techniques, women and demons could conceive, according to their preference, children who would be either giants or pygmies. Some writers dared not mention how this was accomplished, but the mystery seems no more odious than others already revealed.

The method was simple. Since it was thought that the amount of semen injected into the womb determined the size of the child, all that was needed was a sparse ejaculation to produce a pygmy, a copious one to yield a giant.

6. *Sexual psychology of demons*

Why, wondered the greatest thinkers of the Church, did demons enter into sexual relationships with humans? Were they erotically stimulated by men and women? and did they derive sensual pleasure from their fornications with them? Was the intercourse merely a device employed by the demon to degrade the human partner and lead him or her the more deeply into sin? Was the sexual relationship the means by which the human was bound to the demon or kept under the influence of his evil forces? Was procreation of monstrous offspring—above all the procreation of the Anti-Christ—the true purpose? These and many other questions were asked and I will consider a few of the typical theories here. Others occur elsewhere in the text to cast additional light upon the problems of the sexual psychology of demons.

One of the weightiest authorities to hold that demons experience pleasure in sexual intercourse with humans, and desire it, was Saint Augustine. However, there was an equally authoritative opinion—that of Aquinas—to the contrary. Saint Thomas asserted that demons are incapable of entertaining erotic desires and that they are motivated, rather, by their wish to lead mankind into abominable sin. The Aquinas version was adopted by most, though not all, later demonologists.

Hincmar, Archbishop of Rheims, was among those declaring that demons lust after mortals. So too was William of Auvergne,[1] who attributed the Christian rule that the heads of women should be covered since lustful demons are powerfully stimulated by the sight of long and beautiful hair.[2] Females were also cautioned against the use of cosmetics, the wearing of jewelry, and too gaudy or elegant attire on the basis that they might thus call themselves to the attention of amorous incubi.

Michael Psellus,[3] in the eleventh century, declared—having been advised by a Mesopotamian holy man knowledgeable about such matters—that demons are capable of sexual desire for human beings. Tauler, a fourteenth-century mystic, described demons as insanely lustful, as well as insane in their fury, malice, and obstinacy. However, Tauler counseled, this insanity in no way interferes with the workings of a demon's intellect or impairs his physical strength. Others thought otherwise, holding that demons are fully aware that they will be punished for their misdeeds in corrupting men and women, yet persist in the corruption because their hatred of mankind is so all-consuming as to cause them to behave irrationally and so bring about their own punishment and torment.

Sinistrari, attributing lust to incubi, noted that they often copulated with animals, especially horses. This being the case, he pointed out, it cannot be reasonably argued that incubi are motivated only by a desire to bring about the ruination of souls (which the lower animals do not possess). We must understand, rather, that the demon's passion is a sexual one. (Sinistrari's remarks apply only to those beings he calls incubi, and he denies that they are evil. He allows, however, for the existence of evil spirits, which are incorporeal by contrast to incubi, which have bodies.)

Sinistrari did not hold that lust is the exclusive motive of the incubus in having sexual intercourse with humans. He said that there are two conditions under which such copulations occur. In his relations with witches, the demon uses the intercourse as a means of binding them to him. Then there are the copulations with humans to whom he is sexually attracted, and to whom he presents himself as a lover.

As for witches, Sinistrari said, after the demon has concluded his pact with them, and after the performance of various rituals, the following occurs:

"The solemn profession being thus performed, each (witch) has assigned to himself a Devil, called *Magistellus* or Assistant Master, with whom he retires in private for carnal satisfaction; the said Devil being, of course, in the shape of a woman if the initiated person is a man, in the shape of a man, sometimes of a satyr, sometimes of a buck-goat, if it is a woman who has been received as a witch." [4]

Where the relationship is strictly sexual:

"At other times also the Demon, whether Incubus or Succubus, copulates with men or women from whom he receives none of the sacrifices, homage or offerings which he is wont to exact from wizards or witches, as aforesaid. He is then but a passionate lover, having only one desire: the carnal possession of the loved ones. Of this there are numerous instances to be found in the authors . . ." [5]—some of which he gives.

The above might be understood in psychological terms as a distinction between erotic phantasies solicited by the individual consciousness, and erotic phantasies that come uninvited. Or, if it is to be maintained that conscious evocation of such phantasies is always illusory, then it is still possible to distinguish between free phantasies which, so to speak, determine their own forms, and circumscribed or delimited phantasies which occur only within forms determined by ritual or tradition.

This last is an important distinction, and in general it may be useful in distinguishing between phantasy material of an occult nature and material arising from natural (though perhaps pathological) causes.

The witch phantasies, for example, occur within the formal framework of incubi and succubi definitions, the Sabbat, etc., and for this reason they are all more or less similar. Nocturnal pollutions, on the other hand, are accompanied by dreams not at all so stereotyped, and much more dependent upon the individuality of the dreamer.

On the negative side of the question of whether demons experience lust were arrayed such formidable witchcraft authorities as Remy and Boguet. Remy recalls that "Plutarch, in his *Numa*, arguing against the beliefs of the Egyptians, says that it is absurd to believe that Demons are captivated by human beauty and grace, and have intercourse with mankind for the sake of carnal pleasure. For nature provides physical beauty as a stimulant to propagation, of which Demons have no need, since they were created in the beginning of a fixed number. . . ."[6]

Boguet affirmed that demons are without lust "since carnal desire is necessary only to those who need to supply a successor to continue their kind." Since angels and demons do not perish, he said, and have no need for successors, "it follows that spirits are immune from the flames of love, and that they are without those members in which sensual desire is generated, namely, the lower parts of mankind."[7] This opinion, that a penis or a vagina would be superfluous equipment for a demon, even if the demon possessed a body, is expressed by some others. It could have been argued, however, that demons are capable of lust and/or possess sexual organs, the better to tempt mankind—such temptation being an important part of a demon's function, according to many authorities.

Some argued that lust could not possibly be the motivation for demons cohabiting with humans for the reason that if demons had sexual desires, then these could be much better satisfied with other demons. And if the human form, by some gross perversion to which demons were prey, attracted them more than the forms of their own kind, then any one of them could assume a human form far more perfect, more beautiful and titillating than that of any existing human being.

According to the Talmud, demons do in fact copulate and procreate with one another. By some accounts, these devils, unlike those usually described by Christian writers, are either male or female, and capable of having sexual relations not only with one another, but also with humans. Wives of demons, certain learned rabbis said, were entirely faithful to their husbands when it came to relations with other devils; but they copulated with human males and did not consider the activity important enough to be classed as adultery.

There was little doubt that individual demons seemed to show preference for certain types of human lovers, but it was difficult to establish the precise basis for the preference. Some witches declared that it was mainly esthetic. Thus, fifteen-year-old Marie de Marigrane of Biarritz informed the judges that demons copulate with beautiful women from the front, but with ugly ones from behind.

However, some held that demons preferred old and ugly hags who would appreciate their lovers more than would other women, and so better do their bidding. (This view of the merits of older women as mistresses is often advanced on the merely human level, and Benjamin Franklin, in a famous letter, indicated that he was a subscriber to it. The most famous of kite-flyers added that in any case all cats are gray in the dark.) The *ugliness* of unions with decrepit and time-eroded ladies was also held to be a source of (esthetic) delight to demons, and they might intensify the effect by themselves assuming hideous or grotesque forms.

Of those who maintained that demons preferred pretty girls and young women, it was customary to point out that this was not an esthetic bias entirely: Such girls and young women, being more attractive to men as well as to demons, were better able to seduce males to wallow in fleshly depravities, and to lead them astray generally, as the demons encouraged the women to do.

That demons sought carnal pleasure was believed indicated by their occasionally tightening up the slack vaginas of their mistresses—sometimes with the consequence that the husband of the witch could no longer effect entry. Since the penes of demons were in some cases no larger than a witch's little finger, even the aforementioned tightening might leave the vagina overly capacious, so that another orifice was required. This may have been the explanation for a marvel that befell Antide Colas, a witch of Betoncourt in the district of Baume.

On July 11, 1598, Antide was thoroughly examined by a chirurgeon called Nicolas Milliere, who discovered that she possessed an auxiliary sex organ just below her navel, and "quite contrary to nature." So far as Milliere was concerned, it was an insensitive sheath, since he pushed his probe deep into it, in the presence of several witnesses, without causing the witch any pain. But Antide admitted that the cavity was used by her incubus to have intercourse with her, while the "natural hole" was used in the usual way by her husband (which might also suggest that Antide's was a more than ordinarily fastidious incubus). There was a most wonderful aspect to all this, since when Antide was taken to the prison at Dôle, medical examination showed that the second vagina had closed up and was covered over with scar tissue. In view of her monstrously dissolute behavior in carnally consorting with a demon, and by way of an unnatural hole at that, she was burned alive on February 20, 1599.

That some demons were jealous of their human lovers was an established fact. This did not necessarily mean, however, that an erotic attachment was responsible for the jealousy. Demons might be possessive on other scores, or it might be simply a matter of pride. But whatever the reason, the wrath of a jealous demon was not to be taken lightly.

A case in point was that of the mother of Guibert of Nogent in the eleventh century. She was loved by a demon, but did not return the affection of the incubus and instead took a human husband. The demon, by way of retaliation, made her husband impotent for a period of seven years, after which the spell was broken by dint of "perseverance." Later, the good woman's husband was taken prisoner, and in the husband's absence the incubus attempted to assault her in her bed. And yet, most wonderful and reassuring to relate, with the help of the Virgin the incubus was forced to remain at a safe distance.

Another case of a jealous and vengeful demon was recounted

by Erasmus. The human mistress of an incubus was having a furtive affair with the son of the local tavern-keeper at Schiltach, near Freiburg. The demon, discovering that he had been cuckolded, rose up in righteous outrage and in April of 1533 burned down the whole village.

Demons might be jealous not only of human rivals, but also of their fellow demons. Then, not even at the Sabbat was the witch-mistress allowed to participate in the orgies or otherwise have lewdly to do with incubi or sorcerers. It also occurred that humans were jealous of their demon lovers, whether incubi or succubi. This is said to be much more common, however, among Moslems, who tend to be insanely jealous of their *jinn* when they suspect them of inconstancy.

When a demon was so attached to his human mistress that he wanted nothing to do with any other mortal, and wished to impregnate his beloved, he was obliged to enlist the assistance of a succubus demon in obtaining some semen for him. This semen, once procured, he would quickly inject into his mistress during copulation—though only, some said, when the stars were propitious and conception so assured.

Of those who held the belief that demon-human unions could be fruitful without benefit of borrowed sperm, some argued that it was just the desire to procreate that most powerfully motivated the incubus. It was believed by some that such offspring of demons, unlike their fathers, would have souls—and presumably even demons enjoy pondering the prospect that their children will have more than they have had. (That unions with human beings will produce offspring possessed of souls, and therefore immortal, has also been held in the case of elementals, or elementary spirits, who are said to copulate with humans on the same basis as the demons just mentioned. There was, however, a risk involved for the humans: They might lose their souls in such contacts, although it is only fair to admit that this happened infrequently.)

Probably the view most widely held by demonologists was that demons cohabited with humans in order to acquire power over them, and then plunge them deep into pits of deadly sin. For example, Boguet said that the incubus futters females "because he knows that women love carnal pleasures, and he means to bind them to his allegiance by such agreeable provocations. Moreover, there is nothing which makes a woman more subject and loyal to a man than that he should abuse her body." [8] After relating that demons serve men as succubi for the same purpose, Boguet adds: "There is also another reason for the coupling of the Devil with a witch, which is that the sin may thereby become more grievous. For if God abominates the coupling of an infidel with a Christian, how much more shall He detest that of a man with the Devil? Moreover, by this means a man's natural semen is wasted, with the result that the love between man and wife is often turned to hatred, than which no worse a misfortune could happen to the state of matrimony." [9]

The sexual act between the demon and the witch also bound the witch to his service in a magical way, while she gained from it an increase in the potency of her supernormal powers. The coition was an essential part of the pact between the two, and some held that in essence it *was* the pact, with the additional ceremonies, oath-taking, etc., no more than mere trappings and folderol.

Where the pleasure of the demon was thought to be bound up with the degradation of the human, it was argued that in this fact lay the explanation of why demons took the forms of beasts, used the bodies of corpses, etc. That was to say, demons forced the witches to engage in bestiality and necrophilia, more grievous offenses than mere coitus. It has been noted that in the latter part of the seventeenth century witch-demon relationships often began with a formal marriage. This was probably regarded as an additional sacrilege and was performed for the reason just cited. Also along these lines, it was the claim of De Lancre that the Devil only rarely copulated with young girls, because He preferred to wait until they were married, when the intercourse would be adulterous. Others, however, asserted that demons especially delighted in the taking of maidenheads—the defloration of a virgin being at least as damnably delicious a sin as adultery. The authoritative Aquinas advised that demons encouraged these human sins because they interfered with human good.

It might be added that where the demon is seen as deriving pleasure from the degradation and damnation of the human, his motive still might be regarded as sexual—sadistic, as we might say of a human engaging in such behavior, and if we were able to demonstrate that the pleasure taken was libidinous.

7. Demoniality: forms of the union

In seeking to understand the erotic pathology of witchcraft one should pay particular attention to the forms of the sexual unions in which witches and demons participated, and to the various roles assumed by the witches and the demons in the different relationships. It is also possible to learn from these much about everyday human desires, especially as they existed at the time, but also as they exist (filtered through the witch era) presently.

Given the peculiar and damaging Christian equation of sex with evil, it should come as no surprise that the Devil may be considered the Ideal Lover, capable of fulfilling the most intense unconscious as well as conscious cravings of women.

With Him, since at the first embrace one has given oneself over completely to evil and damnation, all restraints may be cast aside, all cravings indulged. There is nothing more to lose, and so all becomes permissible—and, with the aid of the Devil's supernatural powers, possible.

What a woman does with her incubus may be what she would wish to do with her man—if she were not a good woman, if she were not afraid, if repression and suppression did not frustrate and inhibit her.

Of course, this unrestrained indulgence exacerbates conflicts and gives rise to guilt, so that the intercourse is held to be painful, and even horrible; but the falsity and profound bad faith of the protestations of suffering and horror as the dominant aspects of the experience stand revealed in the obstinacy with which the relationship continues to be pursued, or in the "futility" of all attempts at resistance.

It seems clear that in the great majority of cases of demon-human sex relations there is neither conscious, unalloyed pleasure nor pure revulsion and pain, but a mixture of the two; as indeed is the case, though much less pronouncedly, with most sexual relationships between humans. And with the average person it is only consciously that pure pleasure is ever desired. The unconscious, mutilated by the blade of humanity's neurotic and savage pasts, lusts after more complicated, and ambivalent, fulfillments. I will have more to say about this in the analysis of medical and psychological theories of witchcraft pathology to follow.

The variations of the intercourse, and the roles played by the demons in it, were many in number and nuance. Demon lovers could be, as few human lovers can, almost all things to those who entered into relationships with them.

Most demonologists believed that there were no perversions in which demons did not engage with their human lovers, and that such couples even managed to invent some enormities previously unknown (and which did the imaginative powers of inquisitors no small amount of credit). However, there were a few who did not think that demons would stoop to perverted practices; while some held that only the "lower type" of demon would engage in any form of intercourse other than coitus.

Martin del Rio, a Jesuit and one of the most renowned, influential, and vicious of the demonologists, remarked of the belief that demons shun unnatural vice, that they seemed to do so in Spain, Germany, and France, but not in Italy. However, this may have been no more than a personal prejudice of the type which holds that Frenchwomen are unanimously given to the practice of fellatio and Arabs, with equal unanimity, to bum-scuttling.

In any case, Peronette de Ochiis, who was no Italian, was executed in 1462 for having relations *contra naturam* with men and demons, and for prostituting herself to them. She was found guilty of other crimes as well, and was made to sit naked for three minutes on a red hot iron before being put to death.

Pico della Mirandola was one of those who believed that copulation with demons gave witches much greater pleasure than they could possibly achieve with human lovers. This, Mirandola said, was because the demon took a form consistent with the witch's ideal of beauty and sexual attractiveness, and because his penis was larger than a man's. This largeness, he continued, caused an intensity of delight in the most private parts. The intensity of delight was caused, too, in Mirandola's opinion, by the sex techniques employed by demons, who could agitate their members inside the vagina, causing them to spin, throb, etc., and so yield titillations no man could hope to rival. Succubi, he noted, similarly affected men by virtue of their great beauty and the skill with which they could control their genitalia and so manipulate the male organ.

It was an established fact that a demon might seduce a man or woman by assuming the form of the individual's ideal lover. Had not Mephistopheles proved that this was the case when he assumed the form of Helen of Troy in order to please Faust?

So far as the pleasure aspect was concerned, even those who insisted that copulations with demons were usually painful, might allow for exceptions. Thus, it was written in the *Malleus Maleficarum* that while the intercourse was usually painful, the demons would make it pleasurable on certain occasions—"the most sacred times of the whole year . . . such as Christmas, Easter, Pentecost and other Feast Days." [1] Sexual acts which were pleasurable (especially if committed on holy days) were considered to be much more offensive to God than those which yielded no pleasure, or were painful and disgusting. Many a person holding similar convictions has become frigid or impotent as a consequence, in our own time as well as formerly. What better defense, after all, against the sin of ecstatic sexual intercourse than a penis that will not fully erect or female genitalia devoid of feeling?

One female who found pleasure with her demon all the year

'round was a nymphet of a nun named Gertrude. Johann Wier says that she found such rapture in the arms of her incubus, and was so wantonly enamoured of him, that she wrote him many passionate love letters—the cause of her downfall.

There are cases where the intercourse is claimed to have been painful, but where in the telling it becomes obvious that the pleasure aspect more than counterbalanced the pain. Surely it was so with Françoise Fontaine. The Devil first appeared to her as a grand gentleman, with flashing eyes and a black beard. So carried away was she by his conquistadorial appearance and manner that she immediately obeyed his imperious command that she remove her clothing. He copulated with her twice (after masterfully throwing her down on the bed), each time for about half an hour. He was extremely passionate, biting her breasts (as she proved to the court by displaying His tooth marks); and his penis was black, thick, and hard as a piece of flint rock, so that the engagements were painful. He took leave of her gallantly, not forgetting to kiss her and fondle her breasts and privy parts. His semen, Françoise said, was cold, as was his member, and on one occasion they became locked together, like a pair of dogs, and had to remain so for some time.

Surprisingly, not a few incubi and succubi inclined to monogamous relationships. Their jealousy of their human partners has been mentioned elsewhere. And sometimes the unholy unions, devilish travesties on the sacred and sublime institution of wedlock, lasted for as long as forty or fifty years. Then, only the death of the human partner separated the lovers.

Men were more given to participation in such long-term relationships than women. Female witches often had successions of demon lovers, or they might even retain several incubi at a time, or whole harems of them. Part of the explanation lay in the fact that relations with a succubus were more exhausting than those with an incubus (although the last-mentioned were exhausting enough). But succubi, like vampires, often drained their lovers dry, reducing them to impotence, and occasionally to such degrees of nervous prostration and debility that death resulted.

To tempt the still uncorrupted, or to fire the jaded and flagging ardors of mortal lovers, demons sometimes turned pornographers, painting erotic pictures, or singing songs. Various obscene writings are also attributed to the Devil, either by direct authorship or indirectly, by inspiring the writers. (Nor is all Devil-inspired writing necessarily obscene or pornographic. In fact, Giovanni Papini, in his book *Il Diavolo*, quotes André Gide as asserting that there can be no great work of art without the collaboration of the Devil.)[2] One piper at a witches' frolic confessed to a clergyman that "the Foul Fiend taught him a Baudy song to sing and play." The song, the piper added, was soon a great hit amongst the teenagers of the area. Bawdy and obscene tunes were also played, sung, and danced to at the Sabbats.

It had long been known that the Evil One was a pornographer. In an infamous incident, He decorated the walls of Saint Anthony's hermitage with indelicate and lust-provoking drawings and paintings. Unfortunately, they were not preserved.

One of the most reprehensible of the Devil's wiles, used by Him to seduce pious but unworldly and gullible maidens, was to approach them quoting Scripture and offering to instruct them religiously. Once He had gained some innocent young thing's confidence by His seeming devoutness and erudition in matters sacred, He would slyly and imperceptibly introduce into His teachings certain subtle and terribly toxic heresies, which would gradually undermine the maiden's moral fibre. At last, she would be as putty in His clutch, and He would lead her to the performance of deeds she would previously never have dared contemplate—perversions so pernicious she dared not reveal them even to her confessor. (Although it should be noted that similar instruction has been given, and with the same end in mind, by both clergymen and the laity who have succeeded by such means where all other methods would surely have failed.)

To summon one's incubus seems to have been a simple matter, and he would come swiftly, before the desire that had moved the witch to beckon him could subside. Johann Klein, in a dissertation that was well received by the august faculty of the University of Rostock, reported that to call her incubus a witch needed only to cry aloud: *"Komm Raster und Knaster mie."* The incubus, appearing almost before the words were out of the witch's mouth, would be fully prepared for intercourse. Klein also conveyed the valuable intelligence that copulations with demons occur at night or by day, indoors or out, and in bed or on the floor.[3]

The position for sexual intercourse favored by demons, or so it was said, was one where the approach is from the rear, and which is referred to by the vulgar as "dog-fashion." Some held that God would not permit demons to use the man-above woman-below position, because that one is reserved for those joined in holy wedlock by the Church. Theologians have traditionally shown a preference for the man-above woman-below position. It will be recalled that this method of copulating is sometimes referred to as the "missionary position" by natives of primitive lands where men of the cloth have labored to convert the heathen.

If it was the case that restrictions were imposed on demons as to which coital positions they might and might not employ, it does not seem that they were otherwise fettered. The diversity of their perversions was great, and sometimes the conditions of their intercourse were also, by everyday standards, unorthodox. According to Martin Luther, for example, the Devil likes to catch young girls in the water and make them pregnant (although Luther says elsewhere that the Devil cannot propagate). Luther himself was sometimes said to be the product of subaqueous fornication, his mother having been visited by an incubus while she was bathing.

An estimate of the frequency with which demons copulate with witches was tendered by "the law-giver of Saxony," Benedict Carpzov, a seventeenth-century monster who was further distinguished by having read the Bible through fifty-three times and for having signed the death warrants of twenty thousands persons. Carpzov declared that witches have sex relations with devils two or three times a week. He added that as a result of such heinous connections they give birth to Elves.

The Devil as rapist

The year 1400 is often given as an approximate turning point in the Devil's career as a carnal consort of human females. Previous to that time, He was for the most part a rapist, prevailing by force, by threat, or by chicanery. But in the fifteenth century and thereafter these tactics became, with a few exceptions, unnecessary. At most, He seduced; and about as often, He was actively solicited by those depraved creatures called witches.

The assertion that women (witches) engaged in demoniality not against their wills but by choice was of course necessary to fix maximum responsibility and guilt (and so justify maximum punishment). That is, the women who freely chose to commit so abominable a sin as cohabitation with a demon were obviously guilty of a greater evil than those women who were victims of rape—even though it might be held that the latter were usually not altogether guiltless since they must in some blameworthy way have aroused the demon's desire. (The idea that rape victims are seldom completely innocent is no new one, and it was even recognized that the state of mind of the victim, as distinguished from any overt word or gesture, might provoke a rape attack.)

The belief that demons committed rapes seems to have been abandoned, as a consequence of the abandonment at about the same time of the belief that demons are sexually attracted to mortals. (If demons experienced no desire, they would not rape.) From the fifteenth century on, and allowing for exceptions, demons were to be regarded as engaging in intercourse with humans in order to lead them into sin, to bind them to Satan's service, etc. And for this it was required that the woman's (or man's) submission be voluntary, and so culpable.

Saint Augustine was an early (fifth century) commentator on rapes of humans by demons, and he makes it plain that early Christian thinkers derived many of their ideas on the subject from pagan mythology. In his *City of God,* Augustine wrote that "It is widely credited, and such belief is confirmed by the direct or indirect testimony of thoroughly trustworthy people, that Sylvans and Fauns, commonly called Incubi, have frequently molested women, sought and obtained from them coition. There are even Demons, whom the Gauls call Duses or Elfs, who very regularly indulge in those unclean practices: the fact is testified by so many and such weighty authorities, that it were impudent to doubt it."

(It should be remarked that the incubi and succubi of the later Middle Ages and after were quite different from the mythological creatures mentioned by Augustine, and which along .with such others as satyrs and centaurs often molested women. As Catholic demonology developed, a quite distinct variety of demon was evolved, and he no more resembled the creations of the Greeks than the Christian sex ethic, guilt-ridden and cast over with a pall of morbidity, resembled the joyous and healthy Greek sex ethic.)

The early writers told of many cases of rapes of women by demons, and advanced theories as to how such demons might best be dealt with. Saint Thomas saved from the unwelcome attentions of a lustful demon a beautiful woman who came to him for help. The demon had raped her nightly for five years, but Saint Thomas "sealed her" in the name of the Father, the Son, and the Holy Ghost, so that the demon could no more penetrate her. Saint Jerome told of a virtuous noblewoman who was visited in her bed by a devil in the form of her archbishop, and who took more vigorous, or at least more physical, action. She screamed at the top of her lungs for the servants, and when they arrived she had the incubus tossed roughly out of the house.

Some said that a virgin was protected by God or by angels from the assaults of incubi, but others denied that this was so, and there were many tales to the contrary (including a large number about children of two to six or seven years, presumably virgins, raped by demons—statutorially, when not forcibly).

It has been mentioned elsewhere that virgins, even though they might have lain willingly with their incubi, were said to be found with the hymen still intact after the intercourse. These were no longer truly virgins, however, since their souls had been soiled despite the fact that their bodies might provide no evidence of the spoliation. And the question of course arose whether virgins, forcibly deflowered by demons (and sorcerers), did not remain virgins by God's grace, for it was already well established that God could miraculously preserve the virginity of those violently and viciously assaulted by men. It will be recalled in this connection that Christian virgins, by Roman law, had to be raped before they could be executed—a function frequently performed by the executioner—since it was not permissible in Rome to put a virgin to death. But Basil the Great, in his book *On True Virginity*, had given assurance that in such cases God "rendered vain the assaults of sinners upon their flesh and kept their bodies unsoiled by the miracle of His divine power."

Demons intent upon having their way with unco-operative females did not hesitate to turn kidnapers. For example, it was said that when women stirred the lusts of demons, the incubi might take them captive and carry them off to some remote place, there to ravish them and keep them as love slaves until they mercifully died. But these demons were prudent and did not wish to call needless attention to their felonies. Therefore, they would leave in the places of the abducted females wonderfully fashioned effigies, which appeared to be the true corpses of their victims. The effigies would be duly discovered, wept over, and buried. However, women on occasion managed to escape from their demon lovers, so that a woman thought dead and buried might be seen by some traveler to a distant land, who would bring the terrible tidings of a fate worse than death home with him. Thus did the foul tactic become known and the priesthood alerted to the menace.

A case reported in the fifteenth century provides an exception to several general rules: that virgins could not be raped, that rapes did not occur after 1400, and that women are assailed only by lone incubi. But in this instance, a virgin was brutally overpowered and molested by three incubi, who assaulted her repeatedly. Another report of a gang rape by demons had a male as its victim—a holy man who was overcome and made to sin most grievously and often by a group of succubi in the forms of beautiful young girls.

It might further be added that demons, diabolically devoid of all goodness and charity, and certainly of all reverence, did not even respect the sanctity of the confessional, and there propositioned and carnally had their way, by force if blandishments proved insufficient, with both virgins and nuns. Such lecherous behavior by priests was also not unknown, so that the victim was by no means able to say with certainty whether it had been a servant of Satan or of God who in clerical guise had so villainously (though perhaps deliciously) abused her.

The Devil as child-molester

The Devil was greatly given to intercourse of all kinds with children (though as might be expected a few denied that such was the case), and thousands of instances of His pedophilia are recorded. Every witch, by some accounts, was continually exhorted to pervert and deprave both her (or his) own children and the children of others, to lead them into fornication with demons, heresy, blasphemy, etc. Some mothers, perhaps of especially incorruptible offspring, were ordered to slaughter them and so provide delicacies for the banquet tables at the Sabbat.

Among those who denied that demons copulated with children were two eminent witch-scourgers, De Lancre and Boguet. De Lancre asserted that the demons much preferred to fornicate with married women—so that the intercourse was adulterous—and for this reason, and not on account of any scruple, scorned children and virgins. Boguet held that "Satan pursues only those who have passed the age of twelve or fourteen; since in his cunning and guile he knows full well that an agreement with those who are younger than this cannot be binding, seeing that such have no judgement or discretion." [4] Apparently the distinguished jurist could not conceive of even a devil who would fail to bow to legalisms.

In any case thousands of children are reported to have been executed for lewdly coupling with incubi and succubi. In Würzburg alone more than three hundred children of such ages as three and four years confessed to sexual intercourse with demons. After age seven, a child was considered sufficiently corrupt and incorrigible to be put to death—an age limitation many judges and attorneys objected to as being unrealistically over-lenient.

One Sabbat was reported at which more than two thousand children were in attendance and became forever corrupted. That children could become debauched and criminalized beyond redemption by such experiences was not to be doubted. After all, theologians pointed out, God permits even infants to die, and without being baptized, so that although seemingly innocent of even the slightest wrongdoing they are denied entrance into heaven. It is not for man to inquire too closely into these mysterious matters. God's goodness is perfect, but assuredly there are times when it transcends all human understanding.

The question of whether children should be executed (or merely tortured or whipped) for witchcraft and other vile dealings with the Devil troubled some of the more humane thinkers,

though probably a majority favored capital punishment whatever the age of the offender. One of these proponents of the
execution of children was Boguet, who was always able to cite
precedents, usually Biblical, to justify his slaughters.

"Thirdly," Boguet wrote, in a lengthy discussion of the problem, "I base my opinion on the law *Excipiuntur*, which punishes with death a child below the age of puberty for not having cried when its master was killed. In accordance with this
law many children of less than twelve years of age have been
sentenced to death.

"Finally, I have the memorable authority of Holy Scripture;
for forty-two children of the city of Bethel were devoured by
two bears because they mocked Elisha. For if God was so angered by the insult to His prophet, how must His wrath be kin-
dled when He is Himself despised and outraged and denied,
seeing that He is jealous of His honour!" [5] Boguet also adhered
to the theory, often used to justify executions of children, that
witches never reform (or: Once a witch, always a witch!).
Since most of the accused youngsters were children of witches,
that was another good reason to get rid of them, since children
of witches always follow in the foul footsteps of their parents.[6]

Most often the children were handed over to the demons by
their own mothers and fathers. Jeanne Harvilliers, condemned
at Ribemont in 1578, was given to the Devil by her mother
when she was twelve, and continued to have intercourse with
the same incubus up to her fiftieth year. The demon was not
jealous and permitted her to marry and also to engage in orgies with sorcerers and other incubi at the Sabbats. But he
amused himself by cuckolding her husband, and would often
copulate with Jeanne while she was lying in bed at her husband's side. She testified that her husband remained unaware
of these repeated adulteries, because the incubus was visible
only to her. One would gather that the intercourse was less
than ragingly passionate to have escaped notice.

Françoise Hacquart related that she was compelled to give
her daughter Jeanne to the Devil when the child was but seven

—and Jeanne confirmed her mother's confession. The court, as was sometimes the case, showed the child mercy and she escaped burning. Such juvenile beneficiaries of the leniency of the court might be stripped naked and flogged three times around the stakes where their mothers were being burned alive.

Guazzo,[7] author of the *Compendium Maleficarum,* told of Dominique Falvet, a girl of twelve, who was out picking rushes with her mother when a demon in human form accosted them. He copulated with the child while her mother (presumably a witch) looked on; and then, with the daughter as a spectator, he did the same with her mother. This voyeuristic-exhibitionistic aspect is present in a great many accounts of intercourse with demons, and at the Sabbats it may have functioned as an aphrodisiac and as a means of breaking down individual resistances by allowing group participation.

When mothers did not surrender their children to demons, the child might still be raped by the incubus (or succubus). Remy took note of the case of Catharina Latomia of Marche, who revealed at Haraucourt in 1587 that she had been the victim of such an assault. Although she was "not yet of an age to suffer a man," Remy said, the demon "twice raped her . . . and she very nearly died from the injuries she received by that coition." [8]

A boy complained to his bishop of a succubus who came into his room through the closed door and forced him to have intercourse with her. The bishop's prescription of fasting and prayer, and a change of rooms, is said to have been efficacious.

There was some dispute about the minimum age at which a child might have relations with demons. Bodin,[9] in his *De la demonomanie des sorciers,* wrote that the Devil seduces girls of six—"*qui est l'aage de cognoissance aux filles.*"

However, a parish priest of a village near Bonn, drawing upon the authority of the Inquisition, said that in the seventeenth century "Children of three and four years have devils for their paramours."

Still, no childish delinquent ever exceeded the record set by a witch who confessed her lifelong depravity in 1674. She had begun her fornications with demons, she said, while still a foetus in her mother's womb, and had never desisted from them. She was married three times, was barren with her husbands, but had children by her incubus. However, a physician who examined her denied her claim that she had given birth to the offspring of her incubus. Those offspring, said the physician, a Dr. Ettmueller[10] of Leipzig, were only fecal discharges laboriously brought forth under conditions of severe constipation.

Incest

While demons could not themselves engage in incest (or at least there is no record of a demon's having done so), they encouraged, and sometimes demanded, that witches participate in incestuous unions. Such unions—earlier attributed by Christians to the Cathars, the Luciferians and other heretical groups —were held to be a customary and even essential aspect of the Sabbat.

The anonymous *Errores Gazariorum* describes a Sabbat the main feature of which was incest: fathers with daughters, mothers with sons, brothers with sisters. There was no intercourse with the demons present, but the Devil presided and was kissed under His tail. Children were eaten, there were dancing and sacrilege, etc. Members were sworn to try to prevent marriages—perhaps to encourage fornication, or to create a group of frustrated persons who would fall easy prey to the proffered orgies of the Sabbat.

According to De Lancre, the incestuous unions of mothers

with sons were a usual Sabbat highpoint, with the aim being the impregnation of the mother. Boguet also mentions this, and explains the purpose:

"After the dancing the witches begin to couple with each other; and in this matter the son does not spare his mother, nor the brother his sister, nor the father his daughter; but incest is commonly practised. The Persians also believed that, to be a competent and complete witch and magician, a person must be born of a mother by her son." [11] (Others hold that the true Persian doctrine was that sorceresses or female witches only are so conceived. If a male child is born of the union he is not endowed with any special magical powers.)[12]

Procuring and prostitution

Demons very frequently acted as procurers, and sometimes they either patronized prostitutes or themselves engaged in prostitution. Many witches were also harlots, but this was rarely if ever at the instigation of their incubi. Demons may have considered the role of pimp to be unworthy of them.

The tradition of the Devil-as-procurer is an ancient one. Usually He performed such services in order to persuade a prospective client to do business with Him—somewhat as industry is said to make use of call girls in our own time. Satan's most famous (or infamous, if you prefer) adventure of this kind was said to have occurred when He attempted to persuade Christ to join forces with Him. The most appealing of women were said to have been offered to Jesus by the Devil, along with such other inducements as riches and power.

Appearing Himself as tempter or temptress, or acting as procurer, the Evil One held out the promise of lavish erotic rewards to Saint Anthony, Saint Benedict, Saint Elizabeth, and Saint Martin, all of whom are reported to have resisted; and to Saint Victorinus, who is said to have succumbed.

In His bargain with Faust, the Devil guaranteed the surrender of the virginity of the fair Marguerite. A stronger bargain was driven by the priest Louis Gaufridi,[13] who concluded a pact with the Devil only after obtaining a promise that he would be able to seduce every woman on whom he so much as breathed.

The Devil might provide women, or succubi, directly, or He might assist a follower in obtaining his or her ends by more devious means. One woman, frustrated by her inability to seduce the handsome youth of her choice, called upon the Devil for help. He ordered her to remove her clothing and then rubbed her all over with a strange ointment, whereupon she seems to have fallen into a sleep or trance and imagined herself to be voluptuously transported in her lover's embrace. Whether the Devil Himself took advantage of her unconsciousness, or merely presented her with a wish-fulfilling dream or hallucination, is not clear.

If a maiden was particularly stubborn in resisting a young man's efforts to have his way with her, he might invoke a demon to accomplish the defloration and so prepare his way. Once the girl had lain with the demon, seduction was easy, because she had nothing more to lose, because her flesh had been awakened to lust, or both. This practice, becoming increasingly common, drew the attention of the Church theorists, who while not approving it were forced to admit that no heresy had been committed by the lad invoking the demon. That was because the demon had only been called upon to do what was in accordance with his nature and his competence.

The above doctrine was further refined by Bernardo da Como.[14] One could without heresy, he said, ask a demon to tempt a woman—because temptation is a function of demons—but heresy might still be committed if one approached the demon in an improper way. That was to say, if the individual *commanded* the demon to function as a tempter, there was no heresy; but if one "adored" the demon, assuming the role of supplicant in soliciting his help, that was beyond question heresy.

Demons, if they desired a woman and she refused to yield to them, might attempt to persuade her to prostitute herself; and there were demons who maintained human mistresses, or concubines, who were regularly paid for their sex services. Early in the fourteenth century, Arnold of Liége described such a demonic whoremonger, who always presented his harlot with rings of gold, jewels, etc., when she agreed to endure his embraces. Another infatuated incubus promised a woman all the world's wisdom if she would but yield to him, and was turned down. He might better, one surmises, have offered her gold and jewels.

Prostitutes who sold themselves to devils did not always profit thereby. One strumpet solicited by a demon, and who gave herself to him for a bag of gold, reported that he paid her what he had promised. But next morning, when she tried to spend some of her ill-gotten gains, she discovered to her outrage that the glittering wealth had somehow been transformed into black dung.

Demons themselves sometimes functioned as whores. At one great gathering of eminent theologians, it was said that demon streetwalkers were everywhere, painted, jewelled, and seductively attired, doing a thriving business amongst the clergy. The Dominican Nider had personal knowledge of a succubus who did so well as a prostitute that she became immensely and indecently vain and amused herself by boasting of the great wealth she had acquired by her iniquitous behavior.

Demons both patronized human brothels and operated bawdy houses of their own. A demon was said to have ejected the human customers from one brothel, so that he could have all of the women for himself. And in 1468, at Bologna, a man was condemned to death for running a notorious house of prostitution entirely staffed by succubi.

Homosexuality

Homosexual relations of humans with demons do not figure prominently in the lore of witchcraft and of Judaeo-Christian demonology. The bisexuality of demons and the preoccupation with change of sex are suggestive of a substratum of homosexual content, but of overt homosexual acts there are comparatively few.

An early instance, cited by rabbinical authors, was the behavior of demons at Sodom. These demons are said to have "changed their nature" and to have lusted for the first time after the sons rather than the daughters, or as well as the daughters, of men. It was held that God destroyed the Cities of the Plain as much to punish the homosexual acts of humans with demons as to punish any other sexual irregularities.

There is also an account of a Witches' Sabbat, held atop Mont Tonale, at which beautiful youths were provided for the sexual pleasures of the all-male gathering.

Bestiality

"For what is there," inquired Boguet, "to prevent the Devil, when he has taken the form of an animal, from coition with a witch?"

The answer of course was that nothing prevented such coitions. They happened every day, if testimony wrung from witches with white hot rods thrust up their rectums could be believed.

The Devil (and demons) in animal form did not merely couple with witches, but also spoke with them and presided over their meetings. That the Devil is able to assume the form of a beast, and in that form converse intelligibly with humans, was early regarded by Hebrew and Christian thinkers as established by the temptation of Eve, with the Devil appearing in the form of a serpent and seducing Eve into eating the apple in violation of God's prohibition. (Those who denied that the serpent was in fact the Devil, in some cases felt obliged to explain Eve's conversation with the serpent on the basis that Adam and Eve and all of the creatures God had made spoke the same language in those idyllic days. It may be, although no theologian said so, that God assigned separate languages to different creatures when he saw that man, far from towering intellectually above the lower animals, could be beguiled by any snake.)

It was also a fact that witches took the forms of animals to cohabit zoophilously with devils, with other humans, and with whatever walked, crept, crawled, swam, or flew. Guazzo, establishing precedents for such intercourse, and for bestiality of a more mundane sort as well, took note of the copulations of women with monkeys, supposedly commonplace in the Middle East, and of the sodomies committed by men upon bovines—no rarity down to the present day. He also told of male witches and werewolves who, in animal form, ravished helpless little girls.

In any case, it was well known that for the abominable intercourse with demons, and for other malign and monstrous purposes as well, a witch might assume the form of wolf, cat, dog, sheep, cow, ass, pig, fox, chicken or insect (a list not at all intended to be comprehensive). In insect form, the witch sometimes appeared as a loathsome black or green beetle. And some chose to appear as moths and butterflies. Serpents and toads, owls and crows—and especially the raven, who might nip off a woman's clitoris with a single snap of his beak—were sometimes witches transformed. In fact, one did well to be suspicious of whatever showed signs of life and a capacity for movement; nor was even motion a sure guide to recognizing a witch. Some practitioners of the black arts assumed the shapes of plants, and of such objects as sticks, brooms, wagon wheels, and old wooden buckets.

Anyone puzzling over the gratification to be obtained from intercourse with a demon or witch in the form of a creature so small as a cat, may be reassured that when the cat form was assumed, the cat would be one of the size of a large dog, or of a goat. And witches reported that their incubi, although they came to them in the shapes of beasts, nonetheless had sexual organs like those of humans—those most excellently proportioned instruments of their kind.

A shape often assumed by demons engaging in bestiality was that of the dog, and a great many such cases are on record. Collette du Mont, who confessed to having participated in an act of coitus with a demon in canine form, said that the dog stood on his hind legs to accomplish the fornication, and that he rested his paws on her belly. It would seem that some special item of furniture would have been required to make such an intercourse possible.

A rare description of witches changing themselves into serpents to engage in bestiality is given by Mantegazza (*The Sexual Relations of Mankind*), who quotes Leandro Alberti: "At night, the males as well as females became frightful serpents, and sibyls as well, and all those who desired to enter there (the Sabbat) must first take their lascivious pleasure with the said loathsome serpents." [15]

But the animal form above all preferred by demons was that of the goat, and it was usually in goat form that the Devil presided over the Sabbat. A great many writers cite instances of this, and to mention only one, De Lancre told of women (witches) at the Sabbat "loving a violently stinking goat, caressing him amorously, becoming intimate and coupling with him horribly and impudently. . . ." [16]

A theory as to why demons prefer the form of the goat was set forth by Remy in his *Demonolatry:*

"It is not easy to conjecture why they (demons) prefer to assume this (goat) shape . . . unless perhaps, as in the Pythagorean theory of metempsychosis, the Demon is most willing to assume that body which is most consonant with his character and nature. For goats are remarkable above all other cattle for their rank smell; and it is this quality in the Demon of his unbearably fetid smell which is the surest indication of his presence. Again, the obscene lasciviousness of goats is proverbial; and it is the Demon's chief care to urge his followers to the greatest venereal excesses; and lest they should lack any opportunity, whenever he meets them he assumes that form which is the most adapted to such work, and does not cease to seduce them to filthiness, until finally he persuades them to commit even the most ungratifying and revolting obscenities. Goats also show great pugnacity towards those whom they chance to meet; and similarly the Demon always attacks any man whom he meets in any part of the world . . . Goats have a fierce and truculent look, their brows are rugged with horns, they have a long unkempt beard, their coat is shaggy and disordered, their legs are short, and the whole formation of their body is so adapted to deformity and foulness that no more fitting shape could be chosen by him who, both within and without, is entirely composed of shame, horrors and monstrosities. It is an old saying that the lips must conform to the lettuce." [17]

A less colorful explanation for the preference of demons for the form of the goat doubtless lies in the fact that much of the behavior charged by Christians to devils is obviously derived from pagan literature, mythology, and history, with the Devil-as-goat a transparent relative of the Goat of Mendes on the one hand, the satyrs on the other. It is also the case that mankind has a long history of actual copulations with goats (and with sheep—the ram being another form often assumed by demons).

To be accused of having engaged in bestiality was of course a serious matter. Even if one could prove, and this was not so easy as it might sound, that the animal was not a demon in disguise, the punishment was still almost certain to be death. (*Leviticus XX:* And if a man lie with a beast, he shall surely be

put to death: and ye shall slay the beast. And if a woman approach unto any beast, and lie down thereto, thou shalt kill
the woman, and the beast: they shall surely be put to death;
their blood *shall be* upon them.) That was why it was essential to make certain that the intercourse had actually occurred,
and that witnesses had not seen merely an illusion created and
employed by the Devil to bring undeserved punishment upon
some good and innocent child of God. That demons resorted to
such fiendish wiles was not to be doubted.

No less a dignitary than the Prefect of Zürich once chanced
to be crossing a field when to his astonishment and horror he
saw one of the most prominent citizens of the community committing an unspeakable and eldritch act with a mare. Fortunately the Prefect was a man of learning as well as piety, wise
in the duplicitous ways of the Devil, and so instead of sounding
a general alarum, as a lesser man might have done, he hastened
to the house of the man he had seen and found that good citi-
zen peacefully at home and behaving himself as usual. This
proved, of course, that it was a false image the Prefect had seen
performing that atrocious deed in the pasture, and that the
Devil had hoped by means of that diabolic effigy to bring low,
yea to ruin and death, one whom He could never hope to be
able to corrupt.

The famous magus Dr. John Fian was almost the victim of a
beast's assault when one of his sorceries was sabotaged. Dr.
Fian lustfully coveted the young sister of a youth in his training, and he ordered the boy to obtain for him a small tuft of
the girl's pubic hairs. Unable to figure out a way to get them,
and hoping his master would never know the difference, the
boy presented Dr. Fian with hairs taken from a heifer, which
the sorcerer used in preparing a potent love charm. So potent
was it in fact that the heifer broke into a church where the
magus was at worship and there attempted carnally to assault
the wizard, who was forced to abandon his usual posture of
great dignity and flee. Thereafter, the enamoured bovine
followed him everywhere through the streets of the town—

though this, rather than being a source of embarrassment, seems to have enlarged Fian's local reputation as a master of the magical arts.[18] Not a few authorities held that devils are attracted sexually to the lower animals, and Johannes Pott, for one, said that the intercourse might be fruitful, with the offspring resembling either humans or beasts. Pott, a seventeenth-century professor of law at Jena, author of the *Specimen Juridicum de Nefando Lamiarum cum Diabolo Coitu*, a work on the sexual relations of witches with demons, confirmed that devils often assume animal form to copulate with humans and noted that among the offspring of such unions are worms most injurious to mankind, which witches introduce into the bodies of their enemies.

Demons committed sexual intercourse with a variety of beasts, but it was said that their greatest passion was for mares. Noted, too, was the fury of the demon when the mare resisted his advances, or showed little enthusiasm for the operation. The mare that thus offended might be savagely beaten, or even slain (by force, or by such trickery as leading the mare over a cliff or into a quicksand). The mare might also be starved, with the demon stealing its food or causing the pastures to dry up. But if, on the other hand, the mare showed proper ardor in copulating with the demon, she might receive lavish caresses and abundant supplies of good things to eat. In some places an unusually lean mare was thought to be one that had spurned the advances of some incubus, while an unusually fat mare was at once under suspicion of being a willing and even enthusiastic recipient of a devil's lustful embraces.

Sinistrari offered data on the treatment received by both women and mares lusted after by demons:

"We read likewise of numerous women incited to coition by the Incubus Demon, and who, though reluctant at first of yielding to him, are soon moved by his entreaties, tears and endearments; he is a desperate lover and must not be denied. And although this comes sometimes of the craft of some Wizard who avails himself of the agency of the Demon, yet the Demon not infrequently acts on his own account; and it happens not merely with women, but also with mares; if they readily comply with his desire, he pets them and plaits their mane in elaborate and inextricable tresses; but if they resist, he ill-treats and strikes them, smites them with the glanders, and finally puts them to death, as is shown by daily experience." [19]

It was Sinistrari, too, who offered a unique theory as to what constitutes bestiality in the sexual intercourse of demons with humans. Whatever the outward forms of the participants, he said, the act is one of bestiality. But the bestiality is not committed by the human; rather, by the demon.

"From all that has been deduced above," Sinistrari wrote in his *De Daemonialitate, et Incubis, et Succubis,* "it is therefore clear that there are such Demons, incubi and succubi, endowed with senses and subject to the passions thereof, as has been shown; who are born through generation and die through corruption, are capable of beatitude and damnation, more noble than man, by reason of the greater subtility of their bodies, and who, when having intercourse with man, male or female, fall into the same sin as man when copulating with a beast, which is inferior to him. Also, it not infrequently occurs that those Demons slay the men, women or mares with whom they have had protracted intercourse; and the reason is that, being liable to sin whilst on the way to salvation, *in via,* they must likewise be open to repentance; and, in the same manner as a man, who habitually sins with a beast, is enjoined by his confessor to destroy that beast, with a view to suppressing the occasion of relapsing, it may likewise happen that the penitent Demon should slay the animal with which it sinned, whether man or beast; nor will death thus occasioned to a man be reckoned a sin to the Demon, any more than death inflicted on a beast is imputed as a sin to man; for, considering the essential difference between a Demon of that kind and man, the man will be the same thing to the Demon as the beast is to man." [20]

8. *The witches' Sabbat*

For the purposes of this book it does not seem necessary to examine at any great length those gatherings of witches known as Sabbats. Sexual intercourse at such conclaves was usually *en masse* and probably promiscuous (with the exception of the required acts of incest and certain other special unions engaged in for magical purposes). Little in the way of sexual behavior occurred there that has not already been described.

The Sabbat is most often represented as beginning with an entrance and procession, followed by the homage to Satan, the banquet, the Black Mass, dancing, and, finally, the sexual orgy. Of these events, the Black Mass is historically the most dubious and the present tendency is to deny that it had any place in the witch gatherings, being an invention of authors. However, there seem to have been rites which travestied Christian, especially Catholic, ones, and which probably formed the basis for the conception of the Black Mass as it evolved.

It was customary for the witches to fly to the Sabbats, although sometimes they walked—leading jurists to debate whether one who walked to a Sabbat was equally as guilty as one who (with the Devil's help) flew there. It was decided that, pedestrian or aviator, the witch's guilt was the same.

Sabbats might be attended by a handful of persons, or by thousands (although some writers refer to the smaller and more frequent gatherings as Esbats, or coven meetings). It was reported that witches attending the larger assemblies sometimes darkened the sky as they passed overhead in hordes. One early account of such a well-attended Sabbat is dated around 1440. Ten thousand witches, all women, gathered, worshiped the Devil in the form of a cat, were supplied with poisons and powders for raising tempests, and were instructed in other criminal techniques. Then they feasted, fornicated with incubi, and flew home on sticks.

Some writers proclaimed that Sabbats were held several times each week, or even nightly; others, that they were held on special occasions. It was sometimes said that the witches could not meet on Saturday, that day being sacred to the Immaculate Mother of God; or on Sunday, that day being sacred to God himself. But it was not an unusual view that the Devil liked to hold Sabbats precisely on sacred and holy days—the better to blaspheme and commit sacrilege—and that the most fiendish of His festivals were at such times as Easter and Christmas. Four other dates are often mentioned: February 2nd, April 30th (*Walpurgisnacht*), August 1st, and October 31st (the Eve of All Saints, or Halloween).

Among those who reported that the Sabbats were held very frequently were nuns of the convent at Lille. Those holy sisters confessed that they had attended Sabbat orgies several times a week, varying their erotic fare in the following manner: heterosexual copulation, Mondays and Tuesdays; sodomy, fellatio, and cunnilingus, with homo- and heterosexual partners, Thursdays; bestiality with domestic animals and dragons, Saturdays.

Sabbats were most often held on mountaintops, the most famous of these being the Blocksberg or Brocken, in the Harz Mountains, and the legendary Venusberg or Mons Veneris. There were other Blocksbergs or Brockens—in Pomerania, for example, there were two or three. Mounts Tonale (in the Eastern Alps), Kopasztetö and Vaskapu (in Hungary), and Meliboeus (in Brunswick) were mentioned as Sabbat sites.

Other Sabbats were held at crossroads, in meadows and forests, in private homes, and especially in deserted or abandoned churches. It was explained by one analyst that the Devil changed the Sabbat sites from time to time in an effort to prevent His own and His followers' boredom.

Sabbats were usually held at night, but as Montague Summers remarks, there is no sound theoretical reason why they could not have been held in broad daylight. The Sabbat most often began at midnight (the "witching hour") and continued until the first cockcrow (which does not take into account what is known to any poultry farmer—that a cock may crow at any hour whatever, be it dark or dawn). It was also said that the reason the Sabbat ended at dawn (and the reason why vampires return to their graves at that time) was because at dawn the Holy Office of the Church begins.

Some witches reported that it was the custom for those attending the Sabbats to wear masks, or blacken their faces, or put flour on them, to prevent identification. Especially the wealthy and the powerful were said to do this, since their faces were well known. But many other witches made no such claims. Obviously, if the witch-hunters had accepted that such a practice was general, their task would have been made much more difficult. Accused witches incriminated thousands of others as a result of having seen them at the Sabbats; that is, under torture they named other persons and said that they had seen them there.

If a witch, because of illness or for some other urgent reason, could not attend the Sabbat in the flesh, she still might be able to participate. Prierias declared that those witches unable to attend could remain in their own beds and still enjoy the celebration. They did this by performing certain required ceremonies and then turning over onto their left sides and calling on the Devil to enable them to witness the proceedings. The method was not without hazard since a vigilant husband who knew what to look for might always catch his wife at such witchery. The witch betrays herself by a bluish vapor issuing out of her mouth, and it is in this vapor that she sees the Sabbat.

It was a rather generally accepted belief of demonologists

that pregnancy—which the peasant woman dreaded for reasons of poverty—could not result from intercourse at a Sabbat.
It was by diabolic intervention that this was so—the Devil
pledging to His followers that no woman would return from the
orgy "heavier" than when she arrived there. (Intercourse of
sons with mothers, aimed at producing sorceresses, seems to
have been the exception to the rule.)

Given the notorious sterility of the intercourse at the Sabbats, one might wonder whether anal intercourse was not practiced there rather than coitus. It has been suggested that this
might be in accord with the satanic principle of doing everything backwards.

Ernest Jones, who took note of the sterility of Sabbat encounters, linked Satan's alleged lack of semen and consequent infertility to the fact that no salt was permitted to be
used on the food consumed at witch gatherings. The Devil's
lack of semen, he said, explains His dislike of salt, which "can
be shown to be an ancient mythological symbol for semen. Bodin was therefore in a sense right when he accounted for the
Devil's aversion for it on the ground that it is 'a symbol of eternity'." [1] (It is not true, however, as Jones wrote, that "all
writers are unanimous about Satan's sterility.")[2]

Generally, accounts of the Sabbats are rather stereotyped,
but occasionally one encounters meaningful deviations. At
some of the Sabbats held in the Netherlands, a female demon
or Queen of the Sabbat reigned alongside of the presiding
Devil. As it was a part of His function to have intercourse with
all of the female witches, so it was a part of Hers to copulate
with all of the males. At these Dutch Sabbats the females kissed
the Devil's anus, as was traditional elsewhere, but the males
kissed the pudenda of the Queen.

In almost all of the descriptions of the initiation rites of
witches, it is said that copulation with demons, which binds the
pact, occurs publicly and as a part of the general orgy. At least
one authority, however, insists that upon taking her (or his)
oath of allegiance to the Devil, the witch retires to a private

place to sexually seal the bargain. Since the spectator-exhibitionist and mass participation aspects of the Sabbats were such prominent and probably important features, the exception is worthy of remark.

Rare, although not unique, are reports of necrophilia committed at the Sabbats. These were not corpses animated by demons, as very often happened, but dead bodies stolen from their graves by witches and borne clandestinely to the Sabbat sites for use in the orgies. Charles Williams (*Witchcraft*) says that "Dead bodies were sometimes said to be used, though they were made to appear fresh and lively." And C. W. Olliver (*An Analysis of Magic and Witchcraft*) speaks of "monstrous hags (who) clasp in gloating frenzy the icy corpses of young men. . . ." (That necrophilia was sometimes a feature of the Black Mass in the eighteenth and nineteenth centuries is well known, the priest copulating with, performing ritual cunnilingus upon, and otherwise sexually using the murdered body of some virgin whose cadaver served as an altar and whose fresh blood, collected in tarnished chalices, was the beverage of the communion.)

Almost all modern and contemporary authorities on witchcraft are in agreement that the meetings called Sabbats were actually held and that at least a part of the time the Devil was represented by a human in appropriate costume who inserted an artificial penis into the vaginas of females in attendance. Michelet (*Satanism and Witchcraft*) thought that a hollow dildo was probably employed and that down it was poured some icy liquid, probably water from a near-by stream. Since this was unpleasant, he theorized, the sorceress usually used an understudy, whose grimaces amused the onlookers, the whole episode being mainly farcical.

Margaret Murray believes that dildos were used and thinks that they must have been made of horn or of stone. Others propose metal, wood, leather, etc. That such phalli were employed is offered as an explanation for the coldness of the intercourse. Unfortunately, that explanation will not do. The artificial penes would soon have become warm, while the witches told of very lengthy copulations and even insisted that their vaginas remained as if frozen for a long time after the intercourse. Also, these same frigid fornications often occurred in situations other than at the Sabbats—when the coition, sodomy, or whatever practice was obviously hallucinatory or very vividly imaginary. The explanation for the coldness of demons is surely to be sought in the psychological and not in the merely physical realm. Dildos may have been in use at the Sabbats, but they shed little if any light on the peculiarities of coition with incubi (while much less do they explain the similar sensations experienced in intercourse with succubi).

9. *Murder and cannibalism*

If one were to credit the confessions of witches, it would have to be believed that infants and young children by the thousands, and even tens of thousands, were slaughtered for magical purposes and—where the witch murdered her own child—as a token of submission to the Diabolic Power.

The corpses of infants and children (and of aborted foeti) were used in the composition of a great variety of magical potions and powders; for purposes of divination (as in *extispicium*,[1] or divining by means of palpitating entrails); as table delicacies at the Sabbats, etc.

The Catholic abhorrence of midwives ostensibly was based in considerable part upon these practices, and in the *Malleus Maleficarum* one reads that "No one does more harm to the Catholic Faith than midwives. For when they do not kill children, then, as if for some other purpose, they take them out of the room and, raising them up in the air, offer them to devils."[2] The belief seems to have been that many witches took up midwifery in order to have access to infants, and not that midwiving was of itself a corrupting occupation encouraging its practitioners to commit murders and consort with devils.

Means of murdering the infants were varied, poisoning and suffocation being among the most favored methods. Another rather common technique of infanticide was that employed by a witch-midwife in the Diocese of Basel, who confessed that she had slain more than forty newborn babes "by sticking a needle through the crowns of their heads into their brains as they came out of the womb."

The accusation of infanticide, like many others made against witches, had been levelled earlier by Christian theologians against other heretical groups. For example, it had been charged that the Euchites and the Gnostics met on Good Friday of each year to commit incest. Nine months later, bearing their newborn infants, they would meet again to murder the babies, collect the blood, and burn the bodies. The ashes so obtained would be mixed with the blood, and this concoction used to season the food consumed at the banquet tables.

This is quite like some of the descriptions of the Sabbats. There, the newborn (and unbaptized) babes were usually cooked and eaten; although sometimes, perhaps for lack of infants to murder, corpses were exhumed from graves and devoured. The cannibalism or necrophagia was accompanied in some cases by vampirism, the infants being decapitated or their veins pierced on the spot, with the blood collected in receptacles and then drunk. The brains of murdered children were also a favorite repast.

Countless witches admitted to engaging in these and similar enormities. A well-known case was that of Jehanneta Relescee, in the fifteenth century, which also shows how readily the Devil was invoked in those Satan-conscious days. Jehanneta, after a squabble with her husband, called aloud for either God or the Devil to deliver her from her domestic miseries. Almost immediately a black man appeared and she fell on her knees and kissed his posterior. After that she attended the Sabbats twice a week, where she ate unbaptized infants and otherwise conducted herself atrociously, after the manner of witches. It is noteworthy that it was the Devil, not God, who speedily answered her supplication. Had God deigned to appear, she might have been spared an eternity of torment, but such was not the way of the times.

One might mention, too, that it was not only the infantophagy of witches that was condemned. Animals as well, it was remarked, were given to this abomination—doubtless egged on to it by the Devil. Thus, Scottish law of the sixteenth century specified that "If a sowe eate her pigges, let her be stoned to death and buried."

Witches caused abortions with the intention of injuring the woman bearing the child, and to bring grief to the bereaved parents, but also in order to obtain the aborted foeti for magical purposes. Remy, Privy Councilor to the Most Serene Duke of Lorraine, remarked in 1595 that "They can have no other reason for possessing themselves of the abortive births of women; for they make from the skin of these a parchment which they inscribe with some barbarous and unknown characters and afterwards use in the attainment of their dearest wishes. As to this, Agrippa and Petrus de Abano and Weyer, three masters in damnable magic, have left instructions which surpass all human nature. Others again cook the foetus in its entirety until it is either reduced to dry ashes or melted into a mass which they mix with other ingredients . . . Pliny wrote that not only midwives, but harlots also, used thus to dislimb abortions for the purpose of preparing poisons for their crimes. And the practice is common today in German Lorraine, as I have often found in my examinations of witches on a capital charge." [3]

The fat of babes was an important ingredient of the ointment used for flying to the Sabbat, and parts of infantile bodies were useful in curing common aches and pains, such as those of rheumatism and arthritis: "Finger of birth-strangled babe/ Ditch-delivered by a drab" had a variety of medical uses, including those just mentioned. Infant cadavers, when available entire, were cooked in cauldrons. The thickest part of the stew was reserved for the medical armamentarium, and for the flying ointments. The left-over broth was drunk as being generally beneficial to a witch. Baby fat was also an ingredient, along with hemlock, belladonna, aconite, etc., in poisons.

The murders and cannibalizings of children most likely actually to have occurred were those charged to werewolves or lycanthropes (who were also, in most cases, witches). A number of werewolves confessed to killing and eating children and infants, though not so often the latter, and adults as well. Often they raped their victims, especially the young girls, first, and then devoured them. Sometimes, in their wolf forms, lycanthropes copulated with one another, and also with real wolves. By some accounts the ointment used for werewolf transformations was pharmacologically similar to that employed by the witches for attendance at the Sabbats. The cannibalism of the werewolves (as historically described) differed from that of the witches mainly in that the witches customarily ate infants, while the werewolves preferred children and adolescents; also, the witches cooked their human flesh while the werewolves consumed it raw, tearing it from the still-warm bodies of their victims.

It seems probable that many of the werewolf crimes are based upon fact, and that the persons accused of lycanthropic homicides were lust murderers, necrosadists, necrophiles, etc., as we would describe them today, who derived sexual pleasure of a direct sort from their cannibalistic and other offenses. (If the witches derived sexual pleasure, it was indirectly—by way of sacrilege. In this perversion, medically termed *satanism,* orgasm is achieved by blasphemy, by desecration of religious relics, by human sacrifices and ceremonial cannibalism, etc.)

A typical lust murderer and necrophage (as he quite likely would be regarded presently) was the lycanthrope Peter Stumpf, who was enabled to assume wolf-form, he said, by means of a magic belt given to him by his succubus. He killed fifteen young boys and ate their brains, and also murdered two of his daughters-in-law, but was apprehended when about to devour them. Another was Gilles Garnier, executed at Dôle in 1574. He murdered a twelve-year-old boy, then a ten-year-old girl, and then a ten-year-old boy. He stripped the bodies and ate portions of the thighs and bellies (meaning, probably, the genitals). These cases sound very much like that of Vacher the Ripper, who roamed France in the nineteenth century, murdering youngsters, using them sexually, and then devouring their genitals, breasts and other body parts. At the time of Gilles Garnier, Vacher would almost certainly have been executed as a werewolf and a witch.

Necrophagy (eating of dead bodies) often and perhaps usually is an aspect of the sexual perversion called necrophilia, as is necrosadism, or mutilation of cadavers. Typical necrophiles excite themselves sexually in all three ways—by having coital or other intercourse with the corpse, by mutilating it, and by eating the flesh. When the victim is murdered by the necrophile, the case may also be one of sadistic homicide. Further, the blood may be drunk, so that vampirism, also sometimes a sex perversion, enters the picture.

It should be affirmed again that these dread perversions seldom intruded upon the witchcraft scene, save in cases of lycanthropy (which, if the offenses were actual, were instances of sex crime and homicidal psychosis, not witchcraft).

10. *Scatology*

hatever came out of the human body—feces, urine, menstrual fluid, vomitus, pus, semen, etc.—was put to some use by the witches, either ritually, as elements of the famous *Dreck Apotheke*, or both.

Demons were held to love filth generally and feces in particular. It was often said of witches that they had a stink about them, acquired from the embraces of demons animating cadavers in decay, or because of their own bodily filth and the excrements with which they worked. Demons encouraged witches to be dirty and stinking, and discouraged them from washing their bodies, especially their bottoms. When a demon gave a present, it was likely to be made of dung. To successfully perform an incantation, the hands should not be washed (this being just the reverse of the practice of the white magician, who cleanses his body, and especially his hands, before setting to work).

When Martin Luther farted to drive away the Devil, it was supposed to be the stench that the Devil found unbearable. But this is strange, since ordurous stenches are characteristic of devils, and Satan Himself is the Prince of Stenches, particularly fecal ones. Luther's practice makes more sense if seen as derived from the old Eastern belief that demons might be ejected from one's body by farting (the same thing the Messalians sought to accomplish by nose-blowing and spitting).

The belief in the magical power of human wastes (and of menstrual juices, semen, and other body substances) certainly goes back to remotest antiquity and is to be found among prim-

itive peoples of the present as well as of the past. In the past, of
course, it was found also among civilized peoples, and abundant vestiges linger in the most advanced nations of the present day.

Somewhat as the old gods were turned by the Christians into
devils, so the excreta, which originally had possessed power for
good, came to be regarded in the West as being in the service
of evil. Havelock Ellis (*Studies in the Psychology of Sex*) wrote
that "It is not surprising that while along the line of orthodox
religion, holy water, with the advance of civilization, has become completely dissociated from urine, along the line of magic
and witchcraft the association continued. Thus in French ritual
witchcraft the Devil used holy water which was sometimes
urine, and with this all present were aspersed." [1]

The evil power of urine was accepted by the Hebrews, who
held that to urinate in a prayer book was to destroy the force of
the prayer. Neither should a prayer book be used in any room
where a vessel of urine is standing; if such use is unavoidable,
then pure water should be sprinkled on the prayer book to
counteract the force of the urine.

But in the world of Islam, on the other hand, urine continued for a long while to be a potent force for good; brides
and grooms were sprinkled with it, precisely to protect them
from the malign powers of devils.

That the holy water used to celebrate the unholy rites at the
Sabbat was urine has been stated by many writers. Boguet
says: "And to make Holy Water, the Devil pisses in a hole in
the ground, and the worshippers are then sprinkled with his
urine by the celebrant with a black asperge." [2]

For a time, reports that the holy water used by witches was
yellow had baffled authorities. So, too, had reports of certain
discolored hosts—a mystery cleared up when it became known
that feces, menstrual blood, vomitus, pus, etc., were used in the
concoction of the sacral wafers. Some of these substances were
also used in the liquor employed to travesty the drinking of the

blood of Christ. The bread and wine of the eucharist were further defiled by obscenities pronounced over them.

It was a common belief that the Sabbats could only be held in places where there was a supply of water, but urine sometimes obviated (or fulfilled) this requirement. The great Bodin, for example, drew upon his experience to (practically) confound those who insisted that a stream or lake must be near the Sabbat site, pointing out that the witches could, if need be, make their own water:

"Yet I shall say that, according to Antoine Gandillon's statement, there must be water in that place; for when she was asked if she had been at la Georgiere, she answered that the Sabbat was not held there because there was no water. And I think that the reason for this is that, in order to cause it to hail, witches usually beat water with their wands; and, when there is no water, they make a hole in the ground and piss in it, and beat their piss."

Another distinguished authority, the seventeenth-century friar Francesco-Maria Guazzo, quoting De Raemond, told of a young girl who confessed that holy water was obtained at the Sabbat by "a goat pissing in a hole in the ground."

A person might be magically murdered or tortured by means of his excreta if it fell into the gnarled hands of witches. Even newly baptized infants were not immune and would suffer terrible agonies if witches boiled their urine. The witch Joanna Meriweather burned a holy candle mounted on the dung of Elisabeth Colsey, her aim being that Elisabeth's buttocks should fall away into separate halves. Feces and urine of hanged felons, who were left at crossroads as a warning to incipient offenders, were especially valuable in the preparation of poisons; and the ejaculate of a hanged man was often an essential of the witches' ointment. If the hanged man was redheaded and devout, the ingredient possessed even greater virtue.

(It has long been known and thought about that men ejaculate when hanged, and there are cases on record of men who have had themselves hanged in order to experience the intense sexual pleasure that was said to result. An assistant would be standing nearby to cut the voluptuary down before he strangled to death. Still others, having no trustworthy aides, have hanged themselves, and then were unable to cut themselves free before losing consciousness. Some apparent suicides by hanging, though perhaps something less than a majority, are in fact pleasure-seekers of this esoteric variety who have bungled —consciously—the job.)

Belief in the aphrodisiacal power of both urine and feces was prevalent among witches (and/or witch-burners). This belief has prevailed up to recent times, and the practice may still be in favor, with some German brides pouring their urine into the coffee of their husbands with a view to intensifying the man's ardor and insuring his fidelity.

An old witch who favored dung as a sex stimulant mixed her feces with the food of four successive abbots of a monastery. She indicated that each one had consumed a considerable portion of the produce of her bowels, showing the judges how much by marking off a place on her arm. Three of the abbots became so ravenously lustful, she said, that they copulated with her until they perished of sheer exhaustion. The fourth, as a consequence of his excessive, even insatiable, venery, went stark raving mad.

Witches in Germany would stand on a dung heap to renounce their Savior and pledge their loyalty to the Devil. Sometimes this could be accomplished very simply, just by saying: "I stand here on this shit and renounce Jesus Christ." But in other cases a more elaborate ceremony was required or preferred.

Feces might also be employed to cause various ills, including demonic possession. Françoise Secretain, one of history's most famous witches, caused demons to possess eight-year-old Loyse Maillat by forcing the child to eat a dung cake.

Semen and menstrual blood will be mentioned here only briefly. Both were sometimes ingredients of the witches' ointment, with the semen of wizards being particularly well suited to this purpose. More often, and as mentioned, these substances were used in the preparation of the eucharistic bread and wine. The inquisitor Jacquier, in the fifteenth century, told of a priest who copulated in a church and, collecting his own semen, mixed it with holy chrism oil.

An early example of such practices was that of the Carthaginian Manichaeans, who sprinkled their eucharistic bread with semen. This accusation against the Manichaeans was made by Saint Augustine, who said that the purpose was to "purge the divine substance from the bread." Augustine added that semen was sprinkled on or cooked into other foods by the foul heretics, and for the same flagitious purpose. The semen used could be that of a man, or it could be obtained from some beast.

The desecration of the eucharist, however, did not reach its full flowering until the eighteenth and nineteenth centuries, when more sophisticated Satanists committed sacrileges that most probably never even occurred to the witches.

At the Black Mass, obscene representations of the saints, of the Virgin, and of the Son of Man were employed. In some cases the image of the Virgin, raddled and dissolute of mien, was equipped with breasts to be suckled, and with a vagina into which the penis might be inserted. In the case of the Christ-figures, there was sometimes a phallus, which Devil-worshipers both sucked and inserted into vagina or anus, depending upon the sex of the communicant. Occasionally, rather than an image, an actual human figure was bound to the cross and fulfilled the Christly role, eventually discharging his semen, which was collected in a blasphemously consecrated chalice and used in the making of the host.

Semen, along with excreta and menstrual blood, was a standard ingredient of these Devil's hosts, which were converted, by the saying of the appropriate words, into the Body of Our

Lord. The hosts were inserted into anus and vagina, urinated and defecated upon, smeared with semen, and finally consumed.

Sometimes hosts of unusual size were prepared, which were slit and used as artificial vaginas. The priests copulated with them, ferociously screaming all the while that they were ravishing the Blessed Mother of God or sodomizing the Savior. Black Christs, heads downward, were hung upon crosses, their bared backsides to the worshipers, and some of these, too, were so constructed as to allow for sodomy by the priests.

De Sade, whose writings owed much to the lore of satanism and witchcraft, described a scene in which a statue of Christ was inserted into a girl's vagina while the host was placed in her anus, the priest crushing it as he sodomized her and shouted various blasphemies—"the foul torrent of his lubricity (surging) over the very body of his Saviour."

The erotic defiling of holy images became so prevalent that a perversion called *Mariolatry* (a term that also has another meaning) came into being. The records of the Paris police (November 9, 1765) preserve for posterity the case of two monks from the monastery at Crépy who entered an inn called The Mounting Deer and vociferously demanded a bed for three. Their companion was an image of the Virgin Mary.

11. *Cruelties and cuckoldries*

Demons were often cruel, but even those writers who attributed sexual desires to them do not seem to have thought that demons found erotic gratification in their cruelties. That is, they were not regarded as sadistic.

The most common cruelty reported was that involved in the demons' sexual intercourse with witches—a cruelty presumably not essential since demons could take on any forms they chose. Usually described as unpleasant, the coition could be agonizing. The penis of the incubus might stab at the female genitals like a knife, or scrape the vaginal walls with iron scales. It might be freezing cold or burning hot. When the incubus withdrew, he might bring blood and flesh out of the vagina. Terrible pains in abdomen, thighs and lower back, as well as in the genitals, were described. The demon, his dual penis interminably erect, might brutally prod at cuneal crevice and anus for an entire night, resisting all pleas that he desist even for a moment. He might present himself in loathsome or terrifying form, forcing the witch to copulate amidst nauseous and suffocating stenches. And if he paused to give the witch something to eat or drink, the food might turn to dung and the beverage to urine in her mouth.

Male witches were not treated so badly in the act of coitus, although the intercourse with a succubus might have serious and even fatal consequences sooner or later. Exhaustion was a grave risk, and there were a number of cases like that of a holy man, fallen prey to a nymphomaniacal succubus, who was drained dry and unto death within a month. Another gentleman engaged in such an amour was reduced to total impotence and could neither sit nor stand, so enfeebled was he by the incessant demands of his voracious demon mistress. Eventual nervous prostration was likely to overtake either male or female witch, and as the process of debilitation progressed the witch would fall into frequent fits of fainting.

Non-witches embraced by demons might become ill at the first contact with the icy and avid organs, or expire in the throes of the initial orgasm, so cementing their damnation. It was said that witches, among the articles of their agreement with the Devil, were safeguarded against any such untimely demise.

Theologians repeatedly asserted that a witch, once incarcerated, was beyond the reach of her incubus. Yet a great many cases were cited, often by those same theologians, of demons who ignored or defied the prohibition and would visit the jailed witches in their cells. There, the incubus would copulate with the witch, threaten her, thrash her, and sometimes break her neck in order to dissuade or prevent her from incriminating other witches.

Demons broke the necks of witches in a characteristic way that became a kind of trademark of demonic assassins: When the body was found, the head would be turned completely around facing backwards. (Margaret Murray, in *The God of the Witches*, plausibly argues that these deaths, accounted as either suicides or murders by demons, were probably assassinations committed by members of the witch coven or persons hired by them, probably jailers. The purpose would have been to silence the witch before she could implicate others under torture. Considering the horrible tortures to which witchcraft suspects were subjected, murder was merciful as well as prudent.)

Occasionally, a demon would help a witch to escape from her cell—an eventuality peculiarly abhorrent to inquisitors, who liked to maintain that God would permit no diabolic interference with the machinery of justice. Another almost equally detestable trick of the Devil's was to give imprisoned witches an ointment that prevented them from feeling any pain while being tortured. The witch could then either endure with apparent indifference, or calmly sleep through, the torturer's best efforts. Similarly, the witch might receive an ointment just previous to her execution. This would enable her to stand jeering and blaspheming amid the very flames that consumed her. These, of course, were not acts of cruelty on the part of demons, but quite the reverse.

Witches were abused by their incubi outside the prison cells. Demons were firm and even fanatical believers in punctuality, and witches who arrived tardy for the Sabbat or some other engagement were likely to receive merciless cudgelings. An offense still more grave and evocative of demonic ire was to cure, without the demon's permission, some bewitched person; or to fail to commit a crime as instructed. For such gross misconduct and omission a witch might have her mouth or her womb torn out, or both, or be savagely beaten on the head with a hammer.

Other cruelties of demons were less brutal and often had what now seems an obvious humorous aspect. For example, demons enjoyed catching men and women illicitly copulating. Finding such a clandestine couple, the demon would cause them to become stuck together like dogs, and so to remain until apprehended by their fellow citizens.

Early writers held that it was a regular function of demons to make false accusations of sexual misbehavior against righteous men and women. A case in point was that of a demon who in 858 at Mainz caused a man to be persecuted by his neighbors when the demon falsely accused him of taking certain reprehensible liberties with an under-age girl. Demons delighted in persuading husbands and wives that their mates had been unfaithful, and then convincing the aggrieved spouse to commit an adultery by way of retaliation.

The cuckolded husband is a stock character in witchcraft testimony, and demons are often depicted as seeming to take impish pleasure in his outrage. Sometimes a demon would force the husband to watch while the wife was engaged in adultery or being ravished. De Lancre related how, enchanted by demons, husbands "became like immovable statues and were forced to watch their honor being violated before their very eyes without being able to prevent it. The woman, speechless, brought to silence by force, in vain implores her husband with frenzied eyes to come to her aid; the enchanted man with folded arms and staring eyes must look on helplessly at his shame." [1]

(The resemblance between this scene and similar ones described in the newspapers from time to time, where sadistic or cruel rapists force husbands and lovers to watch the rapes of their wives or loved ones, will at once be noted. Phantasies of such behavior, like phantasies of other prohibited behavior, seem to have become palatable to consciousness when the active agent was imagined to be a devil.)

Kramer and Sprenger, in the *Malleus Maleficarum,* told of demons who embraced women in their beds while the husbands slept, and continued the intercourse when the husbands awakened: "Husbands have actually seen Incubus devils swiving their wives, although they have thought that they were not devils but men. And when they have taken up a weapon and tried to run them through, the devil has suddenly disappeared, making himself invisible. And then their wives have thrown their arms about them, although they have sometimes been hurt, and railed at their husbands, mocking them, and asking them if they had eyes, or whether they were possessed of devils." [2]

Husbands were at a great disadvantage in attempting to deal with the demon lovers of their wives. The incubus might come to the wife in a dream, or while the husband slept. And if the husband did not sleep soundly enough, then the demon might cause a profound slumber to fall upon him so that he would snore tranquilly through the adultery. Moreover, the demon could place in the husband's bed an effigy of the wife, who thus seemed to recline in all innocence at her spouse's side while in fact she was miles away taking full part in the orgies of the Sabbat.

Wives who went to the Sabbat only in spirit, leaving their bodies behind, were sometimes found out by their husbands. This was because even spiritual copulations with incubi (or succubi) caused the physical body of the human participant to grow icy cold. More cautious wives, whether going to the orgies bodily or otherwise, drugged their husbands or put them into trances by tweaking their ears and muttering appropriate magical phrases. Some left dummies in their beds, or other objects intended to deceive: Eller of Ottingen, a pillow; Sinchen May of Speirchen, a bunch of twigs; Maria Schneider of Metzerech, a bundle of broomstraws, etc.

Husbands failing to note the difference between their wives and such feeble simulacra must have been more than usually wanting in perceptive powers, and even at the time there were a few skeptics. For example, Felix Braehm, in a dissertation written for his doctorate in 1701,[3] suggested that a husband who awakened to find his wife missing from the bed might more wisely suspect her of infidelity than of witchcraft.

Father Adam Tanner,[4] in his *Disputatio de Angelis*, proved himself another more than commonly practical man. It was unreasonable to suppose, Tanner wrote, that night after night, month after month, year after year, a witch could arise from the side of her sleeping husband, take a trip to the Sabbat, and not get caught at it. Neither, he said, did it seem likely, as some argued, that a dummy or block of wood could be left in the bed and the husband so deceived. And besides, he inquired, how could the witch unlatch and raise the window without making enough noise to awaken her spouse?

12. *Devils in the convents*

Incubus demons sometimes invaded convents and there fornicated with the nuns, but it was a more usual occurrence that nuns became obsessed or possessed by demons. Then the holy sisters would discover that strange and unaccustomed fires burned in their bellies while harsh but seductive voices whispered inside their heads, exhorting them to limitless lewdness.

Nuns (and monks) were also especially prone to being raped by demons. If the nuns were very virtuous, and in particular if they defended themselves with the true cross, the devils were not likely to be able to consummate the attack. But demons sometimes set the conscious resistances of even the most devout to nought, rendering the nuns unconscious and then molesting them while they lay asleep or entranced. Many good sisters were known to have been put to sleep by incubi who then abused them, and there was the well-known case of a holy man who was deprived of consciousness by sweet music and who awakened to find himself polluted like any wanton whoremonger.

In *obsession*, the demon tortured his victim from without, constantly muttering and hissing obscene suggestions and relentlessly urging carnal acts until irresistible and atrocious ardors had been aroused and fanned to holocaust proportions. In *possession*, the demon actually entered into the possessed person, who was called an *energumen*, and became the controlling personality. However, the terms obsession and possession are often used interchangeably.

The phenomena of possession were well known to the early Christians. Lewd rolling on the ground with coital movements, obscene language, etc., were described in the seventh century. Saint Hilary,[1] in the fourth century, reasoned that demons possess the bodies of humans in order to be able to use them as if they were their own. Saint Hilary also proved beyond all dispute that demons possess the bodies of animals. This he did by exorcising a camel.

Demons entered the bodies of men and women in various ways. Saint Gregory[2] told how a demon entered into a nun on a piece of lettuce she was eating, which the demon was able to do because the nun had imprudently neglected to make the sign of the cross before taking a bite out of the lettuce. Another nun had been possessed since age seven, demons entering into her on a bread crust.

Possessing demons also departed the bodies of humans by way of the mouth, or by the vagina or the anus. Sometimes there would be only a single possessing demon; in other cases, thousands, or even millions. The departure of the demon through the vagina recalls the traditional function of that aperture in many occult matters—for example, in prophecy, where the voice of the oracle issues out of the vaginal orifice.[3]

One of the most notorious of all possession cases was that of a nun named Madeleine de Demandolx de la Palud, who was accused by a sister nun of being possessed by Ashtaroth and 6,661 other devils. (Some said later, Beelzebub, Leviathan, Baalberith, Asmodeus, Ashtaroth, and 6,661 other devils, but that seems a formidable and indeed superfluous array of demonic dignitaries to be involved in a single case.) However, the number reported was, even if valid, by no means a record. One Joanna Seiler was exorcised of more than one hundred million devils (although according to Wier, an eminent authority, there are only 44,435,556 devils, not counting Satan, in existence).[4]

Madeleine, who came into court in 1673 to testify against the priest who allegedly had seduced her and caused her to give herself up to the Devil, told her examiners that at the Sabbats she attended with Father Louis Gaufridi (her seducer) little children were eaten and sodomy committed by the celebrants. It will be recalled that the nuns from the convent at Lille reported bestiality, sodomy, coitus with devils, and other enormities to have occurred at the Sabbats they attended.

There were a few authorities who questioned the notion that an incubus could prevail over a nun if she were truly unwilling. However, Prierias, in the sixteenth century, held that God permits incubi forcibly to violate even virtuous and virginal nuns. Moreover, the demon may increase or intensify the sacrilege, waiting until the nun is at her prayers, or has taken the host into her mouth, to poke her in her private parts.

In the seventeenth century, erotomanias and epidemics of possession swept the convents of France, with dramatic outbreaks erupting in such nunneries as those of Aix-en-Provence, Loudun, Louviers, and Auxonne. Most of these have been exhaustively dealt with by other writers and I will barely touch upon them here.

Especially ill-starred was the Ursuline convent at Loudun, about which several books have been written. And even after Loudun's major scandal had passed, the convent continued to be a tourist attraction of considerable value to itself and the town. The nuns, still possessed, were the drawing cards. Fits of erotic abandonment might come upon them at any time, but particularly when a large audience was on hand.

One young nun called Sister Claire, whose behavior was not atypical, would regularly fall upon her back among a host of spectators, lift her habit to expose her genitals, masturbate frantically with both hands, and call upon all nearby males to "Fuck me! Fuck me!" Other nuns did the same, and revealed such extensive acquaintance with current linguistic obscenities that it seemed a wondrous mystery where they had acquired their knowledge. (Although of course it was the demons, not the possessed nuns, who were speaking.) It was said that the frenzied eroticism of the holy sisters, and their depraved and importunate advances to males of all ages and degrees of desirability, would have brought a blush to the face of a hardened harlot from Paris or Marseilles.

The nuns of Louviers were possessed by demons who were in league with the father confessors of the convent. Many marvelous things happened in that cloistral climate during the period from about 1628 to 1642.

The nuns fornicated with black cats, which had penes like those of robust men. They attended Sabbats and participated in orgies with devils, clerics, and the ghost of the dead priest who had been their first seducer.

The father confessors gave them instruction in the techniques of lesbian intercourse and then looked on with delectation while the nuns availed themselves of their knowledge. An artificial penis was sometimes used in these orgies and the nuns would circumcise it before inserting it into their genitals (a different dildo presumably being used on each occasion).

Nuns wandered around the convent, confessed themselves, and took communion in a state of nakedness. At blasphemous rites staged by the priests, one of the fathers would attach a host to his penis before engaging in coitus or sodomy. This was all brought to light in a trial which did not fail to engage the public interest.

For more than five years, demons possessed the Ursulines of the convent of Auxonne. A charge of witchcraft was brought against Sister St. Colombe, the Mother Superior. She was also accused of introducing lesbian intercourse into the convent, although what she seems really to have done was to interrupt the sexual affairs going on between a number of young nuns and their confessors.

At any rate, the sisters testified that she stuck her tongue into their mouths, fondled their breasts and their genitals, introduced them to tribadism, etc. She appeared to them in dreams and in visions, as well as in the flesh. Sometimes she carried a human phallus in her hand, and she was said to be the owner, as well, of an artificial one which she used to masturbate herself and the nuns.

All of this, it was charged, was done with the aid of the Devil, who possessed the nuns, afflicting them with heated and itchy organs and making them helpless to resist Sister St. Colombe when she wanted to have her way with them.

No doubt, convents are still plagued by waves of erotomania today, though the epidemics may take a somewhat different form, and the Church is able to keep the embarrassing incidents quiet. But it is well known that Catholic exorcists still cast out devils, and the *Rituale Romanum,* bearing the endorsement of Cardinal Spellman, gives the rite for driving out evil spirits from possessed persons.[5]

One of the most recent instances of convent infestation by demons to have been reported was that discussed by Laurent and Nagour (*Magica Sexualis*), and it occurred within the memory of living persons:

"Late in the nineteenth century the case of Cantianille turned not only the city of Auxerre, but the whole diocese of Sens, upside down. This Cantianille, placed in a convent of Mont-Saint-Sulpice, was violated when she was barely fifteen years old, by a priest who dedicated her to the devil. The priest himself had been corrupted in early childhood by an ecclesiastic belonging to a sect of possessed which was created the very day Louis XVI was guillotined. What happened in the convent, where many nuns, evidently mad with hysteria, were associated in erotic devilry and sacrilegious rages with Cantianille, reads for all the world like the procedure in the trials of wizards of long ago."[6]

A convent of a much earlier day that was sore oppressed by incubi was in the Diocese of Cologne. There, investigators searching for forbidden works on black magic found among the effects of one fourteen-year-old nun a packet of love letters, ardent in the extreme, written by the girl to her incubus. And the nuns, in addition to copulating with demons in the forms of handsome youths, were forever being assaulted by a big black dog which would knock them to the ground, lick their privates, and then copulate with them. When this happened, the Devil always rendered the nuns quite powerless to resist.

The nuns of Cologne had as their counterparts in such bestiality the holy sisters of Nimeguen, who were victimized by a dog that assaulted them in their beds.[7] Similar erotic manias, replete with hallucinations of rapes by devils, livened the convents of Kentorp and St. Bridget.

Another famous possession was that of Angela de Foligny, who became a raging nymphomaniac as the result of appetites implanted in her by demons. Later, like one Jeanne de Cambray, Angela claimed to have copulated with Christ—not too uncommon a craving at the time. And one remembers that Saint Mechtildis, not possessed by any devils, said that Christ appeared to her and "He kissed my hand, pressed me to Him, whispered to me to give Him my love, and I surrendered my all to Him and in return tasted of His divine essence."[8]

It might be well, before closing this chapter, to mention certain problems involved in the casting out of devils from the possessed, whether nuns or mere members of the laity. Not all incubi could be exorcised, and there were those who said that incubi could not be exorcised at all.

Theorists who maintained that incubi were not susceptible to exorcism believed, therefore, that incubi (and succubi) were a special class of devils. Some suggested that they are relatives of poltergeists, supernatural beings also immune to exorcism. And there was the hypothesis that the incubi resisting exorcism were foreign devils.

Since Christian exorcists were effective only with Christian demons—because of their ritual, which was the only one they were permitted to use—serious problems could occur if a foreign or pagan devil possessed a Christian. This was held to be —thank God!—a rather rare occurrence; but when it did occur, the demon would only laugh derisively at efforts to evict him. Poltergeists, who behave similarly, could usually be counted upon to voluntarily depart the energumen after a while; but a pagan demon might linger on for years, hideously blaspheming and causing the possessed to engage in behavior all the more intolerable because the demon could not be reached and made to suffer for it.

There was the grave risk that the exorcist himself might become possessed and this was considered to be a hazard of the profession. A few intrepid priests would even volunteer to take into themselves the possessing demons who tormented their patients, hoping to be able to oust the demons later by dint of piety and strength of faith, and possibly with an assist from some other exorcist. The offer was not always declined by the demon, and more than one rash cleric lived to rue the day when he agreed to play host to the devils who swarmed out of the energumen and into himself—then refusing to be driven off by piety, faith, prayers, or any other weapon in the priestly arsenal.

13. *Defense and counterattack*

After it had been decided that women (witches) gave themselves to demons willingly, or because they had bound themselves by agreement to do so, the matter of defense against seductive and rapist devils no longer seemed especially urgent. There were some cases, mostly in convents, of assaults by impassioned incubi; but more often nuns were possessed and then driven to erotic excesses with priests and with one another. Then, the remedy was exorcism.

In early Christian times, however, demons habitually assaulted or sought to seduce both men and women, particularly the most pious, and there is a considerable literature of such attacks and of methods of preventing or defending against them. Crosses, holy water, prayers, horseshoes, and garlic are often mentioned, as are techniques such as calling upon God, the Virgin or some one of the saints to directly intervene. The burning of incense was sometimes recommended, the ingredients prescribed being in more than one case narcotics with alleged aphrodisiac properties.

Martin Luther, in the sixteenth century, suggested baring one's buttocks and breaking wind—a risky business, since Hebrew writers had long since established that some demons are sodomists. However, Luther, often visited by devils, is said to have employed the method successfully. (There is another version, or perhaps there were two different incidents, in which the Devil bared *His* buttocks and farted at Luther.)[1]

Sometimes the preventive measures were inadvertent. Thus, the incubus might be incapacitated if the lady happened to be wearing or to otherwise have about her some St. John's grass and vervain. As one demon lover poetically put it to his would-be mistress: "If you want to be a mistress of mine/Get rid of the St. John's grass and the vervain."

There were other herbs, as well as precious stones, symbols, relics, etc., which possessed such guardian virtue.

Prayers, hymn-singing, and simple stout resistance sufficed in some cases. Thus, the blessed and strong-willed Angela de Foligny withstood a devil's attempts on her, but only by calling repeatedly upon her Lord and with considerable distress. The incubus rained heavy blows upon her recalcitrant body and caused her privy parts to ache with lust, yet she stood resolute in her resistance:

"His member is not yet in me!" she exulted, "although I am beaten black and blue by demons, and have been laid low by his blows for many days, and all my privates seem to be bursting." [2]

Nuns, holy men, and saints were always, of course, top priority targets of incubi and succubi, doubtless on the ground that those sworn to chastity would sin more grievously if they entered into fornications with devils than would ordinary persons. Lewd demons, as everyone remembers, disguised themselves as naked and beauteous maidens to tempt Saint Hilarion and Saint Anthony the Great, striving by lustful grimace, lascivious gesture, and opprobrious oral overture to undermine the stout virtue of those dedicated servants of a cunctipotent Creator. Another saint so beset was Margaret of Cortona, who was tormented in her cell by a devil who made obscene and venereal advances and sang dirty ditties whilst she was at her hymns, even making so bold as to demand that she join with him in his blasphemies. By piety and purity she repulsed him at last, but the trial was a sore one.

Saint Caesarius [3] told of a penitent harlot who entered a convent and was at once approached by a lustful incubus. She crossed herself and fended him off with holy water, whereupon he left, only to return shortly and resume his salacious enticements. On this second occasion, she recited the Angelic Salutation, and he vanished "like an arrow shot from a bow." He returned yet a third time, but her *Ave Marias*, while they could not banish him permanently, kept him at a safe distance until finally he wearied of the unfruitful endeavor. Saint Caesarius also told of a most devout nun who was always being approached in her bed by an incubus, even, and with hateful irreverence, while she was at her prayers. She took the good advice of a certain erudite holy man and the next time the incubus came she pronounced the word "Benedicite," which put him to precipitate rout. Caesarius added that a man bothered by an insistent succubus rid himself of the foul whorish creature by means of Sacramental Confession.

Some held that demons are frightened of swords, and most that the threshold of pain of a demon is very low, so that the question posing itself was how to inflict pain on the evil spirit and so send him on his way. Certain authorities suggested beating him—difficult, since in many cases he would, when cornered, resort to invisibility—or, in lieu of that desideratum, beating the object of his lusts in hope of somehow reaching him by that means.

Saint Bernard[4] is said to have helped a woman who had copulated nightly with a demon for six years, and whose husband had finally left her after learning of the adultery. The Saint gave this woman, who lived at Nantes, a stick to take to bed with her, and so long as the stick was in her bed the demon dared not invade it, although he flew into a towering rage and filled the air with his threats and fearsome oaths.

Thomas of Cantimpré[5] was a strong believer in thrashing demons and recommended clubs and other weapons for the purpose, though only if more religious methods failed. He told of a young monk who was visited in his bed by a succubus demon in the form of a toothsome wench. The monk was about to defend himself by making the sign of the cross, but found that the succubus, anticipating that maneuver, had caused both of his arms to become paralyzed. Nothing daunted, the monk kicked her, first in the face, and then in an unspecified location, whereupon she disappeared.

Exorcism was usually employed in those classical cases of possession where the lust of the possessed was directed toward human sex partners. Sometimes, however, it seems to have been used as a weapon against visiting incubi, when the priest would wait with the woman in her room (usually, with the nun in her cell) for the expected incubus to arrive, and then perform the exorcism before the devil could make his assault. It was well recognized that exorcists, in such situations, are exposed to the gravest risks, since the demon may use the body of the female, if he succeeds in possessing her, in the most outrageous manner with a view to seducing and so disarming the man of God.

Unfortunately, at least from the official point of view of the Church, possessing demons seem to have become much more difficult to handle by the end of the Middle Ages than they were in early Christian times. Nuns possessed by demons had often found the matter a simple one to deal with in the fourth century, when it was only necessary to spit or to blow one's nose to evict the malign and unwelcome tenant. In fact, and as briefly mentioned earlier, incubi often refused to respond to exorcism at all, blaspheming and mocking the priestly exorcists, jeering at the sign of the cross, encouraging acts of gross impudicity on the part of the energumen, and otherwise displaying a devilish intractability. This inefficacy of exorcism in dealing with incubi and succubi confirmed the Reverend Father Sinistrari of Ameno in his suspicion that incubi and succubi are not demons at all, but higher beings, intermediate between humans and angels. As such, he said, they degrade themselves in their fornications with mankind, although humans are honored by the contact. They would not, of course, respond to exorcism, which is intended for application to demons. (Sinistrari was able to reconcile these ideas with those of the Church concerning intercourse with incubi and succubi

by stating that most humans who entered into sexual relationships with them *believed* them to be demons, and so were just
as guilty as if the higher beings *were* demons.)

It would not do, however, to conclude these remarks without
remedying any impression the reader might have that exorcism
is always inefficacious, or to be despised. Not so very long ago,
Franz Hartmann told of a vampire-incubus who was handled
quite satisfactorily by exorcism, and after medical interven-
tions had proved wholly useless.

Hartmann related the case of a girl who rejected a young
man's proposal of marriage on the ground that he was a drunk-
ard. She subsequently married another of her suitors and the
man she had rejected shot himself.

A short time afterwards, an invisible being described as a
vampire, and who she was certain was the deceased lover, began visiting her in her bed at night, usually when the husband
was absent, and making his presence felt "in a way that could
leave no room for doubt."

Dr. Hartmann says physicians diagnosed the case as "hysterics" and "tried in vain every remedy in the pharmacopoeia."
He adds that where medicine failed, an exorcist "of strong
faith" succeeded, and the troublesome vampire-incubus was
banished and came no more.[6]

The psychological interpretation to which this case lends itself is so obvious as to need no stating. Commonplace, too, is
the cure by a faith-healer (exorcist) where the physicians
failed. Anyone who has seen the evangelist Oral Roberts casting out devils on television should well understand that in
such (functional, not organic) cases the prestige of the healer,
and the forcefulness of his mumbo jumbo, is more important
to a cure, or at least a temporary remission, than all but the
most extensive psychotherapy which does not take into account the peculiar need for magical trappings of the individual
involved.

Most therapists will oppose the idea, but exorcism as a form of shock therapy should not be lightly rejected in cases where the traditional symptoms of possession are present. Results may be produced very quickly (as compared to psychotherapy) in some cases, and there is much evidence that the remission of symptoms is not always less permanent.

14. *Points of law and order*

It would be possible without any great amount of sleuthing to extend to book length, and beyond a cataloguing of the legal and other casuistries, dialectical degeneracies and piddling disputations concerned with witchcraft and intercourse with demons. For my part, I would much enjoy composing such a book; but there are probably an insufficient number of aficionados to justify the effort. Here, I will be brief.

One of the first theologico-legal problems to arise in connection with the abominable intercourse with demons was what to call it. Such connections were probably most commonly punished under a charge of *sodomy*—sodomy being used as a general category comprehending all "crimes against nature." Not infrequently, however, the charge was one of *bestiality*. The death penalty was authorized by the Scriptures for either of these offenses, and so either was adequate to the ends of justice (as they were seen).

A formidable minority of Catholic theologians preferred the term *bestialitas*—a category considerably broader than bestiality (understood as referring only to sexual intercourse with animals)—under which, from time to time, the Church prosecuted carnal couplings with Jews, Turks, and Saracens. Generally, *bestialitas* might be understood to refer to all intercourse between humans and beings of some other kind or order.

The term *demoniality* was also proposed, and sometimes used, and at first consideration might seem to be most appropriate because most specific. However, the Scriptural authority for punishing sexual relations with demons was less clear than where sodomy and bestiality were concerned, and *demoniality* was opposed on that basis.

The Church held for a time to the doctrine that an incubus was a demon in human form whereas if the demon appeared in animal or some other non-human form he was no longer an incubus but "some other kind of devil." However, this distinction does not seem to have played any important legal role in the witch trials, where demons were described as appearing in all manner of forms and were still regarded as incubi. That is, the charge was still fornication with an incubus (or succubus) and was prosecuted as sodomy, bestiality, or demoniality, depending upon the preference of the tribunal, regardless of the form taken by the incubus.

On the other hand, the form in which the demon copulated with the witch might have some significant bearing upon the degree of her sin. At least many writers seem to have believed that demons assumed certain forms, or made use of particular dead bodies, in order to heighten the severity of the offense against God. Thus, the demon might use the body of a deceased near-relative (when the offense would be demoniality-incest-necrophilia); that of a dead nun (demoniality-necrophilia-sacrilege); or that of a dead beast (demoniality-necrophilia-bestiality).

The sexual debaucheries charged to the witches, even if they had been with men rather than with demons, and even if no perversions had been involved, would still have provided ample grounds for their extermination—as clergymen and demonologists were wont to point out. Many precedents were cited to prove that fornication alone merits the death penalty. A favorite was the incident recorded in Numbers XXV, where Phinehas, outraged that Zambri should copulate with the harlot Cozbi, took a dagger (or a spear) "and thrust both of them through together, to wit, the man and the woman, in the genital parts." This same chapter advises that God, by means of a plague, wrought the execution of 24,000 Israelites for having fallen into illicit copulations and other delinquencies.

After all, it was possible to sin sexually, and by coitus, even if one were married and faithful to one's wife, by indulging too often, or by enjoying it too much. Saint Jerome, for example, had held that: He who loves his wife to excess is an adulterer.[1]

It was usually argued by inquisitors that those who copulated with demons did so voluntarily (although it was necessarily acknowledged, in view of Church history and the experiences of a good many Church luminaries, that in days past there had been good women, even saints, who were ravished by demons). Some distinguished between three types of persons who engaged in demoniality: the willing partners (witches and possibly a few disordered voluptuaries); the unwilling victims (who were carnally assaulted); and those who were forcibly conducted to the Sabbats by witches and there compelled to participate in the orgies. Naturally, degree of guilt was somewhat diminished if the victim was unwilling, although guilt might not be dispelled entirely, since it was a widely accepted doctrine that no person may be tested by a devil beyond his or her capacity to resist.

It was required of those assailed by lascivious demons that they put forth every effort to frustrate the intent of the incubi, and if they failed to do this, they could not be regarded as guiltless (recalling the present-day requirement that a rape victim put up a reasonable struggle). For example, there was a youthful nun who said that she always knew ahead of time when her incubus was coming to (forcibly) molest her. Her sexual organs would become heated and engorged, whereupon she would feel herself irresistibly obliged to run to her cell, lock the door, and lie down on the bed. An exorcist assigned to her case sternly remarked that this must be understood as at least partial encouragement, since forewarned is forearmed, and the nun should, when her genitals got into such a tumultuous state, have resorted to prayers, hymns, invocations of the saints, and all other possible methods to still her excitement.

A troublesome legal problem occasionally presented itself

when an individual maintained that he or she was not aware that the sex partner was a demon (as when, for example, the incubus appeared to a woman disguised as her husband). This seems to have been resolved differently from case to case, though seldom ever was the result the complete exoneration of a witch.

Another defense sometimes offered by an accused was that the witness or witnesses had not actually seen what they reported (and thought they had seen), but had been deceived by the Devil. Probably most thinkers were agreed that a truly innocent person would not be permitted by God to suffer as a consequence of a deception by the Devil leading to false accusations. Some, however, like Sinistrari, urged that all possible precautions be taken to avoid condemning the innocent. After relating the tale of a nun seen copulating with an incubus (by other nuns who had bored a hole through the wall of her cell in order to peep), Sinistrari wrote:

"When, therefore, indications are forthcoming, such as those recited above, a charge might be brought after a searching inquiry; yet, without the confession of the accused, the offence should not be regarded as fully proved, even if the intercourse were testified by eye-witnesses; for it sometimes happens that, in order to undo an innocent female, the Devil feigns such intercourse by means of some delusion. In those cases, the Ecclesiastical Judge must consequently trust but his own eyes." [2]

Was the judge, then, exempt from diabolic delusions? Some said yes, because God would not permit that a judge should be deceived, and justice, derived from divine and immutable principles, set at nought. Similarly, judges were held to be immune to the maleficia, or evil-working magic, of witches—essential if judges were to be able to function in the face of the threats witches made against them. Others were not sure, citing possible exceptions, that judges enjoyed either exemption or immunity. In any case, the precautions advised by Sinistrari were worthless. This was so because a confession would be extracted by torture or by some other pressure the witches could not resist. The insistence upon torture, before a confession could be regarded as acceptable, was also a common one, insuring that individuals would be tortured not to bring them to confession of their crimes, which they were willing to make, but that they might not avoid the suffering.

Sexual witchcraft or magic was deserving of pitiless retribution in its own right, even if it were not proof of something still worse. Speaking of love potions, the *Malleus Maleficarum* set forth that those who by means of witchery "turn the passions of women to lusts of every kind," are dastardly criminals and "are to be thrown to the wild beasts." Young girls suddenly turned promiscuous might, when caught, successfully blame a witch for their behavior, but this did not necessarily mean that the girl making the accusation would be spared punishment for her sexual escapades: If she had been sufficiently virtuous, God would probably have nullified the love potion, or provided an antidote.

To make a man impotent, to make a man or woman sterile, to cause abortion or stillbirth, to dry up the milk of a mother or a wet nurse, to make the milk poisonous or deprive it of its food value so that the infant would starve—these acts were murder by the Devil's black magic. Starving of an infant and the causing of abortion and stillbirth were obvious homicides and required no legal or theological subtleties to make the point. But causing impotence and sterility, and so preventing conceptions which might otherwise have occurred, were deeds where the case against the defendant was less clearcut. However, skilled attorneys would find a way.

Impotence produced by witchcraft gave rise to a variety— indeed, a labyrinth—of problems. In the fifteenth century it was already well established, on the authority of Saint Thomas Aquinas and others, that impotence brought about by sorcery could be a legitimate basis for the annulment of a marriage. This was the case where the witchery occurred before the marriage had been consummated and was sufficiently severe to prevent consummation. Ecclesiastics disputed, however, the length of time which should elapse before the marriage could be voided—some saying, for example, a year, and some holding out for three years. This was based on the belief that the spell might be impermanent and wear off in time so that the husband could perform his connubial duties in the interest of procreation.

It was Christian doctrine that fornication with an incubus provided ground for divorce. Jewish thinkers allowed that such fornications might justify divorce, but did not necessarily do so in every case. It depended upon the circumstances of the intercourse.

That demoniality was cause for divorce is illustrated by the case of Curt Puchenss of Meiningen, whose wife confessed to perniciously frolicking with a demon. The court ruled that in such cases adultery has been committed and the wedlock is dissolved—though in some cases the question was academic since the aggrieved party soon became a widower or widow anyhow, with the felon burned at the stake or otherwise eliminated. However, the right to remarry might be involved.

Marriages of witches to demons were not infrequently described, and the legal status of such unions was pondered; also, in some cases, the marriages seemed to be bigamous. Some said that the unions had no validity for the reason that the demon, instead of placing a ring on the finger of his bride as ceremony required, would merely stoop over and blow on her bunghole.

A very serious and important question was whether intercourse with an incubus constituted of itself a pact with the Devil. Some weighty authorities said that it did, but others of equal ponderosity thought a more formal agreement was required. Those leaning to the last-mentioned interpretation said that the intercourse "cemented" but did not constitute the pact.

The age of consent for atrocious couplings with demons was another vital issue and was heatedly disputed. Peter Binsfeld,[3] sixteenth century author of a *Treatise on Confessions of*

Malefactors and Witches, wrote that girls should be understood to have reached puberty at twelve and boys at fourteen, and that thereafter they should be held *doli capaces*—liable for their acts (such as lewd and unnatural cohabitation with demons). Binsfeld noted, however, that some children are unusually precocious, so that the law should take care to preserve its flexibility, set no rigid minimum age for liability, and thus avoid the horrendous prospect of permitting some sin-saturated little bawd to slip through its over-lenient fingers. He recommended that children under sixteen should, in general, not be executed, though he left abundant room for exceptions. Even so, his position was a liberal one since some writers thought girls to be sexually mature at as young as five years, and from that age on held them responsible for their carnal misbehavior. In a few cases girls of two years were put to death for demoniality, although they seem to have been regarded not as responsible but as corrupted beyond all hope of redemption.

Sinistrari, holding that incubi and succubi were not devils, was faced with a problem unique to his beliefs, or almost so: What of those who copulated with beings they supposed to be demons, but which were not? Such persons, said Sinistrari, sin by intent, and the grievousness of their crimes is equally as great as if the incubi and succubi were in fact the devils the offenders believed them to be.

Nocturnal pollutions also gave rise to a variety of problems, ethical and religious. Were they caused by intercourse with demons, and if so, were the sleepers guilty in the same way as those who fornicated with demons while awake? If wet dreams were not caused by demons, were they still sinful? Were they the result of evil thoughts, or did they happen merely because of an excessive accumulation of semen in the vesicles? And so on.

Daniel Defoe (*The Political History of the Devil*) told the following story, which shows the moral problem considered posed by nocturnal pollutions even in the eighteenth century:

"I knew a Person who the *Devil* so haunted with Naked

Women, fine beautiful Ladies in Bed with him, and Ladies of his Acquaintance too, offering their Favours to him, and all in his Sleep; so that he seldom slept without such Entertainment; the Particulars are too gross for my Story, but he gave me several long Accounts of his Night's *Amours,* and being a Man of a vertuous Life and good Morals, it was the greatest Surprize to him imaginable; for you cannot doubt but that the cunning *Devil* made every thing to be acted to the Life with him, and in a Manner the most wicked; he own'd with Grief to me, that the very first Attack the *Devil* made upon him, was with a very beautiful Lady of his Acquaintance, who he had been really something freer than ordinary with in Conversation; this Lady he brought to him in a Posture for Wickedness, and wrought up his inclinations so high in his Sleep, that he, as he thought, actually went about to debauch her, she not at all resisting; but that he wak'd in the very Moment, to his particular Satisfaction.

"He was greatly concern'd at this Part, namely, that he really gave the Consent of his Will to the Fact, and wanted to know if he was not as Guilty of Adultery, as if he had lain with her; indeed he decided the Question against himself, so forcibly, that I, who was of the same Opinion before, had nothing to say against it; however, I confirm'd him in it, by asking him these Questions.

"1. Whether he did not think the *Devil* had the chief Hand in such a Dream? he answer'd, it could certainly be no body else, it must be the *Devil.*

"2. I then ask'd him what Reason the *Devil* could have for it, if his Consent to the Fact in Sleep had not been criminal? *That's true indeed,* says he, *I am answer'd:* But then he ask'd another Question, which, I confess is not so easy to answer, namely, how he should prevent being serv'd so again.

"Nor could all my Divinity or his own keep the *Devil* from attacking him again; on the other Hand, as I have said, he worried him to that Degree, that he injur'd his Health, bringing Naked Women to him, sometimes in one Posture of Lewdness, sometimes in another, sometimes into his very Arms, sometimes with such Additions as I am not merry enough, and sometimes such as I am not wicked enough to put into your Heads; the Man, indeed, could not help it, and so the *Devil* was more Faulty than he; but as I hinted to him, he might bring his mind to such a stated Habit of Virtue, as to prevent its assenting to any wicked Motion, even in Sleep, and that would be the Way to put an End to the Attempt; and this Advice he relish'd very well, and practised, I believe, with Success." [4]

15. *Sexual magic*

It might be said that there are two general kinds of sexual magic: sexual acts aimed at achieving magical ends; and magical acts aimed at achieving sexual ends. While the first-mentioned certainly had at least a secondary place in witchcraft, data are scant; and it is with magical acts aimed at affecting sexual behavior and capacities that I will mainly deal here.

Much of the magic or witchcraft of the witches was aimed not just at sexual acts, but also at reproduction. Magic was used to inflame erotic passions or to suppress them; to cause impotence and frigidity; and to cause sterility, abortion, and stillbirth. Humans were the usual victims, but animals might also be targets.

Witches could also disrupt or block the passage of feces and urine from the body. This they accomplished in various ways: causing rectum and urethra to clench, or to flesh over at their openings; or wastes might be caused to pass out of the mouth of the bewitched person.

Sometimes, too, victims of witchcraft were made to void all manner of oddities, such as stones and balls, hair and pig's bristles. In one famous case in France an adolescent boy "urinated" not water but a half dozen pieces of paper inscribed with "strange characters," and some peas. (Interestingly, this event followed what seems to have been some homosexual activities between the youth and his schoolmaster, who was then branded a witch.)

One of the techniques used by witches to prevent urination was the same employed to make men impotent—the tying of knots in a cord. Many men, unable to pass water because of such hexes, suffered greatly and at last died.

Witches dried up the udders of cows and also stopped the flow of milk in lactating mothers, the aim of course being to starve the calf or the infant. But the witch, paragon of sexual evil, might be successfully opposed in such cases by the virgin, epitome of sexual (or sex-*less*) good. Whatever the witchcraft employed, the virgin might overcome it by means of a counter-agent as simple as the utterance of the Angelical Salutation. (Since witches could, in the first place, only dry up udders *Deo permittente*, it would seem that God was amusing himself in such cases by playing games.)

That witches concocted love potions (using semen, human and animal genitalia, the multivarious items of the *Dreck Apotheke*, etc.) is well known. But there were other methods of arousing lust, some by means of witchcraft and some by direct intervention of demons. For example, De la Torre said that the demon, to awaken strong desire, could introduce sex stimulants into the human stomach. Sex depressants (anaphrodisiacs) might also be introduced, with the result that the genitalia became anesthetic. (Some witches were also anesthetized by demons, or their body temperatures drastically but painlessly raised, so that when they were consigned to the flames the blaze that consumed them felt cool and even pleasant.)

It is certain that as early as the twelfth century witches were using images of wax, as had the pagans before them, to incite voluptuous passion in men and women (as well as to injure them—the purpose with which we are more familiar today). Spells were pronounced over the images, caresses were lavished upon them, and in a variety of other ways the images were magically manipulated so as to produce the desired effect, up to and including nymphomania and satyriasis, depending on sex, in the intended object.

Sexual bewitchments sometimes took strange and imaginative forms. Thus, the *Malleus Maleficarum* preserves for a grateful posterity the following bizarre case:

"There is in the town of Coblenz a poor man who is bewitched in this way. In the presence of his wife he is in the habit of acting after the manner of men with women, that is to say, of practising a coition, as it were, and he continues to do this repeatedly, nor have the cries and urgent appeals of his wife any effect in making him desist. And after he has fornicated thus two or three times, he bawls out, 'We are going to start all over again'; when actually there is no person visible to mortal sight lying with him. And after an incredible number of such bouts, the poor man at last sinks to the floor utterly exhausted. When he has recovered his strength a little and is asked how this happened to him, and whether he has had any woman with him, he answers that he saw nothing, but that his mind is in some way possessed so that he can by no means refrain from such priapism. And indeed he harbours a great suspicion that a certain woman bewitched him in this way, because he had offended her, and she had cursed him with threatening words, telling him what she would like to happen to him." [1]

Change of sex operations, performed on both human and beast, were known to have occurred by witchcraft and by the intervention of demons.[2] Moreover, there were claims that witches possessed a drug which had the capacity to reverse the sex of the taker.[3] There seems to have been a keen interest in this subject (as of course there is at the present time, and probably has been at most or all other times). Some said that males could be transformed into females and females into males, but it was also argued that the sex change worked in only one direction. Thus, Mirandola declared that the Devil could make males of females, but could not transform men into women, because it is the method of nature to add on rather than to take away.

But the sexual magic of witches in which the authorities took the greatest interest was *ligature,* or the production of impotence by magical means. It seems apparent that the fear of impotence was widespread; and this in its turn probably indicates a high incidence of potency disturbances—no surprise when one considers how licentious the times were on the one hand, and how thoroughly sex was damned on the other (not to mention such likely contributory factors as poor diet and hygiene).

Robbins (*The Encyclopedia of Witchcraft and Demonology*) says that Ivo of Chartres, who died early in the twelfth century, was the first Catholic theologian to deal at any length with ligature. However that may be, medieval executions of witches for the offense go back much earlier. In the seventh century in France a renowned witch was executed. The woman, Brunehaut, was put to death in 613 by order of Clothaire II. She was especially feared for her ability to inflict impotency on men. (Her execution was also, it is prudent to add, for political reasons.)

Aquinas stated in his *Quaestiones Quodlibetales* "that demons are something and that they can do harm by their operations and impede carnal copulation." Aquinas noted various methods by which demons produced impotence and various forms the impotence might take. One procedure of demons, he said, is to make a particular woman, perhaps a wife, so unattractive to a man that he will have no desire for her and hence be unable to copulate with her. The statement of Aquinas was very frequently cited by subsequent authorities.

(It is worth remarking at this point that impotence was frequently held to be a characteristic of Satan. Psychoanalysts note in many of the tales about the Devil symbolic attempts to castrate Him, or to affirm His impotence. Thus, as an architect or engineer, the Devil is never able to complete the buildings and bridges He begins. His plans and projects are never finished. His deals always fall through, or at least' they fall through in most cases. Even when He has contracted for a soul, employing neither coercion nor skulduggery, He is often denied payment. He has no semen, and if He wants to copulate He is obliged to steal the penis of some man or beast.)

Early Christian authors, regarding impotence as more blessing than curse, had declared that angels could take away a man's virile powers, although this was something they usually did only on request and as a token of particular esteem for the individual to be unsexed. Saint Gregory told of the Blessed Abbot Equitius,[4] incessantly distracted and tormented by the provocations of the flesh, who called upon God to set him free from this great evil. An angel came down one night and removed all sensation from his genitals, so that he was as if sexless, which enormously increased his influence as a preacher. God similarly answered the prayers of Saint Serenus, sending down an angel who "seemed to open his belly and take from his entrails a burning tumor of flesh, and then to replace all his intestines as they had been; and said: Lo! the provocation of your flesh is cut out, and know that this day you have obtained perpetual purity of your body, according to the prayer which you prayed, so that you will never again be pricked with that natural desire which is aroused even in babes and sucklings."[5] (The sexuality of infants and children was very well known in the past, was later denied in the interest of the myth of the "purity" of children, and had to be discovered all over again.)

It is plain that castrating angels took away not only the capacity for sexual intercourse, but also the *desire* for it. Witches and demons were of course less charitable. Only the wherewithal for achieving gratification was interfered with, while the lust not only remained but presumably raged all the more fiercely since the hunger could never be even slightly assuaged.

Different theorists mentioned various forms the impotence inflicted by demons and witches might take. Peter of Palude, for example, said that devils have five ways[6] of preventing husbands from doing their duty by their wives:

1. They interpose themselves between the man and the woman so that no contact of the flesh is possible.

2. They "freeze" desire.

3. They make the woman appear loathsome to the man.

4. They act directly on the penis, making erection impossible. (It might be noted here that Hostiensis, in his *Summa,* said that when the impotence is due to a natural defect, or to "coldness of nature," the penis lies limp and no stimulus suffices to rouse it. When the impotence is by witchcraft, however, the organ "becomes stirred and erect, but yet cannot perform." This would seem to conflict with Palude's view. And one wonders if the distinction was not between organic and functional impotence, however vaguely understood.)

5. They "prevent the flow of the vital essence to the members in which lies the motive power; by closing as it were the seminary ducts, so that it does not descend to the generative channels, or falls back from them, or in any of many ways fails in its function."

Peter of Palude neglects to mention a technique which was the most fearsome and drastic of all—the "theft" of the penis or testicles or both, or the causing of those organs to "disappear."

Whether devils and witches might steal a man's privy parts, and whether they could then restore what they had taken away, was much disputed by savants. It was commonplace, it would seem, for the sexual apparatus to turn up missing, and priests wrote of seeing with their own eyes good church members so mutilated. Some held that devils could in fact rob a man of his generative parts, but it was more generally believed that the goodness of God was such as to forbid so desperate a depredation. Those inclining to this last-mentioned position could not deny that penes and testicles sometimes mysteriously vanished, leaving shamefaced and grieving eunuchs where stout fellows well equipped as any had been; but they explained that this was illusion only. Priests might sometimes restore the "missing" organs, as might sorcerers, but to enlist the aid of miracle-workers other than God's own servants on earth was strictly forbidden, and violators were subject to grave penalties.

Still others held that devils could actually remove the sex organs from the human body, but that witches, being of inferior powers, could only create an illusion—real enough to the victim—that the phallus had been removed. One picturesque manner of making the penis *seem* to have disappeared was mentioned by Kramer and Sprenger. Demons, they said, could interpose between the body of the victim and his senses of sight and touch some smoothly fashioned body in the color of flesh, "so that it seems to him that he can see and feel nothing but a smooth body with its surface interrupted by no genital organ." [7]

(I have myself, experimenting with various witchcraft phenomena—that is, seeking to duplicate them—produced the same effect in a good hypnotic subject. That is, by suggesting a negative hallucination I have so managed it that the subject could neither see nor feel his sex organ. That is not to say, however, that the effect was similarly produced in witchcraft, though in some cases it might have been.)

Those who thought that witches actually stole away the penes of males provided many "case histories" to substantiate their claims. One case offered in evidence was that of a man who prevailed upon a witch to return the organ she had pilfered. The crone took him into the woods and led him to a large nest containing a dozen or more male organs. The man, whose own instrument had been of modest size, identified as his the largest of the lot, a truly formidable engine, which later turned out to be the much exercised property of the parish priest.

Where it was believed that witches only made the genitals invisible, it was sometimes added that the enchanted organs might still be seen by some person of unusual purity, such as a saint, or a virgin of extraordinary piety. A fairly typical case of a male organ made invisible by witchcraft was cited by Remy:

"An old man, the porter of the Fortress of Bassompierre, had married a young wife, but continued to maintain connubial relations with a woman who had been his mistress before his marriage. His wife was indignant at the presence of this adulteress, who was not to be compared with her for youth or comeliness, and (as is usually the case) went and told her trouble to a neighboring woman and asked her to advise her what to do. Her neighbor (whose name was Lahire) told her to be of good cheer, for she had ready a remedy for that misfortune; and she gave her a herb plucked from her garden and said that if she put the juice of it in her husband's food, he would immediately forget his other love. So she seasoned his next meal with this juice; and at first his head grew very heavy, and then he sank into a profound sleep, on at last awaking from which he found, not without shame, that his whole masculinity had been taken from him. Being unable to conceal the fact any longer, he told his wife of his misfortune; and she, seeing that she had been deceived by her own imprudence and thoughtlessness, and that in begrudging the part to another she had herself lost the whole, told her husband how it had all happened; begging him to forgive her, since she had acted out of her great love for him. The husband readily pardoned her, since he knew that he had brought the misfortune upon himself by his lecherous lasciviousness: and laid the whole matter before the Lord of the place, François de Bassompierre . . . He, considering it to be his business to take care for the health of one of his servants, and to punish the witch in exemplary fashion for so shameful a crime, had that woman brought before him, and so terrified her by his threats that he compelled her to restore to the man that of which she had by her evil arts seemingly robbed him. This she did by giving him another herb; and so, being convicted by her own act, she was cast into prison and soon afterwards met the fate she deserved in the flames. It is perfectly clear, then, that there was no actual loss of the man's generative organs; but that a false glamour was drawn over the eyes of those who imagined them to have disappeared. For how should it be more possible for that member to grow again once it had been cut off than for the head or any other limb to be renewed after it had been amputated from the body?" [8]

(That witchcraft can result in psychical impotence is not to be doubted, and among primitive peoples such witchcraft is widely practiced even today. It is of rather common occurrence also among American Negroes. In Shreveport, Louisiana, only three or four years ago, a Negro was sentenced for attempting the murder of another Negro who allegedly had put such a hex on him. The assailant stated that he believed that he could recover his lost potency by killing the witch—something he strove manfully to do, beating that sorcerer savagely on the top of the head with a thick board.)

Boguet's experience with the forms of impotence resulting from witchcraft generally confirms what has been said:

"They also cause a man's virile member to disappear and be concealed, and then to reappear at their own pleasure. This is widely practised in Germany.

"At times also they prevent carnal copulation between a man and a woman by relaxing the nerves and depriving the member of rigidity: at other times they prevent procreation by turning aside or blocking up the seminal ducts so that the semen does not reach the generative cells. And they hold a married couple thus bound for as long as it pleases them, sowing ten thousand other seeds of discord between them besides." [9]

Sometimes a man's semen was made to congeal and become hard as rock, so that it could not flow out of his urethra. A penis might be reduced to a mere shriveled shred of flesh, and the female genitals caused to dry up and wither, or to close tightly (vaginismus?) so that penetration became impossible. Not infrequently a man's organ was made to withdraw up into his belly, whence it might with luck be recovered by medical, rather than magical, intervention. (MD magazine, in an article on Singapore, took note of a current medical curiosity that is worth mentioning here: "The oddest medico-cultural phenomenon is a psychiatric syndrome called *koru* which appears among Chinese men. The victim becomes convinced that his genitals are retracting into his abdomen and that final retraction will bring death; to combat his panic the family clings to the genitals until a physician arrives to administer psychotherapy.") [10]

Although there were a number of ways of inflicting impotence, tying a knot in a cord was by far the most common. Women were made frigid by the same sorcery, and there were at least half a hundred different knots, each inflicting a different degree or form of impotence or frigidity. One knot was especially designed to prevent conception, and also to keep the witch advised of how things were going: each time a coition took place and a pregnancy was thwarted, a "wart" would appear on the knotted cord.

The witch might seek to inflict a permanent impotence or she might inflict impotence only for a stipulated period. That was why, as mentioned elsewhere, divorces and annulments were usually granted only after a considerable lapse of time, often three years, at the conclusion of which the impotence was presumed permanent. Frigidity of wives, even though inflicted by witchcraft, was usually no basis for terminating a marriage since coition could still occur, and it was not thought that conception was interfered with by such a condition.

Witches were frequently employed by other women to make males impotent. A woman whose lover was about to marry someone else might turn to a witch and pay her a fee to prevent the marriage or its consummation. The penance for soliciting a witch to inflict ligature for a purpose of that kind was forty days on bread and water.

That was one penalty. The canons held that anyone who through desire for vengeance or because of hatred prevented a man and woman from begetting a child was to be classed as a homicide. (Use of any contraceptive device was also sufficient to brand the users as homicides. It was not essential that demons and witchcraft should be involved.)

Happy to relate, there was an abundance of remedies and preventives for impotence, frigidity, and sterility induced by the magic of witches. Sometimes God would himself take a hand and restore a man's potency when he had been deprived of it by ligature. One approached the Almighty prayerfully, promising never to engage in adultery or sodomy or zooerasty or any other prohibited erotic activities if only the missing or debilitated part should be returned to good working order. Married men had also to reassure the Deity that in wedding their wives they had not entered into the union merely for the purpose of indulging base fleshly appetites.

Confession, the shedding of many tears, plentiful use of the sign of the cross, humility, meditation, and a pilgrimage to a holy and venerable shrine might undo what witchcraft, fell and felonious, had wrought. Most efficacious of all, some clergymen declared, was a large contribution to the churches.

Sometimes a wife could undo the ligature that penalized her no less than her husband by having him urinate through her wedding ring. Going to the woods and there looking at a pie's nest might also turn the trick.

Those who preferred prevention to cure sometimes fell back upon the (forbidden) use of pagan amulets and charms, usually representations of the sexual organs, to thwart attempts to unman (or unwoman) them, whether by demons or witches. Ernest Jones mentions symbolic amulets: upright knife and broomstick (phallic symbols); a horse's skull, a goblin's foot and a pentagram (bisexual symbols); and horseshoes and hag stones, or rocks with holes bored through them (vulva symbols).

Witches themselves could in most cases counteract or nullify the witchcraft, supplying an antidote, or a love potion or philtre so powerful as to override the impotence or frigidity. It was also said that if a man would spend the night in the bed of the witch who had hexed him, she would restore his potency in order to enable him to copulate with her, and then permit him to retain it if his performance was satisfactory.

Much more might be said on this subject, but I will conclude by taking note of a most appropriate question raised by Johann Klein. Why, Klein wondered, since witches could make some men impotent, and since witches hated the whole of humanity, did they not render *all* men impotent and so do away with mankind entirely? Klein found the answer to his own question: God in all his divine love and mercy would never allow such universal impotence or permit his beloved children to perish by so odious a means.

Everyone shits; only Zola bothers about it.

GAUGUIN

16. *Sources of the witch belief*

|

Witchcraft, as dealt with in this book, was a systematized delusion of monstrous proportions; but it was not only that. Many factors conspired to create, to expand, and to maintain the belief.

In approaching, for example, the Witches' Sabbat, a psychological theory unmindful of the history of group sexual practices, including orgies, will almost certainly stray far from the mark. One must have more than a nodding acquaintance with such forerunners of the Sabbat as the orgiastic worship, many centuries before Christ, of Baal and Osiris and other antique deities. One should be familiar, to mention but a single Roman example, with the Bacchanalia—those revels that caused the Senate to be deluged with complaints about "the noises and shrieks resounding through the city by night," and that were said to include wild dancing, the sacrifice of children, incest, and promiscuous copulations.

It should be known that the Salic Law of the Franks, as early as the fifth century, punished sorcery and secret rites, taking note of cannibalism allegedly practiced at the gatherings, and imposing punishments on those who accused others of witchcraft and then could not prove the truth of their accusations. The code of the Visigoths also punished witches, sometimes with death, for such offenses as blighting the crops, raising tempests, and consorting with demons.

As Montague Summers has remarked, the Manichees[1] burned in 1022 described meetings quite like the later Sabbats. The Devil presided there in the form of a beast, infants were murthered, and there was a sexual orgy. Elsewhere in the preceding pages I have mentioned other predecessors of the witches and antecedents of the Sabbats. The Witches' Sabbat was not entirely an invention of the witch-burners, though undoubtedly their febrile imaginations contributed details, as did the imaginations of accused witches, eager to tell an exciting story and so escape further torment.

Erotic sects of various sorts were in existence at the beginning of the witch mania and continued to exist throughout the period of the persecutions. The Flagellants were said to number eight hundred thousand[2] in fourteenth-century France —possibly an exaggerated estimate. The nudist Adamites, and their offshoot, the Picards, flourished in the early fifteenth century and then were crushed by the Inquisition. In Italy the Fraticelli were charged with holding sex orgies in the dark, with various sacrileges, and with the murder of children. Cathar gatherings similar to the later Sabbats were described in the thirteenth century, and Waldensian ones in the fourteenth. Some said that the Waldenses specifically worshiped the Devil; others that the "King of Heaven" presided over their debaucheries.[3]

The Waldenses of Vaudois, known also as the Vaudois, were accused in the fifteenth century, when they were targets of a brutal persecution, of holding Sabbats not essentially distinguishable from some of those later attributed to witches (and in fact members of such heretical sects were often considered to be witches).

To the Vaudois, Satan offered a conclave with but little to recommend it. The Devil appeared in the form of a beast, with flames shooting out of His ears, and so horrible was His voice that many celebrants went mad with terror while others fell into fits of trembling that lasted for hours. Sexual intercourse, with incubi and succubi, was either pleasureless or painful, and food and drink alike were so unpalatable as to cause the diners to vomit. Meetings were held once a week and there were also special gatherings for the holidays.

Other practices of the Vaudois sound equally unpleasant. They would steal wine from cellars, but only drank from the stolen casks after urinating into them. For worshiping Him, the Devil promised them money; but the coins received would usually turn into black dung or else vanish completely.

Women who attended the Vaudois sociables reported that the presiding devil would copulate with them from behind while they were obliged to uncomfortably support themselves on the balls of their feet and the palms of their hands. Moreover, the penis of the demon was almost always soft, or insufficiently rigid, and when he ejaculated, first into the vagina and then into the rectum, his semen was old, yellow, and little short of sere. After such uninspiring fornications, the witches would have intercourse with other demons and among themselves, with homosexual relations as commonplace as heterosexual ones, and no person present was permitted to refuse anything to any other person. (One exception should be noted. Special allowance was made for those so sunk into lewdness and depravity that they could find no delight with others of their kind and craved intercourse only with demons. This was abominable perversion even among the Vaudois, but the demonophiles were not forced to go against their inclination.)

In the case of the Vaudois, much phantasy has already been superimposed upon what may have been fact (meeting and orgy). Basic elements of the Sabbat are already present, needing only to be refined and elaborated, as witches and witchhunters would do during the several succeeding centuries. Practices attributed to all of the sects and cults I have mentioned are doubtless in large part phantasy and deliberate calumny. It is impossible to determine where fact ends and fancy begins. However, the claim of orgiastic behavior is not implausible in most cases.

Not everyone was persuaded that Christian theologians held the key to the mysteries or the solution to the problems of mankind. Many were faithful to the non-Christian religions of their fathers, and some joined new heretical movements either in protest against Christian, especially Catholic, tyranny, or as converts of the usual sort. In some cases the old pagan gods, branded devils by the high-handed pundits of the Church, were represented at the illicit gatherings. Sometimes the representative of the god appeared wearing furs or otherwise in the guise of some beast. If the representative of the god copulated with a member or members of the congregation, the copulation was, by Catholic lights, with a demon; or with a demon in the form of a beast (if the heretic priest was so attired).

This element of fact, combined with the demonological theories of Augustine, Aquinas, and others, helped shape and give some measure of credibility to the belief in witchcraft. Later, as (tortured) witch after witch confessed guilt and described carnal and other dealings with demons, the delusion came increasingly to be supported by a voluminous mass of pseudo-evidence that "no reasonable man could challenge."

As witch belief and witch persecutions increased in scope and intensity, so did the general terror increase, spawning mental illness, particularly hysteria. It seems certain that hysteria reached epidemic proportions; that hysteria explains, or could explain, much of the witchcraft phenomena will be shown.

Nocturnal pollutions, viewed since the dawn of history with superstitious awe, became visits of incubi and succubi; and nightmares, too, were erotic encounters with demons. Some dreamed of Sabbats. These dreams, vivid and made more so in retrospect by superstition and dread of being found out, were often mistaken for reality. Visions induced by alcoholic and more potent narcotic intoxications were similarly transmuted. The dividing line between real and imaginary experience thinned, became blurred, and in some cases was erased. Delusion was the order of the day.

Women, denounced by the Church as wicked and excessively sensual, and in any case falling far short of the ideal of both mental and physical chastity, were ridden by guilt and prepared to believe themselves capable of any enormity. Hysteria and other disorders encouraged noctambulism (sleep-walking), and if a noctambulist awakened away from home, or at home but bearing traces of having been abroad, she was at once convinced that she had been to the Sabbat. Michelet (*Satanism and Witchcraft*) describes such an occurrence:

". . . there was, over and above the actual objective Witches' Sabbath, an imaginary *Sabbath*, which many terrified individuals believed themselves to attend, especially women somnambulists (sleep-walkers), who would get up in the night and scour the country. A young man, crossing the fields at the first peep of dawn, and following the course of a brook, hears a very soft voice hailing him, but in timid, trembling accents. Looking, he sees a pitiful sight—a woman's white body almost naked, save for a scanty pair of drawers. Shuddering and shamefaced, she was hiding among the brambles. He recognizes a neighbor; and she begs him to rescue her. 'What are you doing there?' 'I was looking for my donkey.' He expresses incredulity, whereupon she bursts into tears. The poor woman, who had very likely in her somnambulism slipped out of her husband's bed and wandered away, starts accusing herself. The Devil took her to the Witches' Sabbath; while conducting her home again he heard a church bell, and let her fall . . ." [4] The youth then tells others in the village what he has seen; and the woman is formally accused, brought to trial, and probably burned for witchcraft.

Hallucinations, apparently more common among non-psychotics than today, were another source of the witch belief and helped to sustain it. It is not surprising, even apart from the apparent high incidence of mental disturbance, that hallucinations should have been commonplace. Superstition (more potent if not more prevalent then than now) is a great producer of phantasms. Who believes in ghosts is likely to see ghosts, especially if he visits some place reputed to be haunted. Those who go out into the woods to watch the fairies or the elves often see those beings. (It is my charitable opinion that such persons as ornithologists, and lepidopterologists even more, are also subject to these hallucinations deriving from suggestion and expectation; and that naturalists generally are often so afflicted. However, when what is "seen" has a known objective existence in the world, it is more difficult to establish whether the particular reported instance of seeing was or was not hallucinatory.)

It is certain that hallucinations played an important role in the development of the Christian belief in incubi and succubi. In the fourth century a great number of persons embarked upon careers as religious hermits, going to live in deserts and caves and other solitary retreats. Sometimes they remained there for years, fasting and praying and scourging their flesh. In their isolation and monomaniacal preoccupation with religion, they developed psychoses and lesser mental aberrations. Especially, they were rich in hallucinations. Since the recluse was tormented by sexual frustration, these hallucinations often took the form of supernatural beings-in human shapes (usually thought of by the eremite as devils), attempting to lead him or her into sinful fleshly indulgence. The holy hermits gave accounts of their experiences, which were taken as factual, and so helped to firmly establish the belief in visitations by lustful spirits.

Looking back upon the sex lore of witchcraft, it is not uninstructive to regard the whole as a vast and complex pornographic phantasy or collective art work. As such, it might be regarded as the ultimate esthetic expression of an era notable for its excesses: the combination of an impossible ideal of asexuality, accompanied by a hatred of the flesh, with a practical libertinism seldom rivaled in all of history. This gigantic phantasy was a delusion insofar as it was mistaken for objective reality, leading to the most savage attempts at suppression of the imaginary offenses accepted as authentic by both the offenders and those who judged and punished them. It may be that largely as a result of intolerable pressures (the antisexual morality) the forces of the unconscious rose up in revolt, overpowering consciousness or threatening so to do, and that the extravagant cruelty of the attempted suppression was in fact an effort of consciousness, battling desperately for survival, to repress the black teeming hordes of the barbarian invaders and restore the forces of the unconscious to their traditional place in the psychic scheme.

All of the elements usually found in the pornographic or obscene work of literature are to be found in the witch lore. Perversions of almost every kind are dealt with and there is a preoccupation with excrements and filth. Rape, defloration, other violence, incest, the profanation of the sacred—all are present. To consider some of the criteria offered by the Kronhausens,[5] we note that the victim is often more or less a "willing collaborator." The sexual organs and physiological sex responses are emphasized—the size of the penis, the feel of the penis in the vagina, the sensation produced by the ejaculation of the semen. There is the "permissive-seductive parent figure"—in this case the parent who hands over the child to the incubus to be sexually used, and who may participate in the orgy. There are "supersexed males"—demons of limitless potency, with outsized penes; and "nymphomaniac females"—witches in perpetual rut, and succubi who drain their human lovers to the point of impotence and even death. Voyeurism and exhibitionism, homosexuality and bestiality, necrophilia and fetishism—all are a part of the picture. Much pornographic writing was produced in Europe during the period of the witch persecutions, but the efforts of no single author could rival in scope and intensity the obscene and pornographic work of art that is witchcraft in its totality.

Before proceeding to a more specific discussion of the roles of drugs and mental illness in the fabrication of the witch delusion, it might be well to say a few more words about why demons, rather than human beings, were assigned leading roles in the phantasy. Looking at the pictures of demons that have come down to us, we note that almost without exception these productions of the witch era are (by the artists' intention) hideous or grotesque. Why then, we are likely to wonder, did the erotic imaginations of the witches and others given to de-moniality seize upon such beings? Why did not these persons exploit for their sexual phantasies more (to us) desirable ob-jects?

It may be that we will not go far astray to consider the ele-ment of masochism implied in such a choice (or the cruelty when the choice was that of a witch-burning demonologist). We understand rather well the masochistic craving for self-degradation, which may manifest itself in the choice of an ugly, deformed, or otherwise seemingly unattractive or repul-sive sex partner. One recalls the life of Baudelaire; and the ad-vertisement of that other masochistic satanist Aleister Crowley for "DWARFS, Hunchbacks, Tatooed Women, Harrison Fisher Girls, Freaks of All Sorts, Colored Women, only if exceptionally ugly or deformed . . ." But masochism was not Crowley's only motivation, nor was it the sole motivation of the witches. Stronger still, in his case and possibly in (some of) theirs, was the desire to do evil—specifically, to sin heinously—and while such a desire may itself have masochistic components, maso-chism is far from being the whole story.

The raptures of sexual love, many a guilt-ridden voluptuary has noted, are intensified by the feeling that one is doing evil. It is this sense of sin, here pushed to its most intense, that does much to explain the sexual allure of demons. For as the officials of the witchcraft tribunals liked to point out, if forni-cations between humans are abominable to God, how much worse must be fornications with devils! And by their loathsome and sinister appearances the demons proved their inward evil, and heightened to its maximum intensity the conviction of the demonophiles that in their copulations they were doing evil to the maximum extent possible. Could it be that this strange ecstasy, beyond the comprehension of those who had never experienced it, explained why the witches persisted in coitions so painful by ordinary standards? But to think so would be to accept in large measure the very portrait of the witches painted by the demonologists; while surely that portrait was the likeness of only relatively few.

It is no more romantic to propose that the incubi and succubi, and the gamut of sexual activities attributed to witches and those demons, were the faultily repressed cravings of the frustrated celibates of the Church, projected in symbolic form upon the people; and that, for the Inquisitor, to kill a witch (usually and appropriately by burning) was to kill also, for the moment, the lust that intolerably tormented him. But only for the moment; and then a new witch had to be found and killed, to put down the resurgent inadmissible desire. Was it this appetite, necessarily insatiable, resembling that of the lust murderer, that at last terminated the witch mania, the people sensing, finally, the truth that all of the rest of mankind could be consumed without ever assuaging that bottomless hunger?

17. Drugs and the witches

Narcotics were employed by the witches for a variety of purposes. For poisons they preferred aconite, used earlier by the Romans, to produce cardiac retardation and arrest; belladonna, which produces fatal exhaustion of the nervous system; and hemlock, which kills by effecting motor paralysis and respiratory failure.

These same plants, and others yielding similar or related alkaloids (atropine, hyoscyamine, scopolamine, and others), were used as ingredients of love potions and of the famous witches' ointment, used for flying to the Sabbats, or for producing hallucinations of the Sabbats.

It has been suggested that a combination of delirifacient drugs with others producing irregular heart action might have yielded the sensation of flying.

It was generally believed that the witch ointment was rubbed over the whole body (or on especially sensitive areas, such as the armpits, the palms of the hands, the forehead, the penis, and the vaginal walls). That the witches' ointment was already well known in the fifteenth century, and that it was thought to produce dreams or illusions of flying and attendance at the Sabbat, is clear from a case cited by Nider. A Dominican had watched a woman rub herself with the ointment and fall into a trance or some unconscious condition. When she awakened she claimed to have been transported to the Sabbat and to have joined in the revels there. Other investigators reported similar observations.

It was also claimed that transportation to the Sabbats was

effected by the drinking of a magical fluid, which some held to be mainly semen. Others asserted that the ointment and the magical fluid both had to be used.

Some enthusiasts have attempted to explain the whole phenomenon of the Sabbat on the basis of drug intoxication. Ludwig Meyer attributed the Sabbat experiences to drunken phantasies produced by a concoction whose principal ingredient was the thorn apple (*Datura stramonium*). J. L. Holzinger agreed that narcotics explain the Sabbat, but claimed to have proved that thorn apple was not known at the time (a view disputed by the writings of many toxicologists and historians).[1]

Ernest Jones notes that Freimark has adduced evidence to show that ointments were used to produce voluptuous dreams, mentioning substances with aphrodisiac, intoxicating, and anesthetizing properties. Jones also reports the experiments of Kiesewetter, who concocted a witches' ointment, applied it to his body, and experienced flying and traveling dreams. However, Jones remarks, "It is known nowadays that no drugs can do this directly, so that the belief in their potency must have been an important factor in the effect." [2]

On the other hand, I have reported in my book *Forbidden Sexual Behavior and Morality* the quite recent experiments of a Goettingen professor who prepared a witches' ointment on the basis of a recipe found in an old book of magical writings. The professor, who was joined in his experiment by a friend, is said to have reported dreams of flying and of attendance at the Sabbat, with suggestion presumably ruled out in the case of the friend. In the same work I reported a minor experiment of my own with thorn apple, which yielded flying dreams on the first night and erotic dreams on the second night—with how much of an assist from suggestion it is impossible for me to say.[3]

That the *solanaceae* (thorn apple, mandragora or mandrake, belladonna, the henbanes, etc.) were the principal ingredients (or at any rate the main effective ingredients) of the witches' ointment seems well enough established. Should there be skeptics willing to settle only for contemporary on-the-spot testimony, an appeal might be made to the findings of Andreas de Laguna, physician to the sixteenth-century Pope Julius III. De Laguna, who personally analyzed a tube of the ointment recovered from a witch, said that it was green in color and contained hemlock, salanum, mandragora, and henbane.[4]

There has been a continuing dispute as to whether dreams or hallucinations or both were produced by the ointment. There is no doubt that the effects of certain drugs include erotic visions or hallucinations. Opium, hashish, mescaline, the *solanaceae,* and others may produce such visions, though much always depends on the individual making use of the drug: his peculiar psychological organization, his expectations, etc. However, the visions produced by these drugs are not likely to be mistaken for real events, are not hallucinations in the usual sense, and in some cases would not be remembered, whatever the content of the vision. With the *solanaceae,* however, vivid sexual *dreams* may occur, and sometimes are subject to recollection. It would seem likely that these dreams, rather than any visions or hallucinations produced by the drugs employed, explain some of the experiences of witches—if in fact drugs played any part in the flights to the Sabbats and the intercourse with incubi and succubi.[5]

According to Michelet, the *solanaceae* were put to other than magical uses by witches:

"They would entice to the festival some ill-advised married man, whom they proceeded to intoxicate with their deadly brews (datura, belladonna, and the like), till he was spellbound and lost all power of motion and speech, but not the use of his eyes. His wife, also spellbound, but in a different way, with erotic beverages and reduced to a deplorable state of self-abandonment, would then be shown him naked and unashamed, patiently enduring the caresses of another before the indignant eyes of her natural protector, who could not stir a finger to help her." [6]

(In this case it would be difficult to say whether the spectators were lustfully entertained by the sexual abuse of the wife, or amused by the impotent misery of the husband. Probably the "comic" aspect was most appreciated, the witnessing of sexual intercourse being no novelty to the witches.)

That the *solanaceae*, especially datura, are capable of producing aphrodisiac and other erotic effects in some cases is also well established. They have been used for that purpose over a period of many centuries (although their vogue has finally, and happily, passed). Assuredly they are not very satisfactory aphrodisiacs, giving rise to mental confusion, severe anxiety, grave illness or the feeling of being gravely ill, and sometimes death. That all of this failed to deter the users testifies equally to the shallowness of man's rationality and to the depth of his craving for sexual excitement and heightened capacity for indulgence.

In *Forbidden Sexual Behavior and Morality* I have cited several reports of the sexual effects of datura:

"Edwardes (*The Jewel in the Lotus*) quotes a Mussulman observer:

" '. . . Opium, arrack, hasheesh: they are of little use save for the imagination. And the imagination works like evil *jinn* (demons) that come in the night and steal the precious seed of virile men, being jealous of their power. Even datura, which makes a man ragingly lustful and exuberant for an entire night, is of little avail. It deceives one, robs him of true courage in lieu of false; and when he possesses reality of manly vigor, he is hopelessly lost in an abyss of bewilderment.'

"Others too have made this complaint about the effects of the thorn apple, pointing to the bewilderment inevitably accompanying the aphrodisiac benefits. But there is worse: The user of datura can recall little, and sometimes nothing, of his experience. And what good is an erotic escapade, however 'ragingly lustful,' that cannot be recollected in tranquility?

"The combination of bewilderment and sex stimulation resulting from the use of datura and allied drugs can sometimes result in antisocial actions creating subsequent woes for the

drug-taker. Hesse (*Narcotics and Drug Addiction*) para-
phrases Riebling, who had encountered such a case resulting
from an accidental atropine-scopolamine intoxication:

"'. . . a fifty-four-year-old woman . . . inadvertently took
too many atropine-scopolamine drops. During her narcotic
psychosis, she attempted to have a Lesbian intercourse with
her landlady, and unashamedly she invited also the fiancé of
the landlady to have sexual intercourse with her. After her re-
covery from the intoxication, she had no memory at all of
these happenings.'

"Asthma patients, who used to be treated with some of these
(*solanaceae*) drugs, have confirmed the fact that they give
rise to hallucinations, delusions, and sexual imagery; and sometimes to considerable erotic stimulation." [7]

Wine, presumably with some secret aphrodisiacal ingredient
added, was also used as a sex stimulant by witches according
to a number of writers.[8] Father Sebastian Michaelis (*Histoire
admirable de la possession*) remarked that when they could
the witches drank wine stolen from cellars by those especially
assigned to that task, and that this wine was intended to inflame their sexual passions ("they drink malmsey to excite
them to venery"). Even if effective it must have been difficult
to stomach, for Guazzo described the witches' wine as resembling clotted and blackened blood; and what was more,
they were obliged to drink it out of filthy and slimy vessels,
while the beverage, as mentioned elsewhere, was often seasoned with urine and particles of dung.

Drugs may have figured in witchcraft in other ways. The
strange behavior of those under the influence of the *solanaceae*
may have caused them to be regarded as possessed by devils,
or as having acquired supernatural powers. It may be that
witches awaiting torture or execution consumed drugs smuggled to them to induce unconsciousness or some degree of
anesthesia. This might explain, as the discussion of hysteria
will further indicate, the curious and often reported phenom-

enon of witches who "slept" while being tortured, or otherwise seemed indifferent to the efforts of the torturers.

That narcotics were believed used by witches, and especially that they were thought to be used to induce sexual excitement and for the purpose of attending the erotic orgies of the Sabbats, led to the denunciation of all "pleasure" narcotics as inventions of the Devil. It is extremely unfortunate that such a view continues to prevail in so many official quarters today, resulting in needlessly harsh punishment and cruel treatment of drug-users, and in the withholding of some drugs that might serve a socially useful, and certainly individually educational, purpose.

18. *Disordered minds*

The statement already has been made that the mental disorder called hysteria *could* explain many and perhaps most of the phenomena of witchcraft; also that hysteria seems to have been extremely prevalent, even epidemic, during the period of the witch persecutions.

The last-mentioned conclusion is more susceptible to challenge than the first and admittedly can never be more than a plausible inference. Classical Freudians might have reason to doubt that "epidemic" hysteria is possible; or at any rate that it is probable. On the other hand, Charcot claimed to have induced hysteria by suggestion. It is my own suspicion that suggestion was largely responsible for the wealth of hysterical phenomena, if they were that, existent among the witches; and Pierre Bayle[1] and some others thought so even at the time. Bayle was of the belief that once the witchcraft literature had become voluminous it influenced many to think themselves witches and develop appropriate symptoms, and to become possessed. Gossip, sermons, fear of the Inquisition and other witch-hunters, along with additional factors, must also have played an important part.

In a sense there arises the question of the chicken and the egg. That is, did the suggestion create the hysteria, or did latent hysteria respond to suggestion which in turn was to some extent based upon observation and misinterpretation of the symptoms of hysterics?

It is generally accepted that hysterics are extraordinarily suggestible. Hysterics also have among their symptoms vivid sexual dreams, sensory hallucinations, erotic "fits" and day-dreams, false pregnancies, frigidity and impotence, spontane-ous trance states, sleep-walking, spontaneous and deep anes-thesia, dermatoses and stigmata, and a wealth of other relevant oddities and wild talents. They over-react in some cases to narcotics, and Palmer (*Psychopathic Personalities*) states that they may "become deeply anesthetised with an amount of anaesthetic which would not affect others."[2] This might pro-vide substantial support for the belief that the indifference to torture manifested by some witches was the result of their having taken drugs smuggled to them by relatives, friends, or other witches.

It should also be noted that the symptoms of hysteria are especially likely to flower when the individual hysteric feels himself to be "cornered" or "trapped," either by some objective situation, such as arrest and interrogation, or by subjection to, for example, a value system approved by the society in which he lives but unacceptable to the hysteric. Some of the above-mentioned symptoms of hysteria call for further discus-sion.

Many women were accused of being witches, and of copulat-ing with incubi, on the basis of so-called erotic fits. Demonolo-gists gave numerous accounts of women found lying on their backs, naked to their navels, in woods and fields, going through impassioned copulatory motions and arriving at last at appar-ent orgasm. The women were thought, of course, to be copulat-ing with invisible incubi. Reports of these incidents, perhaps more than any others, have persuaded later medical writers that the witches were mentally ill, since such phenomena have often been observed in hospitals, with hysterics and others. Sinistrari gives a rather typical description of such behavior and gives a theologian's verdict as well on the proper handling of cases of the sort:

"Sometimes, it is true, women have been seen in the woods, in the fields, in the groves, lying on their backs, *ad umbilicum tenus nudatae, et juxta dispositionem actus venerei*, their legs *divaricatis et adductis, clunes agitare* . . . In such a case there would be a very strong suspicion of such a crime (fornication with an incubus), if supported by other signs; and I am inclined to believe that such action, sufficiently proved by witnesses, would justify the Judge in resorting to torture in order to ascertain the truth; especially if, shortly after that action, a sort of black smoke had been seen to issue from the woman, and she had been noticed to rise . . . for it might be inferred that that smoke or shadow had been the Devil himself, *concumbens cum foemina*. Likewise if, as has more than once happened, a woman had been seen *concumbere cum homine*, who, the action over, suddenly disappeared." [3]

(One might be almost willing to concede that should a cloud of black smoke arise from a woman at the termination of her coital movements, or a seemingly solid human lover abruptly vanish into thin air, then something out of the way could at least be suspected. Unfortunately, however, such "additional evidence" was seldom demanded; and where supplied, was accepted without much attempt to verify the truthfulness of the witness or whether he was subject to hallucinations—as seems often enough to have been the case.)

The situation was greatly complicated by the fact that the women themselves, after such experiences, often believed that they had been copulating with demons. Where the accused, the witnesses, and the judge were all equally convinced of the accused's guilt, there was of course not a chance of establishing innocence—and there must have been many cases in which the defendant no less than the prosecutor and the judge believed herself (or himself) guilty as charged.

The painful character of the coitions with incubi and succubi is intelligible in terms of hysteria if it is granted that the experiences occurred in dreams or were hallucinatory. Pitres (*Leçons cliniques sur l'Hysterie, Vol. II*), a famous pupil of Charcot's, said that sexual dreams, similar to those of the witches, are common among hysterics. Such dreams (and hallucinations), Pitres said, are rarely pleasurable; rather, the illusion of intercourse provokes extreme pain in many cases.

The same might be said, however, of illusory intercourse experiences in mental disorders other than hysteria—schizophrenia, for example. Schizophrenics frequently report imaginary copulations and rapes, and that they were painful.

Laurent and Nagour observe that "These statements on the pain of coition with the devil coincide so remarkably with descriptions of lunatics . . . that it appears quite probable that the first acount of infernal copulation was given by a female lunatic.

"This theory is not disproved if later, when the peculiarities of the infernal embraces were made known to the witches' judges, the same accounts were given by women who underwent torture and did not suffer from hallucinations." [4]

Laurent and Nagour cite various relevant erotic hallucinations and delusions of psychotics, including one case of an old woman who complained bitterly "that a certain physician would visit her every night and inject his penis into her ear, penetrating down to her throat.[5] Staff members of almost any large mental institution could give similar examples.

It is also the case that even conscious objective coition may be extremely painful if there is sufficient mental conflict about it, especially if that conflict is based on deep-rooted antisexual values and consequent moral-sexual inhibitions. Even so, it seems to me that the pain aspect of intercourse with incubi and succubi is probably the single most significant fact to be offered in refutation of those who, like Margaret Murray, would attempt to convince us that the Sabbats were no more than the orgiastic rites of some pagan religion. I have already offered reasons why the argument that the pain of the coitions is intelligible in terms of the use of artificial penes is unacceptable. An explanation in terms of moral conflict would be acceptable only if the witches were subscribers to the Christian antisexual ethic—as the evidence suggests that they were (in some and possibly most cases). But if they were believers in an antique religion, as the Murray school would have us suppose, then such conflicts would probably not have been present, and there is no reason why intercourse at the Sabbats should have been less pleasurable than it was at the orgiastic rites of Bacchus, Faunus, and comparable deities.

In those cases where the witch copulated with some human male representing the Devil, or some other supernatural being, the resulting lack of pleasure might possibly be explained by the frigidity often encountered in hysteria when guilt is attached to the act of sexual congress. It is not unlikely that an hysterical anesthesia of the genitals occurred in some cases. Where the copulation was painful, it is possible that there was a constriction of the vagina, or vaginismus, requiring the use of considerable force to effect penetration. Vaginismus is another condition not uncommon in hysteria. And the sensation of coldness could have been yet another hysterical reaction; or it could have resulted from the use of one of several narcotics capable of yielding that effect.

What may be regarded as a classical Freudian explication of the unpleasurable and/or painful character of incubus and succubus visitations (in dreams) is presented by Jones:

"We may make an interesting contrast between these pleasant and unpleasant experiences, with all their intermediate types, from several points of view. Psychologically the matter is, thanks to Freud's investigations, very simple. His doctrine of intrapsychic repression gives us the full explanation. As was pointed out in the preceding chapter, the wishes culminating in unpleasant experiences differ from those of the opposite kind merely in being subject to internal repression or condemnation, so that they are unconscious. Another way of putting this is to say that the erotic wishes in question may be compatible with the standards of the subject's ego, and therefore accepted by it, or not . . ." [6]

Presumably those who found the intercourse with demons most pleasurable would be those least troubled by guilt and consequent anxiety, while those who found it most painful would be the ones who were the most guilty and the most anxious. In between, probably, would be the great majority of witches whose ambivalence enabled them to derive both pain and pleasure, in varying degrees, from the experience.

Analgesia, or insensitivity to pain, has been mentioned frequently in the foregoing pages. It occurs spontaneously in the cases of both hysterics and hypnotic subjects (and it is usually taken as axiomatic that any and all of the phenomena of hypnosis may occur in hysteria cases).[7]

Anesthesia of the genitals, varying in degree from total insensitivity to a mild inhibition of sensation precluding orgasm but not excluding pleasure feelings altogether, probably occurred rather often among the witches. It has also been suggested that spontaneous analgesia might explain in some cases the ability of witches to withstand torture. The hysteria hypothesis serves further by affording a possible explanation for the "Devil's Mark" and for the fact that witch-prickers were able to probe those marks with needles without causing any pain or even awareness of what was being done on the part of the (blindfolded) witch.[8]

It has been noted that the hysteric develops not only spontaneous analgesias, which may cover a large or a very small area of the body, and which may appear in several areas simultaneously, but also curious dermatoses and stigmata. Warts, for example, may come and go. Bleeding may start and stop. A prison psychologist a few years ago described a prisoner who, while in self-induced hypnotic trance, could cause the signs of the zodiac to appear and disappear on his flesh. Everyone is familiar with the much publicized cases of persons who bleed from appropriate places during the season of the crucifixion. Fakirs of all sorts produce comparable phenomena. That the mind may so affect the body seems to have been demonstrated beyond all possibility of further doubt. Given these data, it may plausibly be argued that witch marks might appear on the body of an hysteric, and that they might be insensitive. One recalls the rather spectacular case of Antide Colas, the witch with a second insensitive "vagina" just below her navel, and which was only a "scar" when examined a short time later. This, too, might be understood in terms of hysteria, and the only reasonable alternative, given the analgesia of the orifice, would seem to be to deny the authenticity of the story altogether.

That some of the witchcraft phenomena, especially those of the Sabbats, may have been hypnotic trance phenomena is another possibility. The dancing at the Sabbats may have been a means of inducing trance in the dancers, as is still done today among some less-than-civilized peoples, for example, the Dervishes, and the Voodoo dancers of Haiti. A kind of hallucinatory intercourse with a god in human or animal form is experienced by some participants in Voodoo and similar rituals. However, hypnosis (induced by music, dancing, a hypnotist, or by means of any other method external to the hypnotic subject) will not do as a general explanation for the demoniality experience because the intercourse with incubi and succubi was not at all limited to the occasions of the Sabbats; while if one suggests spontaneous trance states, then the likelihood is that those, if they occurred, would best be understood as part of an hysteria syndrome.

That sleep-walking is common in hysteria has been mentioned, and the role of sleep-walking in witchcraft has been discussed elsewhere. The occurrence of false pregnancies among witches has also been discussed, and such false pregnancies, with distention of the abdomen and even the vivid sensation of the infant stirring in the body, occur in hysteria.

One of the more interesting phenomena is that of stenches and other odors associated with both witches and demons (and the sweetly perfumed aromas associated with those theological opposite numbers of witches and demons—saints, mystics, and angels). Persons given to experiencing apparitions have often described the foul odors of demons and the nose-pleasing smell of angels. Those having to do with witches and saints and mystics described similar (foul and sweet) aromas emanating from their bodies. We have to do here, of course, with two distinct types of phenomena.

When the sense of smell seems to be involved in the apprehension of apparitions, the most acceptable explanation is that the hallucination is olfactory as well as visual. Some hallucinations may also be auditory and tactile, as is well known; and such hallucinations occur in hysteria and in some other mental disorders. Hypnotic trance hallucinations may also involve any or all of the senses.

Less familiar to most persons is the fact that the mentally ill are sometimes able, by an inadequately understood process, to give off a variety of body odors. The process is almost always unconscious, but it has sometimes been claimed that certain individuals (accomplished Yogins, for example) are able to control the production. The distinctive aromas described in the cases of saints, prophets, witches, etc., are presumably not to be accounted for by physical dirtiness, recent consumption of food or beverage, or any other obvious way. Some mystics, mediums, and other occultists are reputed to be able to produce a whole bouquet of odors at will, but it is known that trickery has often been involved (in the form of concealed atomizers and other gadgets).

Those tormented by sexual guilt, typically, when they produce olfactory phenomena, emanate fecal stenches (the unconscious making the equation of sex with filth and representing filth with feces). Saints and mystics, identifying themselves with goodness or purity, are more likely to smell of flowers. Lilacs and roses—ironically, since the rose is a vagina symbol and lilacs are associated with homosexuality—seem to be the plants of preference.[9]

Among others of the mentally ill who produce body odors on the one hand and are subject to olfactory hallucinations on the other, are schizophrenics whose hallucinations may additionally be haptic (tactile), visual, and auditory. Schizophrenics share with hysterics a variety of symptoms relevant to the study of witchcraft phenomena and there is no reason to doubt that the ranks of the witches probably included a fair number of schizophrenics.

The "burning glance" attributed to witches (and to prophets, messiahs, etc.) may be a symptom of schizophrenia. Schizophrenics may be pathological liars, as some of the witches, and accusers of witches, seem to have been. They are also given to erotic visions and daydreams of great vividness, and to claims (on the basis of these) of having been sexually assaulted. Moreover, schizophrenia, like hysteria, may be "infectious," the sick individual causing others to share in his (or her) delusions. "Infections" of this sort seem definitely to have been responsible for some epidemics of incubus visitations and possession, such as those that raged in convents, and which were noted to have begun with the behavior of a single individual.

Medical analysts of the witch persecutions have occasionally disputed contentions that the witches were mentally disturbed, advancing as a reason for their skepticism the fact that self-accusations and confessions (except under torture or other powerful coercion) were rare; whereas presumably they would have been commonplace had the witches been mentally ill. However, it would seem highly probable in the light of the foregoing discussion that mental illness had at least some part in the witch persecutions.

Before closing this chapter, it might be well to take further note of the theory, advanced by some psychologists and others, that most or all of the incubus and succubus experiences are to be understood in terms of particularly vivid dreams. Jones, for example, suggests that many who confessed to sexual relations with devils may have experienced these in dreams and then, because of the intensity of emotion involved, persuaded themselves that they had had such intercourse in fact. He advances numerous instances of persons who have confused dream happenings with real events.

No doubt such confusion occurs occasionally, but today at least the occurrence is scarcely common enough to afford much help with an attempted explanation of the incubus experiences of thousands of witches. On the other hand, it is possible that dreams were more readily confused with objective experiences at the time.

Early in the fourteenth century Jean de Meung[10] took the position that some other reasonable men were to take (though they seldom dared to give tongue to their beliefs) throughout the witch persecutions. It was that such experiences as night-flying are in fact particularly vivid dreams, or possibly hallucinations, resulting from sexual frustration. Because of their vividness, De Meung said, the dreams or hallucinations were accepted by the ignorant and the superstitious as real events.

The philosopher Hobbes (*Leviathan*) expressed a similar opinion in the seventeenth century, embracing not only incubi and succubi but other supernatural beings: "From this ignorance of how to distinguish dreams and other strong fancies from vision and sense," he wrote, "did arise the greater part of the religion of the Gentiles in times past that worshipped Satyres, Faunes, Nymphs, and the like; and nowadays the opinion that rude people have of Fayries, Ghosts, and Goblins, and of the power of Witches."

It should be kept in mind in evaluating the dream theory that "rude people"—i.e., the very superstitious and ignorant—are more likely to mistake dreams for objective reality than are better educated and more civilized people. Even presently there exist primitives and savages, highly superstitious and living in a world peopled with all manner of devils and other strange and menacing spirit entities, who display the tendency to mistake dreams and other subjective experiences for objective reality to an extent far in excess of any similar tendency found among civilized peoples, especially in the West.

The dreams supposedly mistaken for physical events by witches were presumably of two kinds: nightmares, and erotic dreams of the sort culminating in orgasm or at least ejaculation. Erotic nightmares specifically seem to have been more common a few centuries ago than they are today. The anxiety of nightmare was similar to the anxiety reported in some cases of incubus visitations, and the conviction of helpless paralysis encountered in nightmare was also reported by some witches relating assaults upon themselves by incubi.

Robbins, however, while noting that the nightmare experience is a projection of repressed sexual desires, like the incubus experience, raises the objection that the latter differed from the former in a crucial respect:

". . . with the mare-demon, terror predominates; but with the incubus-demon, the main element (although mingled with dread) is pleasure."

That frustration or "repressed sexual desires" lay at the bottom of the dreams mistaken for objective incubus visitations was recognized by some even at the time, as the previously quoted theory of De Meung makes evident. There is an old Abyssinian proverb, "When a woman sleeps alone, she sleeps with the Devil," that perhaps sums up the theory well enough.

It must be admitted that even after due weight has been given to the likelihood that hysteria, hypnotic trance, schizophrenia, dreams, etc., explain, or could, a large part of the witch phenomena, there remains an unexplained residue, including testimony which seems to refer to objective events and not to have been only fabrications. This is not at all to suggest that the residue is "supernatural," only that a completely satisfying analysis, no matter how eclectic, is scarcely likely at so late a date.

19. *Eros and evil*

There remain to be set down a few speculations concerning the Christian equation of sex with evil and of sexual intercourse and its pleasures with sin. This was the poison that Christianity gave to Eros. How different the world might be, how much healthier, and how much human misery might have been avoided—including the horrors of the witch persecution—had reasonable men of authority decreed that: *The sexual appetite is a normal and healthy one; only Paul bothers about it.*

"The God of one religion becomes the Devil of the next." Was it a part of this process of deicide and resurrection to degradation that sexuality, reverenced by pagans and celebrated with orgiastic festivals, became a force to be hated and despised, still orgiastically celebrated, but by evil and degenerate spirits, and by those human servants of the Father of Evil, the witches?

Was it understood by the priests, intuitively if not intellectually, that to assert control over so powerful an appetite and so intense a pleasure was to stifle human freedom and to produce slave-men submissive to an autocratic Church dispensing earthly punishments and heavenly rewards while holding exclusive power to grant or deny absolution to carnal transgressors?

Why did the belief in the evil and debased character of matter become reduced for most practical purposes to a belief in the evil and debased character of human sexuality?

Why was God's particular authority over the sexual organs

and sexual functions of mankind, well established in the *Old Testament*, handed over to the Devil so that the authors of the *Malleus Maleficarum* should write:

". . . yet their (demons') power remains confined to the privy parts and the navel . . . For through the wantonness of the flesh they have much power over men; and in men the source of wantonness lies in the privy parts, since it is from them that semen falls, just as in women it falls from the navel." [1]

And again: "God allows more power of witchcraft over the genital functions, on account of the first corruption of sin which came to us from the act of generation; so also He allows greater power over the genital organ, even to its total removal." [2]

(The interference by witches and demons with potency and the capacity for sexual gratification assuredly testifies to conflict and ambivalence; for why should the Devil, Prince of Fornicators, wish to prevent sexual intercourse? There are answers in terms of procreation and the preservation of marriages, but the reasoning is confused, contradictory, and inadequate.)

The sexlessness of demons, affirmed by most authorities, seems perplexing. They engage in sexual relationships of every sort, but they have no sexuality. The solution to the riddle of their sexlessness is bound up, it would appear, with the abhorrence of matter. Being immaterial, or much less material than men, demons, like other supernatural beings, must be held to be "above" sexuality and the lust of the flesh—that ultimate and monstrous efflorescence of the material. But then why do they engage in sexual acts? Because they are evil, and because they know that mankind may be seduced to no greater abomination than sexual intercourse. That was the theologians' answer. It may be that to impress upon men and women the sinful character of sex intercourse some additional element of horror was felt to be required—an element provided by the terrible and God-loathing demons. Yet the question of why it should have been felt to be required remains, since even mortal fornications were held to be so iniquitous as to warrant execution and, on the metaphysical level, damnation. The addition must have been necessitated by repeated failures successfully to repress or suppress the free exercise of human sexuality.

Religion, like all superstition, is made possible by man's penchant and capacity for objectifying the subjective. God and Devil, angels and demons, are examples of the objectification of the subjective. They are also symbols, and far from immutable ones. Demonologists of the witch era considerably narrowed the symbolism of these supernatural entities, especially the demonic ones, by vastly increasing the importance of sexuality within the framework of their concerns. The result was that the Devil became, and has remained, popularly identified mainly with sexual and a few other pleasures while the role of God became an increasingly negative one—that of a proclaimer and *post mortem* enforcer of anti-pleasure prohibitions. So far has that process advanced at the present day that to the popular mind "morality" refers almost exclusively to sexual matters.

The forms of demons are instructive as to both the conscious and the unconscious sexual attitudes of their creators. They illuminate the equation of sexuality not only with sin and evil, but with ugliness and filth. It would be interesting to know at just what point in man's development the initial and pre-antisexual equation was made between flawlessness (and sometimes symmetry) on the one hand, and beauty and goodness (and later chastity—desire being imperfection) on the other. From such equation—unless, as is unlikely, the order should be reversed—evolved the further identification of the imperfect (and sometimes the asymmetrical, or distorted) with the ugly and the bad. (It might be added that symmetry, a much more recent ideal than that of flawlessness, of which it purports to be an example, is also an example of absolutist rigidity.)

In demonology such ideas achieve perhaps their ultimate representational symbolic form. Demons are ugly and imperfect (in their "true" though not always in their illusory or "glamorous" forms)—visible tokens of their evil nature; while angels are beautiful and perfect of form—badges of goodness.

The typical witch who has come down to us is old and ugly and often deformed; or, less often, she is beautiful in a not altogether wholesome sort of way, but is sensual and wicked, her imperfection and deformity being mainly of the soul or of the mind. No doubt, the beautiful but wicked witch represents something of an advance and a refinement over the ugly witch, since blatant signs of iniquity are no longer required. In a bow to probability, the beautiful witch tempts men to lust while the crone is more likely to be an enemy of procreation, interfering with potency and conception, and murdering infants. Both witches are sex symbols—foes of marriage and friends of fornication—further stimulating the identification of sexual acts (when not the passionless unions of married couples laboring only to procreate children) with sin and evil. Demons have the same functions, and to the same end.

(The ugliness and deformity attributed to witches for ideological reasons resulted in accusations of witchcraft being made against the ugly and the deformed. Women with strange eyes —"mirroring the rot of their souls"—were likely to be accused. Feet with only four toes were a sign of the witch. Supernumerary nipples were especially incriminating [since "familiars" surely suckled them], while an hermaphrodite or a person with unusual growths on his or her genitalia was almost certain to be suspect. Bites [and scratches and other lesions were often termed "bites"] were also incriminating, especially when in the region of the genitalia or breasts or anus. One woman, whose vagina had lesions, testified under torture to what her examiners had surmised from the start—that a little demon had crawled up into her and nibbled at her vaginal walls. Yet in the final analysis no one was safe. If a woman were young and beautiful, she was almost certainly in the service of the Devil, Who exploited her charms to seduce good men and lead them through their frailty into damnation. And if a woman's appearance were plain, or seemed to suggest exceptional piety and strength of character—how infernally clever of the Devil! and what a diabolic disguise for the witch and harlot lurking beneath!)

We recall that woman was lust incarnate, and a morally feeble creature easily seduced to evil, so that Jofreu estimated that female witches outnumbered the males by one hundred-to-one. Pythagoras, philosopher and mathematician, had summed it all up centuries before the birth of Christ: There is a good principle which created order, light, and man, and an evil principle which created chaos, darkness, and woman.

How drastically it all changed with the decline of witch-craft and the reaction against the excesses committed by the religious in the name of struggle against witches and demons!

The angel, for centuries thoroughly masculine, was trans-formed into a woman.

Woman, noted for the insatiability of her carnal appetites, became the ideal of purity—meaning chastity—and so far was this carried that she was even denied a capacity for sexual de-sire and an appreciation of sexual pleasures.

A complete reversal? But only in a superficial sense. Each of these views of woman serves a single purpose: to excuse male sexual inadequacy (as males have seen it).

When woman is regarded as a creature of bottomless carnal appetites, it is not to be reasonably expected that any man will be able to satisfy her; when woman is regarded as having no sexual appetite whatever, then, man is not even obliged to make the attempt to satisfy her. She has been *reduced* to moral, instead of sexual, superiority, and so is less threatening.

The physiology of the male, with its tumescence-detumes-cence mechanism, has endowed man with a permanent sense of sexual inferiority. Woman may engage in a "limitless" num-ber of copulations, but man's capacity is strictly, all-too-strictly, limited. One or two sexual acts, in some cases a few more, and he is finished for the night. But he is well aware, or supposes himself to be, that the woman could go on and on, receiving him (with gratification) as often as he could achieve erection.

It is always he who is obliged to call the halt, and often it is a fact that the woman (though not because she is insatiable) is left unsatisfied. This is a potent source of sexual inferiority feelings, and it would not be difficult to elaborate a theory to the effect that most of the perversions, and all of the refinements of love-making, have as their fundamental aim compensation for the sexual inadequacy of the male, or are a flight from that inadequacy. The insistence upon the general all but moral superiority of the male as it equips him for dominance in man-woman relationships—and perhaps the actual traditional superiority of the male in artistic and intellectual and some other fields—might be seen as further compensation. And where might it all end?—with the equation of sex with evil!—man damning that relationship in which lies, as it seems to him, the final and greatest proof of his inferiority.

Or (to indulge in one last brief bit of theoretical play), might we better propose that the true purpose of the equation of sex with sin was *aphrodisiacal!* We have it in the words of Baudelaire, the poisoned, the satanic man: *The sole pleasure of love lies in the knowledge that one is doing evil.* .

Celebrities of demonology

The more systematic demonologists were of the belief that not all devils or demons are concerned with sex. There are individual devils, and even whole classes of devils, who are assigned to specific types of work, and only some of these seduce men and women or incite them to fornication and other illicit sex behavior with their fellow humans. Some encourage and coerce mortals to engage in different misbehavior—greed and gluttony, heresy and blasphemy, sloth and drunkenness, for example.

Since one witch sometimes injured another by means of her demon, the question arose as to how the demon of one witch might prevail over the demon of another. This question did not trouble the jurist Boguet, who explained that just as there is a hierarchy of angels, with some angels more powerful than others, so there is a *cacarchy* of demons; and if one witch injured another, the fact indicated that the victimized witch had the less powerful demon, one who ranked lower in the cacarchy.

The cacarchy, or organization of Hell, was differently rendered by various demonologists. Investigation of the demonic authority structure would contribute nothing to this volume, but it might be worth while to mention a few of its chief dignitaries, limiting the very brief and arbitrary selection to some of those devils concerned with human sexuality.

Erotic celebrities of Hell

The first incubus was said by some to have been (the diabolized) Pan. The first succubus, according to the same version, was Lilith. Perhaps by virtue of seniority, this pair ruled over all the hosts of incubi and succubi.

Lilith's title as Queen of the Succubi was assigned by other writers to Nahemah. Presumably Nahemah is that Naama who (again like Lilith, and like Igereth and Machalath) was said by the Jews to be the Mother of Demons. Particularly it was believed that Nahemah or Naama was the mother of those female devils (succubi) who seek to seduce sleeping men. Other Jewish authorities credited Lilith with primary authority over dream fornications (the induction of nocturnal pollutions).

According to Sayed Idries Shah (*Oriental Magic*), Lilith is of "Accadian (Far Asian) origin—Gelal, or Kiel-Gelal—and her name in Hebrew and English is derived from the Assyrian Lil or Lilit." The origin of Lilith is, however, unresolved and has been the subject of an extremely extensive debate.

Belial, sometimes referred to as the Evil Spirit, presides over devils whose mission it is to incite men to do wickedness, in particular, to fornicate and to engage in sexual perversions. He it was, it is said, who corrupted the peoples of the Cities of the Plain, and who caused Potiphar's wife to lust adulterously after Joseph.

Belial is sometimes equated with Satan Himself, but more often is mentioned as one of Satan's chiefs. He is to be cast into the eternal fire at the Second Coming of Christ.

Belial is also sometimes equated with Beliar, who is said to have power over men and women only when they succumb to lust: "If fornication overcomes not the mind, Beliar cannot overcome man." As that versifying demonologist Milton singeth:

"Belial, the dissolutest spirit that fell,
The sensualest, and, after Asmodai,
The fleshliest Incubus."

Asmodai, or Asmodeus, King of Demons and husband of
Lilith in Hebrew legend, is also sometimes reputed to be the
demon in charge of tempting humans to the deadly sin of
lechery. The authors of the *Malleus* say of him:

"But the very devil of Fornication, and the chief of that
abomination, is called Asmodeus, which means the Creature of
Judgement: for because of this kind of sin a terrible judgement
was executed upon Sodom and the four other cities. Similarly
the devil of Pride is called Leviathan . . . And the devil of
Avarice and Riches is called Mammon." These were the three
cacarchical commissars most instrumental in tempting the
witches to give themselves to Satan, by some accounts.

It was this very devil of Fornication, Asmodeus, who loved
Sara, the daughter of Raguel, and who in his fierce jealousy
murdered her seven bridegrooms in turn, each on the wedding
night, before the husband could lie with her. The account, as
rendered in *Tobit*, is in part:

"It came to pass the same day, that in Ecbatane, a city of
Media, Sara the daughter of Raguel was also reproached by
her father's maids; because that she had been married to seven
husbands, whom Asmodeus the evil spirit had killed before
they had lain with her. Dost thou not know, said they, that
thou hast strangled thy husbands? Thou hast had already
seven husbands, neither wast thou named after any of
them . . ."

The sorrowful Sara, hearing these stinging reproaches, considers suicide; but instead she prays to God, who sends down
the angel Raphael to bind Asmodeus and give Sara for a wife
to Tobias, son of Tobit.

Her father's maids' accusation suggests that Sara had lain
with Asmodeus, but there remains some doubt. Sara does not
specifically deny such an offense in her prayer, saying only

that "I am pure from all sin with man," but she adds that "I never polluted my name, nor the name of my father," and this might be understood as a denial of intercourse with the demon.

It may be added, too, that Asmodeus (or Asmodai) seems to have been insecurely bound, since he was soon at work again making more mischief. Among the Christian demonologists he is usually a somewhat lesser power than with their Jewish counterparts; but his especial province is fleshly lust.

According to that school of demonology which lists Lucifer as Emperor and Ashtaroth as Prince of Hell, Satan is the chief general whose assignment it is to seduce and corrupt women and maidens. His principal aides include Pruslas, Aamon, and Barbatos. Another subordinate is Sidragasum, whose function is to "drive women sex-mad with dancing."

Another demonic dignitary is Belphegor. Worshiped by witches and Satanists, his tongue is a male organ of copulation. He is said to be the counterpart of the Hindu's Rutrem, who is represented by an erect phallus.

Not only the fallen angels, converted into demons in the Legions of Hell, had sexual relations with humans. Saint Justinus and Tertullian, among others, advised that the angels of the Christian God sometimes assumed human form to copulate with mortals. The *Apocrypha* also makes mention of such angels.

In *Enoch*, God sends two angels, Uzza and Azael, to earth to see if mankind may be seduced by them into succumbing to lustful temptations. But instead, the angels themselves fall into such temptation, conceiving carnal lust for mortal women, and God punishes them. Azael stands further accused of having taught women to paint their faces.

Cabalists provide the names of a number of angelic luminaries concerned with human sexuality. Among them are Aniel and Anael, Rachiel and Sachiel, Sarabotes and Amabiel, Aba, Abalidot, and Flaef.

The Cabalists add that in addition to the good angels there are evil ones, not to be mistaken for demons. One such is Isheth

Zemunin, the Angel of Prostitution, who is the wife of Samael, Angel of Poison and Death.

Those demons who have sexual intercourse with mortals, who encourage licentiousness and perversion, and who are patrons of various forms of sexual behavior, are in many cases (malign) replacements for the (mainly benevolent, or amoral) gods who had previously carried out such functions, and who continued to do so amongst the heathen. Since all such deities are no more than devils according to the most authoritative demonological thinking, it is appropriate to mention (a very few of) them here. As with other devils, some protect, or are patrons of, human sexuality and sexual practices; some participate in erotic acts with humans. Some, of course, do both; but such deities still are likely to have as their primary function either participation or the role of patron.

Sexual deities

In Persia, Scythia, Armenia, and Lydia, the goddess who was patroness of love and of sex cults was Anaïtis. Young virgins performed holy prostitution as an act of devotion to her. Her male counterpart, in the sense of being a patron of sex cults, is the Scandinavian deity Yarilo, God of Carnal Pleasures.

In Egypt, the cat goddess Bastet or Bubastis was also a patroness of sexual love. An Egyptian deity or semi-divinity closely allied to the incubi was Bes, a dwarf of hideous mien, who provided the sleeper with delicious erotic dreams while protecting him or her from nightmares and other unpleasant nocturnal occurrences. It is said that Bes still haunts the southern gate of Karnak, where he sometimes loses his temper and strangles those persons so imprudently impudent as to poke fun at his grotesque body and bestially ugly countenance.

Baphomet is an androgynous deity sometimes considered to be a patron of homosexuals. He is very old and many attempts have been made to ferret out his origins. By some accounts he was the deity worshipped by the Templars, who committed ritual sodomy and fellatio in his honor.

Backlum-Chaam was the Mayan Priapus or Penis God. His co-worker in provoking Mayans to venereal excess was Chin, God of Vice.

Among Moslems a kind of counterpart of Backlum-Chaam is El-A'awer, sometimes known as the Penis Genie. He is the patron saint of rapists, but advocates "estimable seduction, subtle enravishment," rather than the "coarse antics of lowly beasts."

"Note thou," El-A'awer pontificates, not unpoetically, "the ardor of ripe fruit when impaled by a vigorous thorn." And: "Rape is glory and guileful conquest."

Eros, God of Love, often merges into Priapus, God of the Phallus, or Penis God. The original Priapus is said to have been a man, noted for his virility and the estimable size of his organ, who was later deified. Priapus is also said to be closely related to, if not identical with, the god Mutinus or Tutinus, although scholars remark that Mutinus-Tutinus was represented by an isolated phallus, while in the case of Priapus (later, some say, Hermes or Terminus) the phallus was attached to a body. Priapus is sometimes identified too with Dionysus, and H. T. F. Rhodes declares that the goat who represented Satan at the Sabbats "is Dionysos, that rustic clod who came out of Thrace, and reached at last the high places of Olympus. He is, symbolically, the tree without arms (phallus) and the patron of fruit, flowers and particularly the vine."

Yet Dionysus seems to have been homosexual. In mourning for the death of his pederastic lover Polymnus, he carried about with him a wooden phallus, which he inserted into his anus, once doing this while squatting over Polymnus' grave, as a token of undying devotion. Cults of Dionysus, with their heterosexual orgies and other rituals and symbols, seem to have misunderstood the significance of the phallus Dionysus carried with him wherever he went. A similar error must probably be attributed to those who have confused him with Priapus.

Freisa (or Frigga or Frida) is a Scandinavian Goddess of Love whose day is Friday—thus linking her to Venus. It is said that the once popular term "frigging" was derived from her name.

Among the Hindus, the God of Self-Contemplation and the Patron of Auto-Eroticism (*Hautrus,* or masturbation) was Krishna. The act of masturbation was performed, with prayers and proper reverence, to win his favor.

P'an Chin-lien was Patroness of Prostitutes among the Chinese. She had been a whore herself, but was murdered by her father-in-law, and became instead a saint and a divinity.

A Phrygian deity, noted as the Patron of Licentiousness, was Sabazius, who is sometimes identified with Zeus, and also with Dionysus. Etymologists have attempted to establish that the term *Sabbat* was derived from his name, but Montague Summers, for one, has raised powerful objections.

Tlazolteotl was the Aztec Goddess of Illicit Passions, Lust, Pleasure and Filth. She is regarded by some as the Mexican counterpart of Venus. Tlazolteotl is further esteemed as Patroness of Prostitutes.

Among the Chinese, boy prostitutes have their own patron, Tcheou-wang, who is also God of Sodomy.

A Patroness of Homosexuals was Venus Castina. Several other Venuses have been distinguished, including one who is Patroness of Wives, another who is Patroness of Virgins, and a third who is Patroness of Prostitutes. Some authorities also mention Venus Illegitima, Patroness of Sexual Perversions.

The Goddess of Love, called Venus by the Romans, was found among almost all of the peoples of the ancient world. She was in fact more accurately to be described as a Goddess of Sexual Desire, or of Lust. As such she was known to the Babylonians as Ishtar, to the Phrygians as Cybele, to the Egyptians as Isis, to the Greeks as Aphrodite, and so on. However, it can by no means be validly maintained that these goddesses are identical, differing in names only. Each has her own peculiar background and identity. To assume that they are identical is a mistake too often made, and the source of further grave errors.

Some other goddesses more or less closely associated with Venus were Milda, Lithuanian Goddess of Love (said to have engaged in an amour with the God of War, Kauas, the result being a son, Kaunis, after whom the city of Kovno was named); and Volupia, Goddess of Voluptuous Desires. Also related to Venus seems to have been Saint Venera (or Venerea or Venerina). Until quite recently there were, and perhaps still are, temples or chapels to her in Italy, located next to sources of brimstone. These Christian chapels were denounced as modern counterparts of the Temple of Venus, and Venera was declared to be none other than Venus herself, the old pagan lust goddess in masquerade.

Other sexual deities of the Romans (listed and their functions defined by Saint Augustine) included Jugatinus, who brings husband and wife together; Virginiensis, who detaches the virginal girdles of brides; Stimula, who fans the flames of masculine desires; Strenia, who gives males the needed vigor to accomplish their desires; Liber, who makes the semen of those who invoke him fertile; and Libera (sometimes identified with Venus), who is able to make women fertile.

Strange sexual beings

In addition to Christian and Hebrew devils and pagan gods, man has crowded his world with a vast number of strange entities who copulate with mortals, either with or without their permission. It is my hope to devote a separate book-length work to these beings, who are of considerable importance to an understanding of man's psychosexual development. However, I should not on that account omit to make mention of at least a few of them here.

'ALUKAH. A Hebrew succubus and vampire derived from Babylonian demonology. The 'Alukah bears a close resemblance to the Arab 'Aulak.

ARDAT-LILE. A Semitic succubus; also a class of succubi. They are noted for the voracity of their sexual appetites, and for the delight they take in doing harm to mankind.

BASILISC. A monster who comes into existence as the result of some deviant sexual act, most commonly, sodomy.

BHOOTUMS. Sexual spirits or incubi who copulate with Hindu women.

BRUXSAS. Portuguese succubi who seduce wanderers and also copulate with other demons. They are vampires as well as succubi and may appear only at night.

CABALLI. Lustful spirits, still possessed of their earthly passions, who instinctively seek out living persons of similar inclination for the purpose of gratifying their desires. Spiritualists believe that they are especially attracted to lustful and salacious mediums, whose powers permit the Caballi to materialize and so experience more intense pleasures than are possible to them otherwise. However, their sexual practices also take place on the astral planes, where they copulate with a variety of astral beings and with humans visiting the planes in their astral bodies.

CAMBIONS. Offspring of incubi and succubi.

CENTAURS. Beings with the upper bodies of men growing out of the bodies of horses. Much more than the Satyrs, usually credited with such traits and behavior, the Centaurs were lascivious, cruel, and drunken. Forever lecherously inflamed, they were rapists by preference.

CHURELS (or CHURREYLS). Hindu succubi who perform fellatio until the very life is sucked out of the enraptured victim. The Churreyl is said to be the spirit of a woman who has died in childbirth (women dying in that circumstance becoming demons and vampires according to the lore of many times and places).

COCHE-MARES. Sexual beings apparently related to both incubi and succubi and to nightmare demons. Coche-Mares were sent by witches to persons whom the witches hoped thus (by sexual pleasure) to enslave or make dependent on them. They appeared only at night, usually while the recipient of their embraces was sleeping.

COCOTO. West Indian deities or demons who have carnal intercourse with human females.

COMPUSAE. Succubus demons.

CORYBANTES. Asiatic spirits noted for their orgiastic rites and wild dances.

DRAGONS. Invisible beings which can under certain conditions become visible and assume human form for the purpose of copulating with witches. The Dragon makes a body for himself out of semen he obtains from masturbators and the intercourse of onanists and fornicators, especially when the woman involved is a prostitute engaged in practicing her trade. In such cases the Dragon becomes an exact replica of the person whose semen he has used and so may be mistaken for that individual or for his Double. Dragons may also copulate with mediums who are able to give them ectoplasmic bodies.

DRUJAS (or DRUJES). Persian succubi noted for their raging lust, deceitfulness and general corruption, rather resembling the human female as medieval Christian theologians saw her. The Drujes continue in the spirit world the pattern of evil they earlier established as human beings. They delight in "crime and pollution," and their main objective is to lure others to ruin, pain and depravity. The resemblance to the Caballi is obvious.

DRUSII (or DUSII). According to the Gauls, demons who copulate with human females.

DUENDES. Spanish incubi.

DVOROVOI. Slavic household spirits of male sex who copulate with the female members of the family to which they have attached themselves. Dvorovoi are extremely jealous and may strangle a human mistress if she proves unfaithful.

EGRIGORS (or THOUGHT-FORMS or, in Tibet, TULPAS). Egrigors created by group effort, and which may be apprehended only visually, are the most common, but most occultists also hold that there may be tangible materialized Thought-Forms, and that these may be created by individuals as well as by groups. Usually they are created by intense concentration, but they may also come into being as the result of very intense daydreams or phantasies.

Egrigors, once in existence, may develop wills of their own, passing beyond the control of their creator(s). Sometimes, it is reported, they turn upon their creators, inflicting bodily harm. There is the story of a young woman driven insane by the physical and mental cruelties of her Egrigor-lover. There are other stories of men driven to crimes of violence because of their jealousy of the unfaithful Thought-Form mistresses they had created. Other accounts tell of Thought-Form replicas (and DOPPELGANGERS), created for homosexual indulgence, who have murdered their creators and slipped unnoticed into their places in the world. It might be noted that some authorities vigorously deny that the Tibetan Tulpas are to be equated with the Thought-Forms of Western occultists.

ELVES. In the Teutonic tradition, Elves court mortal women, seduce them, and sometimes, if the women resist their advances, become kidnapers and rapists. The Elves are the offspring of the unions of demons with mortals and their gestation period may be as brief as four weeks or as long as one year. They may be born singly, as twins, or in litters. They are inclined to mischief of all sorts and often assist their witch-mothers in injuring human adversaries.

EMPUSAE. In ancient Greek lore, malevolent and sensual female demons. They could assume the forms of animals or of beautiful girls, and in the forms of young girls they copulated as succubi with men. Mentioned by Aristophanes and other writers, they were said to be the daughters of Hecate, Patroness of Witchcraft.

EPHIALTES and HYPHIALTES. Greek equivalents of incubi and succubi.

ESTRIE. A medieval demon; also, a witch. A night-flier capable of changing form at will, the Estrie drinks the blood of humans and has sexual intercourse with them.

FAIRIES. That fairies, both male and female, wed and/or had sexual congress with humans of their opposite sex was a firmly entrenched belief in the Middle Ages and beyond. There was no problem of anatomical discrepancies to cast doubt upon reports of such unions. Fairies, while of less than average (human) stature, were of approximately the same size as mortals. As Margaret Murray has remarked, it was only after the appearance of Shakespeare's *A Midsummer Night's Dream* that the fairies of literature and folklore began to dwindle to their present tiny stature.

FAUNS. Beings with the lower bodies of goats, and with tails, horns, and furry ears. They resemble, in other words, Satyrs. Fauns copulate with women and were sometimes regarded, as has been noted, as incubi.

FIG FAUNS. Fauns or Satyrs of the desert, so called because they supposedly subsisted on figs. The *Malleus Maleficarum* holds that Pans, Incubi, Satyrs, Fauns and Dusii are all the same beings.

FIRE SPIRITS. Elementals said to cohabit with old women who

are witches, or who are obsessed by evil spirits. Fire Spirits are reported to have a fiery shape, though whether they are hot, and burn the women who enter into intimacies with them, I have been unable to discover.

FRIDAY SPIRITS. Friday's star is Venus, and the Spirits of Friday incite sexual desires. When called up, these spirits may appear as naked girls or as she-goats, and in these forms they may act as succubi. They sometimes take other forms as well.

GANDHARVAS. Blood-sucking Hindu incubi.

GNOMES and GNOMIDS. Elementals who dwell in the earth but come up onto the surface for various purposes. Gnomes are the males and Gnomids the females. They are small of stature but well formed and the Gnomids are extremely attractive sexually to men. They sometimes mate with mortals as do Sylphs (air elementals), Melusines (water elementals), and, by some accounts, Salamanders (elementals of fire).

GOBLINS. This term was often used as a synonym for incubi, or for other spirits who have sexual intercourse with humans. For that purpose a Goblin could assume a variety of shapes. Like the Poltergeist, the Goblin was unimpressed by and entirely resistant to the efforts of exorcists.

KOSTCHTCHIE. Russian Goblins, hideous in appearance, who live in the mountains of the Caucasus and are especially lustful after young girls.

LAMIAS. Greek and Roman succubi-vampires. The Lamia steals children and sucks their blood until they are completely drained. Lamias are occasionally reported to be bisexual, having intercourse with both men and women.

LARVAE. Lewd spirits conceived when humans phantasy sexual intercourse with imaginary partners and so reach the orgasm. Larvae are not, however, born of the physical sperm, but of a sperm secreted by the aroused imagination. It is said that continued loss of this sperm of the imagination, as a result of over-indulgence in erotic phantasies, will make a man physically impotent and a woman sterile. Creative powers of the intellect and the imagination may also be impaired and even destroyed, and such imaginary venereal excesses are further said to cause moles, miscarriages and malformed offspring. More, night-wandering spirits may carry off the imaginary sperm to their nests where they hatch them out, producing horrible and homicidal monsters. The hatching may also be done by witches, with physical sperm.

LEMURES. Beings similar to Caballi.

LESHY. A Slavic woodland demigod who is born as the consequence of the lustful coupling of demons with women.

MERMAID. She is in some respects the counterpart of the Water Nymph, who lures men down into the water to drown; and of the Siren, who also lures men to their doom by her beauty and/or singing. The Mermaid was often beautiful from her waist up, but her lower body was that of a fish. However, some authorities supplied her with two fishtails, like legs, with a vagina in between.

MERMAN. The male counterpart of the (presently better known) Mermaid. Some held that Mermen were conceived as the result of humans copulating with large fishes; or that fishes were impregnated by the sperm of cadavers tossed into the sea, giving birth to both Mermen and dreadful Sea Monsters. The Merman was said to be sexually attracted to human females, though his body from the waist down was that of a fish and he was not usually provided with an organ suitable for copulation.

MOLONGS. Malayan incubi-vampires.

NIXIES. Beings similar to Water Nymphs, Undines, etc. They sit naked by ponds and streams, combing their long golden hair, and entice men to follow them into the water, after which the men are usually not seen again.

NOSFERAT. A Rumanian (Transylvanian) vampire. Any person killed by a Nosferat becomes one. The vampire also acts as both incubus and succubus. Its twin missions are to suck the blood of its victim and to cause nocturnal pollutions. It is the spirit of the stillborn bastard of two parents who were also illegitimates (or, as mentioned, it may have been the victim of another Nosferat). When a woman is impregnated by a Nosferat the child is a witch. Young persons are especially attractive to it and are approached with such insatiable and overwhelming ardor that the boy or girl dies of exhaustion. The Nosferat also causes sterility and impotence in humans.

NYMPHS. Elementals (usually) of various sorts, living in forests, at the edges of streams, etc., who may assume human form and even dress as humans and move in human society without being recognized as supernatural beings. They frequently enter into sexual relationships with men; also with Satyrs, Fauns, Pans, etc.

ORNIAS. A vampire; also a succubus demon. In the form of a human female it copulates with men.

PANS. A class of demigods or spirits derived, it would seem, from the god Pan. They resemble traditional representations of Pan and of Satyrs. They copulate with both humans and nymphs, and also, on occasion, with animals, particularly she-goats.

PISÁCHAS. Incubi who specialize in raping drunken, psychotic, and sleeping women.

PISHAUCHEES. Hindu succubi who cause men to have wet dreams. They are probably female counterparts of Pisâchas.

POLUDNITSA. A beautiful Russian succubus encountered in rustic regions.

PREYTS. Hindu incubi.

RAUKSHEHS. Hindu incubi.

RHAGANA. A Lithuanian Hamadryad. They reward with delightful sexual pleasures those persons who prevent the cutting down of the trees to which their existences are mystically connected.

RUSALKI. Beautiful but cruel Slavic spirits with eyes that burn as with a green fire. Men die in their embraces, but it is said to be worth the price.

SATYRS. Beings physically similar to Fauns. They were extremely lustful (so much so that the medical term *satyriasis* is derived from them), copulating with women, nymphs and animals, especially goats. There is a remarkable statue of a Satyr copulating with a goat at the Museo Nazionale in Naples. (Some say that the Satyr is Pan himself.) This admirable work of art is pictured in Hans Licht's *Sexual Life in Ancient Greece*.

SE'IRIM. Demons resembling Satyrs and having similar (sexual) inclinations and habits.

SILVANUS. A Latin divinity (and also a class of beings) who physically resembles Pan. He was an agricultural, or arboricultural, god whose father, a shepherd, sired him with a she-goat. According to Saint Augustine, the Silvanus lived in the woodlands and consorted wantonly with women.

SIRENS. Their practice was to seduce men and then destroy them.

SPIRITS OF THE DEAD. There are prohibitions, said often violated, against raising the dead and providing them with material bodies for immoral purposes. This *sexual necromancy* is definitely an abomination of the Left-Hand Path, and is rigorously condemned by white magicians.

TROLLS. According to the *Malleus*, Trolls are the Scandinavian equivalent of Fauns. (Others, however, identify them with Gnomes.) Trolls were said to abound in Norway, and in addition to seducing and raping mortals might also, in time of wrath, inflict grievous bodily injury.

UNDINES. Elementals who cohabit with human males and may even enter into marriage relationships with them. The children of such unions receive souls from their human fathers and so are to be considered human beings. The Undine is a kind of Water Nymph, derived from many related water goddesses. She is beautiful, stirs great lust in men, and is renowned for her possessiveness and jealousy. If her human lover or husband should be unfaithful to her even once, she will disappear and he will never see her again.

UPIERZYCA. Ruthenian succubi who visit youths in their beds when the moon is full and "consume them" with hot and ravenous embraces.

VAMPIRE. Most commonly known as a blood-sucking spirit, usually animating a cadaver. The earliest known representation of a Vampire is found on a prehistoric bowl and establishes the link, often present, between Vampire and Succubus. On the bowl, the Vampire, headless, is copulating with a human male. (Summers suggests that the Vampire is headless—Vampires are destroyed by beheading—as a threat to her of what would happen if she engaged in the sexual act depicted. Probably the man drank from the bowl and so protected himself from a visit by the succubus.) There is some question as to whether Vampire or Succubus is the older conception, and as to whether the two functions were originally combined in a single entity.

With regard to the succubus function of the Vampire, Summers quotes the *Malleus:* "Is it Catholic to affirm that the functions of Incubi and Succubi belong indifferently to all unclean spirits? . . . It *seems* that it is so; for to affirm the opposite would be to maintain that there is some good order among them."

Summers himself comments: "Now the Vampire is certainly an unclean spirit, whether it be that the body is animated by some demon, or whether it be the man himself who is permitted to enter his corpse and energize it, and accordingly it is Catholic to believe that a Vampire can copulate with human beings. Nor are there lacking instances of this."

Certainly there are not lacking instances. Vampires are to be found in the traditions of almost all of the peoples of the world, many function also as succubi, and sometimes as incubi. The better known Vampires include the AKAKHARU (Assyrian), BRUCO-LACAS (Greek), DEARG-DULS (ancient Irish), EKIMMU (Assyrian), KATAKHANES (Ceylonese), MURONY (Wallachian), PONTIANAKS (Javanese), RALARATRI (Hindu), STRIGON (Indian), SWAMX (Burmese), TII (Polynesian), UPIOR or WAMPIOR (Polish), UPEER (Ukrainian), VRYKOLAKA or VURKULAKA or WUKODALAK (Russia, Morlacchia, Montenegro, Bohemia, Serbia, and Albania), VAMPYR (Dutch), WAMPIRA (Servian), PENANGGLAN (Malayan), and PANANGGLAN (Indian). The Penangglan and Panangglan seem to differ in that the former, contrary to most conceptions of the Vampire, is a living witch. Deserving of special mention is the MORA, a Slavic Vampire, who falls hopelessly in love with any man whose blood she has tasted.

VIECHTITSA. A succubus with fiery wings who descends on sleeping youths to overwhelm them with lustful caresses and rouse them to fearsome heights of venery. The preferred lover of the Viechtitsa, however, is said to be the Voukodlak, a human somnambule, who drinks blood after the fashion of the Vampire and ravens after flesh like the Werewolf.

VOUKODLAKS. (See above.) Somnambules (occasionally regarded as possessed by demons) who ravish young girls and drink their hot nourishing blood. While in trance the Voukodlaks are exceedingly dangerous and attack with tooth and nail any living creature they may meet (save for the Viechtitsas, with whom they mate).

VODYANOI. A Slavic water spirit capable of assuming a variety of forms. One of these is that of an alluring and naked girl. In such a form the Vodyanoi lures men into the water and there drowns them.

WATER NYMPHS. Water Nymphs were especially lustful of handsome young men, whom they dragged down into the depths of ponds and lakes and held captive there as their lovers (though by some accounts the humans ran out of breath and drowned). When a youth of comely appearance leaned over the water to drink, or to admire his reflection, he always took the risk of calling himself to the attention of some Water Nymph who would rise up out of the waters and drag him down; or she might appear in the middle of the body of water, perhaps taking a seat on some large lily pad, and lure him by her beauty to his fate. Some said that youths who vainly admired their own reflections and so attracted the attention of amorous Water Nymphs got no worse than they deserved.

WENDIGO. A huge and horrible being with a heart of ice who roams the wilds of northeastern Canada. The Wendigo may be either male or female but does not mate with his kind. He is clearly related in many ways to Vampires, Werewolves and other cannibalistic monsters, and the belief in the Wendigo (like the belief in the Vampire and the Werewolf) gives rise to human psychoses in which the behavior of the mythical monster is imitated. The nature of the psychosis leads to the hypothesis that repressed incest desires are at the bottom of the conception of the Wendigo (or Windigo or Wee-Tee-To or Weendegoag, etc.). The monster does not sexually assault humans, but victims of the psychosis may. Moreover, their violent assaults have overtones of sadism, necrophilia, and other perversions.

WEREWOLVES (or LYCANTHROPES). The Werewolf, a human in wolf form, sometimes copulates with humans and beasts, but its primary craving is to mutilate, kill and devour. (This is also true when, more rarely, the Werewolf is not a human but an evil spirit animating the body of a real wolf.) Like the conception of the Vampire, that of the Werewolf is bound up with sexual perversions— sadism, necrophagia, necrophilia, etc.—and the Werewolf is also a creature of castration anxieties and incest desires. There are many animals besides the wolf to whom the prefix *were-* has been applied. These include Werefoxes, Werebadgers, Wereleopards, Weretigers, Werebears, and others. Not all have identical functions or behave similarly. The Chinese Werefoxes, for example, seem to be much closer to the Western incubi and succubi than to the Werewolf. Male and female Werefoxes, in human or animal forms, mate with women and men, respectively. The Werebears of Baluchistan are another variant of the succubus idea. By day they are huge black bears, but by night they become beautiful women who solicit the embraces of men and sometimes hug their human lovers to death during the frenzy of the coition.

Some propose that Werewolves are especially motivated by *parthenophagy*, or an appetite for the flesh of young girls, which may be sexual as well as cannibalistic. In a rare pamphlet (called "A True Discourse. Declaring the damnable life and death of one Stubbe Peeter, a most wicked Sorcerer") that predilection of Lycanthropes would seem to be exemplified:

". . . he would walke vp & down, and if he could spye either Maide, Wife or childe, that his eyes liked, or his hart lusted after, he would waite their issuing out of ye Cittie or town, if he could by any meanes get them alone, he would in the feeldes rauishe them, and after in his Wooluishe likenes cruelly murder them; yea often it came to passe that as he walked abroad in the feeldes, if he chaunste to spye a companye of maydens playing together, or else a milking of their Kine, in his Wooluishe shape he would incontinent runne among them, and while the rest escaped by flight, he would sure to laye holde of one, and after his filthy lust fulfilled, he would murder her presentlye, beside, if he had liked or knowne any of them, look who he had a minde vnto, her he would pursue, whether she were before or behinde, and take her from the rest, for such was his swiftness of foot while he continued a woolf: that he would out-runne the swiftest greyhound in that Countrye: and so much he had practised this wickedness, that ye whole Prouince was feared by the cruelty of this bloody and deuouring Woolfe. Thus continuing his diuelish and damnable deedes within the compas of a fewe yeeres, he had murdered thirteene yong Children, and two goodly yong women bigge with Child, tearing the Children out of their wombes, in most bloody and sauedge sorte, and after eate their hartes panting hotte and rawe, which he accounted dainty morsells & best agreeing to his Appetite."

YUKSHEE. The most beautiful, voluptuous, and sexually insatiable of the many Hindu succubi. Her lovers become erotically exhausted and not infrequently impotent as a result of her gluttonous demands. Only Kokah Pundit, an immensely virile minister of state in the eleventh century, is credited with having been more than a match sexually for a Yukshee.

APPENDIX B

*Demoniality**

Ludovico Maria Sinistrari

INTRODUCTION†

Ludovico Maria Sinistrari, of the Order of Reformed Minors of the Strict Observance of S. Francis, was born on the 26 February, 1622, at Ameno, a small town some few miles from Orta, in the diocese of Novara, Piedmont, a suffragan of Vercelli, during the episcopate of Carlo Bescapé, a Barnabite, who is honourably known in letters as the elegant and learned historian of his see.

The young Sinistrari received a liberal education, and with great distinction pursued the course of Humanities in the ancient University of Pavia, which even in Roman times was a literary centre; and, later, as the capital of the Lombard kingdom boasted its "grammar" schools, whilst the Emperor Lothair erected a "college" there in 825. Pavia, famous in every branch of scholarship, especially excelled in Roman Law, even rivalling (her sons declared) the proud Bologna. The professors were often religious, as, for example, the Servite Filippo Ferrari (1646), a mathematician of no mean renown, whose lectures Sinistrari most probably attended; and Fra Giovanni Battista Drusiano of the same Marian Order, who was the first to teach military architecture (1645), and who assisted so nobly in the defence of the city when it was besieged by the French during 1655.

Eminent doctors filled the Chairs of Theology and Philoso-

---

* The complete text originally written sometime late in the 17th century by Ludovico Maria Sinistrari (Friar Minor), translated into English from the Latin by Montague Summers, 1927.
† Abridged.

phy, whilst Astrology had been taught at Pavia since the year 1374. In Sinistrari's day the great reputation of Gerolamo Cordano, naturalist and occult astrologer (died 1576), was yet green.

In the year 1647 Sinistrari entered the Order of Franciscans. No doubt in his boyhood he had come under the gentle influence of the Franciscan Fathers of Miasino, where there is a famous convent of the Greyfriars, yet visited by the traveller if only for the sake of the fine sunset view of Monte Rosa which may be thence obtained. Hard by his native Orta, also, is the Sacro Monte, a sanctuary dedicated to the stigmatized Patriarch of Assisi, a retreat beautifully situated upon a well-wooded promontory, approached by some twenty chapels or oratories, where the sweetly languorous magnolia and the tropical cactus bloom amid open gardens in fullest luxuriance and florid loveliness.

Acting under the shrewd direction of his Superiors Sinistrari now applied himself with whole-hearted intenseness to pedagogics and the practice of tuition. So keen a psychologist as he soon excelled in these infinitely difficult, but most profoundly human, acquirements, and he was shortly nominated Professor of Philosophy at Pavia. After a little while he proceeded to a yet more onerous task, and for fifteen years he taught Theology to the admiration and applause of Italy's most learned masters and scholars. His lecture room was crowded month after month by throngs of students who were attracted from all parts of Europe owing to his high repute and the fame of his encyclopaedic knowledge.

At the same time he preached courses of Lenten and Advent sermons in many of the principal cities of Italy. The cathedrals, when he occupied the pulpit, never failed to be filled from end to end with multitudes who hung upon his sacred eloquence, whilst the Missions which he held in country towns and even in smaller villages, for he deemed no labour of the priesthood to be unworthy of his utmost care, reaped their own reward, a rich harvest of glowing piety and innumerable conversions.

A scrupulously exact religious, he was none the less an ur-
bane and cultured man of the world. His fine bearing and
courteous manners made him as agreeable at the sumptuous
table of prelates and princes as at the humble and scantier
board of the refectory and convent cenaculum.

In person he is described as being well-built and athletic,
with a singularly graceful gait, tall, of an open and comely
countenance, with a high, broad forehead, bright lively hazel
eyes that flashed with intellect, and a somewhat ruddy com-
plexion.

His conversation was remarkable for its easy sallies of wit,
whereby he could attract and hold the attention of the most
desultory or careless listener, and awaken a yet warmer enthusiasm in the heart of the devoted and eager scholar. Among
his companions of the cloister he was, moreover, remarkable
for a very real devotion and a truly humble spirit, which enabled him to sustain without any fretful complaints or grum
parade of mortification, but with unconquerable patience and
a placid composure, frequent attacks of gout that severely
tormented him, sufferings which were far from relieved by his
constant study and ceaseless labours, often protracted into the
midnight hours after a long day of almost unbroken academic
toil. His contemporaries, indeed, especially noted the mildness
of his temper, his candour, and, so his brethren tell us, the perfect observance of his religious rule in every minutest particular. He was in truth, as they loved to call him, *omnium scientiarum uir*. Such leisure moments, or, rather, such rare respite
as he allowed himself from his unwearied research into pro-
founder authors, he gave to the study of languages other than
his own, many of which he mastered without the help of any
formal teacher, reading them with great facility, and even
speaking them with fluency and precision, and, so keen was
his ear, he was acknowledged by the native professors of the
several tongues to be gifted with a singularly pure accent and
enunciation.

It was hardly possible that so famous a scholar should not

soon attract the notice of the highest authorities, and accordingly we are not surprised to find that Sinistrari was summoned to Rome to fill the position of Consultor to the Supreme Tribunal of the Most Holy Inquisition. The chief official of this Congregation is the *Commissarius Sancti Officii,* a Dominican of the Lombard province, and there can be no doubt that it was owing to the Commissioner of the day, who, coming from Lombardy, must have known Sinistrari well, that this important appointment was made.

For some years Sinistrari acted as Vicar-General to the Archbishop of Avignon, whose see comprises the territory embraced by the department of Vaucluse. The prelate in question, whose episcopate lasted from *1673-84,* was Hyacinth Libelli of Tiferno, O.P., Master of the Sacred Palace to Clement X. "Non in theologia tantum sed in omnia quoque scientiarum genere fuit uersatissimus," says Sainte Marthe. Sinistrari was appointed as a coadjutor to Claude Pertuyse, now an old man, worn out and broken with some thirty years of ceaseless anxiety and gravest responsibility. This was then no enviable position, but an outpost needing the continual exercise of the nicest tact and most skilful diplomacy. The Houses of Valois and Bourbon had more than once endeavoured to subject the papal territory to the French crown, and in *1663* Louis XIV., in consequence of an unfortunate attack made upon the mohocking attendants of the overbearing and arrogant Duc de Créqui, his ambassador at Rome, swooped down upon Avignon, which was forthwith declared an integral part of the realm of France by the jingoistic Parliament of Provence. Nor was the sequestration raised until Flavio Chigi, the Cardinal Padrone, nephew of Alexander VII., had tendered an ample apology. In *1688,* during the reign of the Venerable Innocent XI., another French attempt at the sudden occupation of Avignon was made, but without success. By this time, however, Sinistrari had long left the troublous Archdiocese, and after a short residence again in Rome was acting as Theologian to Federico Caccia, the Cardinal-Archbishop of Milan.

From Rome, where he could find no leisure owing to the constant press of visitors, many of whom being of noble birth and highest rank, both ecclesiastical and lay, could not be denied, Sinistrari had withdrawn to the Franciscan retreat of the Sacro Monte, hoping that here he might complete his great work *De Delictis et Poenis* undisturbed. But the summons to Milan forced him back into the busy world. A year's illness also intervened, and it was only by dint of sheer dogged work and hours stolen from sleep that he was able to put the finishing touches to his noble volume.

At the suggestion of José Ximenes Santiago, who, upon his retirement in 1682 from the office of Minister-General of the Franciscan Order, had been obliged by Innocent XI. to accept the mitre as Bishop of Placentia, the plenary Chapter of Franciscans, which met in 1688, entrusted Sinistrari with the compilation of the statutes of the Order. This formidable task he performed in his treatise entitled *Practica criminalis Minorum illustrata*. Ever a student and lover of books, pen in hand to the last, he died in the pontificate of Clement XI. on 6 March, 1701, at the ripe old age of seventy-nine, honoured and regretted by all.

His several tractates were more than once reprinted early in the eighteenth century, and his complete works have been collected, 3 vols., folio, 1753-1754: *R. P. Ludovici Mariae Sinistrari de Ameno Opera omnia, Romae, in domo Caroli Gianniani*. Herein are included the *Practica criminalis Minorum illustrata; Formularium criminale; De incorrigibilium expulsione ab Ordinibus Regularibus;* and the *De Delictis et Poenis*.

The *De Daemonialitate*, the manuscript of which was discovered in London in 1872, was printed for the first time in the year 1875.

When we consider how acute and how accurate a theologian Sinistrari was, how great was his first fame during his lifetime, and what high positions he held with credit and applause both at the University of Pavia and at the Roman Court, it will come as something of a surprise to many to learn that one of his books, or rather the first edition of one of his books, was actually placed upon the Index. It must at once be pointed out that the *Index librorum prohibitorum* is a highly technical codex or catalogue, and that, generally speaking, books are only included therein for highly technical reasons. The curious inquirer who imagines that he has got hold of a guide to knowledge in the shape of a copious list of those volumes which book-sellers of the meaner sort are apt to dub "Facetiae," that is to say undiluted pornography, when he eagerly turns the pages of the Index will be most woefully and grievously disappointed. Instead of salacious titles to thrill his jaded fancy with some new arcana of phallism, instead of lewdness and lubricity, he will read long columns of dusty names of dead and gone heresiarchs, men whose works have left not an echo behind them, he will read the dreary captions of Lethean volumes, "Dry Bodies of Divinity," of pseudo-philosophy, whose pages have gone to wrap up as many mackerel and bloaters as did the *Annals* of Volusius in ancient Rome long centuries ago.

Yet on the Index is filed: Sinistrari (Ludovicus Maria) de Ameno, De Delictis et Poenis Tractatus absolutissimus. *Donec corrigatur. Decret. 4 Martii, 1709. Correctus autem iuxta editionem Romanam anni 1753 permittitur.*

The *De Delictis et Poenis* was published for the first time at Venice in *1700, Venetiis, apud Hieronymum Albricium, MDCC.* It is a treatise, extraordinarily complete, dealing with all imaginable crimes, sins, and offences; and in most cases it discusses the punishment due to the crime, the penalities inflicted both by the ecclesiastical and by the civil law.

The closing decades of the seventeenth century were a time of great and perplexing intellectual difficulties. In Moral Theology Rigorists (even Jansenists), Probabilists, Aequiprobabilists, Probabiliorists, and Laxists were putting forward conflicting views; they contended for their opinions with the utmost pertinacity, and it is hardly to be wondered at that, in their revolt from the bitter severities of Port-Royal, the spiritual harshness, and the pessimism which, however unintentionally,

none the less inevitably, this narrow attitude of mind was bound
to produce, some few theologians went perhaps a thought too
far in the opposite direction.

As early as *1653* Innocent X. condemned the five propositions which had been taken from the *Augustinus,* published
after the death of its author, Jansen, folio, *1640,* and another
blow was dealt at rigorism in *1657* by Alexander VII., but this
school did not seem absolutely forbidden and completely
banned until *1690,* when Alexander VIII. in uncompromising
and directest terms condemned the proposition of Sinnichius,
a leading rigorist: *Non licet sequi opinionem uel inter proba-
biles probabilissimam.* On the other hand, for fear of the
least shadow of scandal the Popes corrected certain tendencies
of Laxism, and thus we find that many leading authorities
were in some small points impugned by the punctilious vigi-
lance of Innocent XI. and Alexander VII. Accordingly there
were censured propositions which had been speculatively approved by the Theatine Antonio Diana (died *1663*), a Consultor of the Holy Office of the Kingdom of Sicily and an ex-
aminer of Bishops; theorems advanced by the famous and
learned Juan Caramuel (died *1682*), sometime Archbishop
of Otranto; by the profound theologian Leander (died *1663*);
by Juan Azor, S.J. (died *1603*); by De Graphoeis; and by not
a few other authoritative names. Nay, more, important books
were actually forbidden. Thus the famous *Aphorismi Confes-
sariorum ex Uariis Doctorum Sententiis collecti,* published
Venice, *1595,* of Manoel de Sa, S.J. (died *1596*), who for his
holy life was held in high honour by Pope S. Pius V., was
placed on the Index in *1603,* and only removed in *1900.* (For
a quarter of a century I have constantly used the *Aphorismi,
Coloniae, sumptibus Petri Amorfortii MDXCIX.,* with the approbation of the Censor Silvester Pardo, a Canon of Antwerp,
and I should indeed find it difficult to say why this treatise
had merited a censure.)

Two works of the great Etienne Bauny, S.J., who died in
the odour of sanctity *1649, Practique du droit canonique*

au gouvernment de l'Église, Paris, *1634,* and *De Sacramentis ac Personis Sacris . . . Theologiae moralis pars prima,* Paris, folio, *1640,* are both on the Index. What seems perhaps even more remarkable, is that by a decree of *4* February, *1627,* there were placed on the Index some editions of Volume III. of the *Disputationes de sancti Matrimonii Sacramento,* first published *1602-3,* the famous work of Thomas Sanchez, S.J., who died in *1610.* But displeasure was caused by his treatment of a highly technical point, the power of the Pope to grant a valid legitimation of the offspring of marriages gravely invalid under Canon Law; Book VIII., disputatio *7.* It is perhaps worth noting that Sanchez also upholds a theory concerning mental reservation, which was the twenty-sixth thesis condemned by Innocent XI.

Since the Supreme Authority from time to time deemed it expedient that in some small point so many and such great writers should have been corrected, it is no real reflection upon the sound erudition and orthodoxy of Sinistrari that on account of some formal small circumstance, a certain numerical ambiguity to wit in one or two paragraphs, his *De Delictis et Poenis* should have been censured. Moreover, it was not until nine years after his death that any fault was alleged, and even then the mitigating rubric *Donec corrigatur,* "Until such time as it be amended," was added; although this, of course, was beyond the author's power.

Sinistrari's *Demoniality,* the Latin text with a French translation, *De La Démonialité et des Animaux Incubes et Succubes,* was first published (Paris, 8vo, *1875*) by the celebrated bibliophile Isidore Liseux, who issued it from his house, *2* Rue Bonaparte. Liseux had discovered the manuscript in London in *1872,* and gives the following account of its provenance. He relates how he used to frequent the shop of a certain Mr. Allen, "a venerable old gentleman, whose place of business was in the Euston Road, close to the gate of Regent's Park." Mr. Allen seems to have sold his stock according to size, folios and quartos at two or three shillings apiece; octavos at one shilling; and duodecimos at sixpence. He methodically bought in his volumes at the book auctions, and among these lots rare volumes not unseldom chanced to come his way for a handful of coppers. On one occasion, from the 6 to the 16 December, 1871, Sotheby was selling the library of Seymour Kirkup, an English collector, who some months before had died in Florence, and Mr. Allen then acquired a number of books and manuscripts which had been neglected by Quaritch, Sotheran, Pickering, and the rest. A little while after, Liseux, who happened to be in the shop, turned over various specimens of these late Italian codices. The title of one was *De Uenenis;* of another *De Uiperis;* of a third *De Daemonialitate et Incubis, et Succubis.* All three were separate, and by several authors. "Poisons, adders, demons," he cries, "what a collection of horrors! Yet, were it but for civility's sake, I was bound to buy something." He decided to choose the last, and for sixpence he became the possessor of Sinistrari's work. In 1879 he was advertising for sale "the original manuscript of *Demoniality,*" for which he asked forty pounds, not a bad return on the humble tester he had originally laid out in Mr. Allen's shop.

The manuscript in Sotheby's sale catalogue is listed as follows:—

No. *145.* AMENO (R. P. Ludovicus Maria [*Cotta*] de). *De Daemonialitate, et Incubus, et Succubis,* Manuscript.

SÆC. XVII-XVIII.

This manuscript, written on strong paper of the seventeenth century, bound in Italian parchment, and beautifully preserved, has eighty-six pages of text. The title and first page are in the author's hand, that of an old man. The remainder is in very clear, and probably professional, calligraphy, made under Sinistrari's direction, as is obvious from the side notes and corrections in his quavering script, which occur throughout the whole work. It was, no doubt, taken down from his dictation, and thus is certainly the original manuscript.

MONTAGUE SUMMERS

In Festo vij Dolorum B.M.V. in Quadragesima, 1927

DEMONIALITY

The first author who, so far as I know, uses the word *Demoniality* is Juan Caramuel,[1] in his *Fundamental Theology*, and before him I can find no one who distinguishes that crime from *Bestiality*. Indeed, all Moral Theologians, following S. Thomas (II. 2, quest. 154), include, under the specific title of *Bestiality*, *"every kind of carnal intercourse with any thing whatsoever of a different species":* such are the words used by S. Thomas. Cajetan,[2] for instance, in his commentary on that Question, classes intercourse with the Demon under the description of Bestiality; so does Silvester,[3] *de Luxuria;* Bonacina,[4] *de Matrimonio,* quest. 4; and others.

2. However, it is clear that in the above passage S. Thomas did not allude to intercourse with the Demon. And as shall be demonstrated further on, that intercourse cannot be included in the particular and peculiar species *Bestiality;* and, in order to make that sentence of the holy Doctor tally with truth, it must be admitted that when saying of unnatural sin, *"that committed through intercourse with a thing of different species, it takes the name of Bestiality,"* S. Thomas, by *a thing of different species*, means a living animal, of another species than man: for he could not here use the word *thing* in its most general sense, to mean indiscriminately an animate or inanimate being. In fact, if a man should fornicate with a dead body, he would have to do with a thing of a species quite different from his own (especially according to the Thomists, who deny the form of human corporeity in a corpse); similarly if he were to have connexion with a dead animal: yet, such copulation would not be bestiality, but pollution. What therefore S. Thomas intended here to specify so exactly is carnal intercourse with a living thing of a species different from man, that is to say, with an

animal, and he assuredly intends no reference to intercourse
with the Demon.

3. Therefore, connexion with the Demon, whether Incubus
or Succubus (which is, properly speaking, *Demoniality*), differs in kind from Bestiality, and does not in conjunction with it
form one particular species, as Cajetan wrongly maintains;
for, whatever may have been said to the contrary by some
early authorities, and later by Caramuel in his *Fundamental
Theology*, by Vincenzo Filliucci,[5] and others, unnatural sins
differ from each other most distinctly. Such at least is the general doctrine, and the contrary opinion has been condemned by
Alexander VII.[6] (No. XXIV. of the condemned propositions):
first, because each of those sins carries with itself its peculiar
and distinct turpitude, opposed to chastity and to human procreation; secondly, because the commission thereof entails each
time the sacrifice of some good by reason of the nature attached
to the institution of the venereal act, the normal end of which
is human generation; lastly, because each has a different motive, which in itself is sufficient to bring about, in divers and
several ways, the deprivation of the same good, as has been
clearly shown by Filliucci, Crespinus, and Caramuel.

4. It follows that Demoniality differs in kind from Bestiality,
for each has its peculiar and distinct turpitude, opposed to
chastity and human procreation. Bestiality is connexion with a
living beast, endowed with its own proper senses and impulses;
Demoniality, on the contrary, is copulation with a corpse (in
accordance at least with the general opinion which shall be
considered hereafter), a senseless and motionless corpse which
is but accidentally moved through the power of the Demon.
Now, if fornication with the dead body of a man, or a woman,
or a beast differ in kind from Sodomy and Bestiality, there is
the same difference with regard to *Demoniality*, which, according to the general opinion, is the intercourse of man with a
dead body accidentally endued with motion.

5. Another proof follows: in sins against nature, the unnat-

ural semination (which cannot be regularly followed by procreation) is a genus; but the object of such semination is the
difference which marks the species under the genus. Thus,
whether semination takes place on the ground, or on an inanimate body, it is pollution; if with a male *in uase praepostero*,
it is Sodomy (*Sodomia perfecta*); with a beast, Bestiality:
crimes which unquestionably all differ from each other in
species, just as the ground, the corpse, the man and the beast,
passive objects of such emission of semen, differ in species from
each other. But the difference between the Demon and the
beast is not only specific, it is more than specific: the nature of
the one is corporeal, of the other incorporeal, which makes a
generic difference. Whence it follows that several emissions of
semen practised on different objects differ in species from each
other: and that is, according to the intention of the act.

6. It is also a common doctrine with Moralists, established
by the Council of Trent, session 14, and approved by S. Thomas,
Gabriel Vasquez,[7] Enrique Henriquez,[8] Bartholomew Medina,[9]
and other theologians, that in confession it suffices to state the
circumstances which alter the species of sins. If therefore Demoniality and Bestiality belonged to the very same particular
species, it would be enough that, each time he has fornicated
with the Demon, the penitent should say to his confessor: *I
have been guilty of the sin of Bestiality*. But that is not the case:
therefore those two sins do not both belong to the very same
particular species.

7. It may be urged that if the circumstances of copulation
with the Demon should be revealed to the confessor, it is on
account of the offence against Religion, an offence which
comes either from the worship rendered to the Demon, or from
the homage or prayers offered up to him, or from the compact
of fellowship entered into with him (*S. Thomas*, II. 2, Quest.
90, art. 2, and Quest. 95, art. 4). But, as will be seen hereafter,
there are Incubi and Succubi to whom none of the foregoing
applies, and yet there is carnal connexion. There is consequently
in that special case, no element of irreligion, no other char-

acter than of plain and simple fornication; and, if it were the same species as Bestiality, it would have to be confessed by clearly stating: *I have been guilty of the sin of Bestiality;* which is not the case.

8. Besides, it is acknowledged by all Moral Theologians that carnal connexion with the Devil, or a familiar, is much more heinous than the same act committed with any beast whatsoever. Now, in the same particular and peculiar species of sins, one sin is not more heinous than another; all are equally grave: it is the same whether connexion is had with a bitch, an ass, or a mare; whence it follows that if *Demoniality* is more heinous than Bestiality, those two acts are not of the same species. And let it not be argued, with Cajetan (II. 2, Quest. 154, art. 2, towards the end of III.), that *Demoniality* is always more heinous on account of the offence to religion from the worship rendered to the Demon or the compact of fellowship entered into with him: since it has been shown above, that these circumstances do not always occur in the connexion of man with Incubi and Succubi; moreover, if in the genus of unnatural sin *Demoniality* is more grievous than Bestiality, the offence to Religion is quite foreign to that aggravation, and accidental, since it is foreign to that genus itself.

9. Therefore, having laid down the specific difference between *Demoniality* and Bestiality, so that the gravity thereof may be duly appreciated in view of the penalty to be inflicted (and that is our most essential object), we must needs inquire in how many different ways the sin of *Demoniality* may be committed. There is no lack of people who, mightily proud of their small stock of knowledge, venture to deny what has been written by the gravest authors and what is, moreover, testified by every day experience: namely, that the Demon, whether Incubus or Succubus, unites carnally not only with men and women, but also with beasts. They allege that it all proceeds from the human imagination troubled by the craft of the Demon, and that it is nothing but phantasmagoria, glamour, and diabolical spells. The like happens, they say, to

Witches who, under the influence of an illusion brought on by the Demon, imagine that they attend the nightly sports, dances, revels and sabbats, and there have carnal intercourse with the Demon, though in reality they are not bodily transferred to those places nor do they take any part in these abominations. But the reality and the truth of all this have been explicitly laid down by Episcopal Capitularies,[10] by the Council of Ancyra, by the Roman synods under Pope S. Damasus I. These are cited by Lorinus of Avignon.[11]

10. Of course, there is no question that sometimes young women, deceived by the Demon, imagine they are actually taking part, in their flesh and blood, in the sabbats of Witches, and all this is merest fantasy. Thus, in a dream, one sometimes fancies that one is sleeping with someone else, and there is an emission of semen, yet that connexion is wholly unreal and imaginary, and often brought about by a diabolical illusion: and here the above-mentioned Episcopal Capitularies and Councils are perfectly right. But this is not always the case; on the contrary, it more often happens that Witches are bodily present at sabbats and have an actual carnal and corporeal connexion with the Demon, and that likewise Wizards copulate with the Succubus or female Demon. Such is the opinion of Theologians as well as of jurists, many of whose names will be found at length in the *Compendium Maleficarum*, or *Chronicle of Witches*, by Fra Francesco Maria Guazzo.[12] It is maintained by Grilland,[13] Remy,[14] S. Peter Damian,[15] Silvester, Alfonso à Castro,[16] Cajetan, Père Pierre Crespet,[17] Bartolomeo Spina,[18] Giovanni Lorenzo Anania.[19] This doctrine is also therein confirmed by eighteen actual instances adduced from the recitals of learned and truthful men whose testimony is beyond suspicion, and which prove that Wizards and Witches are indeed bodily present at sabbats and most shamefully copulate with Demons, Incubi or Succubi. And, after all, to settle the question, we have the authority of S. Augustine, who, speaking of carnal intercourse between men and the Demon, expresses himself as follows, book xvth, chap. 23rd, of the *City of God:*

"*It is widely credited, and such belief is confirmed by the direct or indirect testimony of thoroughly trustworthy people, that Sylvans and Fauns, commonly called Incubi, have frequently molested women, sought and obtained from them coition. There are even Demons, whom the Gauls call Duses or Boggarts, who very regularly indulge in those unclean practices: the fact is testified by so many and such weighty authorities, that it were impudent to doubt it.*" Such are the very words of S. Augustine.

11. Now, several authors assert, and it is confirmed by numerous experiments, that the Demon has two ways of copulating carnally with men or women: the one which he uses with Witches or Wizards, the other with men or women who know nothing of witchcraft.

12. In the first case, the Demon does not copulate with Witches or Wizards until after a solemn profession, in virtue of which such wretched creatures yield themselves up to him. According to several authors who have related the judicial admissions of Witches when on the rack, and whose recitals have been collected by Francesco Maria Guazzo, *Compendium Maleficarum*, book 1, chap. 7, that profession consists of eleven ceremonials:

13. Firstly, the Novices have to conclude with the Demon, or with some other Wizard or Magician acting in the Demon's place, an express compact by which, in the presence of witnesses, they enlist in the Demon's service, he giving them in exchange his promise that they shall enjoy honours, riches and carnal pleasures. Guazzo; *loc. cit.*

14. Secondly, they abjure the Catholic Faith, withdraw from their obedience to God, renounce Christ and the protection of the most Blessed Virgin Mary, and all the Sacraments of the Church. Guazzo; *loc. cit.*

15. Thirdly, they cast away the Crown,[20] or Rosary of the most Blessed Virgin Mary, the girdle of S. Francis,[21] or the Cincture of S. Augustine, or the Scapular of the Carmelites, should they belong to one of those Orders; the Cross, the Med-

als, the *Agnus Dei*, whatever other holy or consecrated object may have been about their person, and trample them under foot. Guazzo, *loc. cit.*; Grilland, passim.

16. Fourthly, into the hands of the Devil they vow obedience and subjection; they pay him homage and vassalage, laying their fingers on some foul black book.[22] They bind themselves never to return to the faith of Christ, to observe none of the divine precepts, to do no good work, but to obey the Demon alone and to attend diligently the nightly conventicles. Guazzo; *loc. cit.*

17. Fifthly, they promise to strive with all their power, and to devote their utmost zeal and care to the enlistment of other males and females in the service of the Demon. Guazzo; *loc. cit.*

18. Sixthly, the Devil administers to them a certain sacrilegious baptism, and after abjuring their Christian Godfathers and Godmothers of the Baptism of Christ and Confirmation, they have assigned to them a new Godfather and a new Godmother, who are to instruct them in the arts of witchcraft; they drop their former name and exchange it for another, more frequently a scurrilous and absurd nickname. Guazzo; *loc. cit.*

19. Seventhly, they cut off a part of their own garments, and tender it as a token of homage to the Devil, who takes it away and retains it. Guazzo; *loc. cit.*

20. Eighthly, the Devil draws on the ground a circle wherein stand the Novices, Witches and Wizards, and there they confirm by horrid oaths all their aforesaid promises. Guazzo; *loc. cit.*

21. Ninthly, they request the Devil to strike them out of the book of Christ, and to inscribe them in his own book. Then is brought forth that foul black book on which, as has been explained above, they laid hands when doing homage, and they are inscribed therein with the Devil's claw. Guazzo; *loc. cit.*

22. Tenthly, they promise the Devil sacrifices and offerings at stated times: once a fortnight or at least each month, the

slaughter of some child, or a murderous act of sorcery, and week by week other vile misdeeds to the bitter hurt of mankind, such as hailstorms, tempests, fires, rinderpest, the destruction of sheep and kine, etc. Guazzo; *loc. cit.*

23. Eleventhly, the Demon imprints on them some mark, especially on those whose constancy he suspects. That mark, moreover, is not always of the same shape or figure: sometimes it is the likeness of a hare, sometimes a toad's foot, sometimes a spider, a puppy, a dormouse. It is imprinted on the most hidden parts of the body: with men, under the eye-lids, or it may be under the armpits, or on the lips, on the shoulder, the fundament, or somewhere else; with women, it is usually on the breasts or the privy parts. Now, the stamp which imprints those marks is none other but the Devil's claw. When all these rites have been performed in accordance with the instructions of the mystagogues who initiate the novices, these then promise never to worship the Blessed Sacrament; to insult all Saints and especially the most Holy Mother of God; to trample under foot and defile Holy Images, the Cross, and the Relics of Saints; never to use the sacraments or sacramentals; never to make a good confession to the priest, but to keep always hidden from him their intercourse with the Demon. The Demon, in exchange, engages to give them always prompt assistance; to fulfil their desires in this world and to make them happy after their death. The solemn profession being thus made, each has assigned to himself a Devil called *Magistellus* or Little Master, with whom he retires aside for carnal satisfaction; the said Devil assuming the shape of a woman if the initiated person be a man, the shape of a man, sometimes of a satyr, sometimes of a buck-goat, if it be a woman who has been received a witch. Guazzo; *loc. cit.*

24. If we seek to learn from these Authorities how it is possible that the Demon, who has no body, yet can perform actual coitus with man or woman, they unanimously answer that the Demon assumes the corpse of another human being, male or female as the case may be, or that, from the mixture of other

materials, he shapes for himself a body endowed with motion, by means of which body he copulates with the human being; and they add that when women are desirous of becoming pregnant by the Demon (which occurs only with the consent and at the express wish of the said women), the Demon is transformed into a Succubus, and during the act of coition with some man receives therefrom human semen; or else he procures pollution from a man during his sleep, and then he preserves the spilt semen at its natural heat, conserving it with the vital essence. This, when he has connexion with the woman, he introduces into her womb, whence follows impregnation. Such is the teaching of Guazzo, book 1, ch. 12, and he proves it by a number of quotations and instances taken from many learned Doctors.

25. At other times also the Demon, whether Incubus or Succubus, copulates with men or women from whom, however, he receives none of the sacrifices, homage or offerings which he is wont to exact from Wizards or Witches, as aforesaid. He is then but a passionate lover, having only one desire; the carnal possession of those whom his lust craves. Of this there are numerous instances to be found in authors of no small repute, amongst whom we read of the case of Menippus Lycius, who long cohabited with a woman, and when she had served him sexually many times and oft, so doted on her that she persuaded him to marry her; but a certain philosopher, who happened to be present at the wedding banquet, having guessed what the woman was, told Menippus that he had to deal with a *Compusa*, that is a Succubus; whereupon the bride vanished shrieking and wailing bitterly. Such is the narrative related by Coelius Rhodiginus,[23] *Antiquitatum*, book xxix., ch. 5. Hector Boece[24] (*Scotorum Historia*,[25] book viii.), also relates the adventure of a young Scotchman, who, during many months, although the doors and windows of his chamber were ever fast shut, was visited in his bed-room by a Succubus of the most enchanting beauty; she resorted to every blandishment, caresses, kisses, embraces, entreaties, to prevail upon

him to fornicate with her: but she could not succeed with the chaste young man.

26. We read likewise of numerous women incited to coition by an Incubus, and who, though reluctant at first of yielding to him, are soon moved by his prayers, tears, and endearments; for he is a desperate lover and must not be denied. And although this comes sometimes of the craft of some Wizard who avails himself of the agency of the Demon, yet the Demon not infrequently acts thus on his own account, as Guazzo informs us, *Compendium Maleficarum*, III. 8; and this happens not only with women, but also with mares; for if they readily comply with his desire, he pets them, and plaits their manes in elaborate and inextricably reticulated tresses; but if they resist, he ill-treats and strikes them, infects them with the glanders and lampass, and may finally kill them, as is shown by daily experience.

27. It is a most marvellous and well nigh incomprehensible fact that the Incubi whom the Italians call *Folletti*,[26] the Spaniards *Duendes*, the French *Follets*, do not obey the Exorcists, evince no dread of exorcisms, and show no reverence for holy things, at the approach of which seemingly they are not overawed. Now they are very different in this respect from the Demons who vex those whom they possess; for, however obstinate those evil Spirits may be, however resistant to the injunctions of the Exorcist who bids them leave the body they possess, yet, at the mere utterance of the Most Holy Names of Jesus or Mary, or the recitation of some verses of Scripture, at the imposition of Relics, especially of the Wood of the Most Holy Cross, or at the sight of pictures and statues of the Saints, they roar fearfully from the mouth of the possessed person, they gnash, shake, quiver, and display fright and terror. But the Folletti show none of those signs, and only desist their vexations after a very long space of time. Of this I was an eye-witness, and I shall relate a story which verily passes human belief: but I take God to witness that I tell the actual truth, corroborated by the testimony of many reputable persons.

28. About twenty-five years ago, when I was lecturer on Sacred Theology in the convent of the Holy Cross, in Pavia,[27] there was living in that city a married woman of unimpeachable morality, and who was most highly spoken of by all such as knew her, especially by the Friars. Her name was Hierónyma, and she lived in the parish of S. Michael.[28] One day, this woman had kneaded bread at home and given it out to bake. The cook-shop man brought her back her loaves when baked, and with them a large cake of a peculiar shape, made of butter and Venetian paste, as is usual for manchets to be made in that city. She declined to take it in, saying she had not kneaded any thing of the kind. "But," said the cook, "I had no other bread save yours to bake to-day, therefore this cake also must have come from your house; you have, perhaps, forgotten." The good wife allowed herself to be persuaded, and partook of the cake with her husband, her little girl who was three years old, and the maid servant. The next night, whilst in bed with her husband, and both were fast asleep, she suddenly woke up at the sound of a very small voice, something like a shrill hissing, whispering in her ears, yet with great distinctness, and inquiring whether "the cake had been to her taste?" The good woman, thoroughly frightened, began to guard herself with the sign of the cross and repeatedly called upon the Names of Jesus and Mary. "Be not afraid," said the voice, "I mean you no harm; quite the reverse: I am prepared to do anything to please you; I am captivated by your beauty, and desire nothing more than to enjoy your sweet embraces." Whereupon she felt somebody kissing her cheeks, so lightly, so softly, that she might have fancied being stroked by the finest feather-down. She resisted without giving any answer, confidently repeating over and over again the Names of Jesus and Mary, and crossing herself most devoutly. The tempter kept on thus for nearly half an hour, when he withdrew.

The next morning the dame sought her confessor, a discreet and learned man, who confirmed and encouraged her in her faith, exhorting her to maintain her stout resistance and to provide herself with some holy Relics. On the ensuing nights she was sore tempted with the same amorous words and loving kisses, and she showed the same constancy in repulsing them. Utterly weary, however, of such painful and persistent molestations, upon the advice of her confessor and other reverend men, she had herself exorcised by experienced Exorcists, in order to ascertain whether perchance she was not actually possessed. Having found in her no trace of the evil Spirit, they blessed the house, the bed-room, the bed, and strictly commanded the Incubus to cease his annoyance. But all was in vain; he kept on worse than before, pretending to be love-sick, weeping and moaning in order to melt the heart of the lady, who however, by the grace of God, remained unconquered. The Incubus then went another way to work: he showed himself in the shape of a lad or little man of great beauty, with crisped golden locks, a flaxen beard that shone like fine gold, sea-green eyes calling to mind the flax-flower, and arrayed in a comely Spanish dress. Besides he appeared to her even when she was in company, billing and cooing gently after the fashion of lovers, kissing his hand to her, and continually endeavouring by such means to obtain her embraces. She alone saw and heard him: to everybody else he was invisible.

This good lady kept persevering in her disdain with admirable constancy until, at last, after some months of courting, the Incubus, angered at her insensibility, had recourse to a new kind of persecution. First, he took away from her a silver cross filled with sacred Relics, and a holy wax or papal Agnus Dei of the blessed Pontiff Pius V.,[29] which she always carried on her person; then, although it could not be found that the locks had been tampered with or opened, he purloined her rings and other gold and silver ornaments and jewelry from the casket wherein they were stored. Next, he began to strike her cruelly, and after each beating, livid bruises and discolorations were to be seen on her face, her arms and other parts of her body, which lasted a day or two, then suddenly disappeared, the reverse of natural bruises which heal slowly and by degrees. Sometimes, too, while she was nursing her little girl, he would snatch the child away from her breast and lay it upon the roof, on the edge of the gutter, or hide it, but without ever harming it. Sometimes he would upset all the furniture, or smash to pieces saucepans, plates, and other earthenware utensils which, in a twink, he restored incontinently to their former whole state. One night whilst she was lying by her husband's side, the Incubus, appearing in his customary shape, vehemently urged his desires, which she steadfastly resisted as usual. He thereupon withdrew in a rage, and shortly after came back with a large load of those flag stones which the Genoese, and the inhabitants of Liguria in general, use for roofing their houses. With those stones he built around the bed a wall so high that it reached the tester, and the couple were unable to leave their bed without using a ladder. This wall, however, was built up unmortared, without lime; and when pulled down, the flags were laid by in a corner where, during two days, they were seen of many whom came to look at them; they then disappeared.

On S. Stephen's day, the husband had asked some military friends to dinner, and, to do fitting honour to his guests, provided a substantial repast. Whilst they were, as customary, washing their hands before taking their places, suddenly the table, just ready laid, vanished clean away from the dining-room; all the dishes, saucepans, colanders, kettles, plates and crockery in the kitchen vanished likewise, as well as the jacks, jugs, bottles, beakers, and glasses. The guests, eight in number, stood, surprised and confounded, in strange amaze. Amongst them, as it chanced, was a Spanish Captain of infantry, who, addressing the company, said boldly: "Do not be alarmed, it is but a trick: the table is certainly still where it was, and I shall soon find it by feeling for it." With these words, he paced round the room holding his arms wide outstretched, and endeavouring to lay hold of the table; but when, after much groping and walking to and fro, it was apparent that his efforts were useless, since he continually grasped nought but thin air, he

was well laughed at by his friends; and it being already high
time and past for having dinner, each guest took up his cloak
and was about to return home. They had already reached the
street-door with their host, the husband, who, out of politeness,
was attending them, when they heard a great crash in the
dining-room. Astonished beyond measure, they paused awhile
wondering what the cause of such a noise might be, and lo!
the servant ran up hastily to announce that the kitchen was
stocked with new vessels filled with food, and that the table
was standing again in its former place. Having gone back to the
dining-room, they were dumbfounded to see the table indeed
was laid, with napery, napkins, salt-cellars, silver cruets, castors,
trenchers and trays that did not belong to the house, and
groaning with rich meats, pasties, pullets and puddings, which
certainly had not been cooked there. On a large sideboard, too,
were arrayed in perfect order crystal, silver, and gold cups,
with all manner of flagons, decanters and lusty bowls filled
with rare foreign wines, from the Isle of Crete, Campania, the
Canaries, and the Rhine. In the kitchen there was also an
abundant variety of viands, fish and game, in saucepans and
dishes that had never been seen there before. At first, some of
the guests much hesitated whether they should partake of that
food; however, encouraged by others, they sat down, and soon
ate heartily, for the dishes proved to be of exquisite flavour. Immediately afterwards, when dinner was done, as they were sitting before a good winter fire, everything vanished away, the
dishes, the very orts and crumbs, and in their stead reappeared
the table of the house, laid with a cloth, and thereupon the
victuals which had been previously cooked; but, for a wonder,
all the guests were fully satisfied, so that no one could think of
supper after such a magnificent dinner. A clear proof this that
the substituted viands were real and nowise fictitious.

This kind of persecution had been going on for some months,
when the lady betook herself to the Blessed Bernardine[30] of
Feltre, whose body is venerated in the Church of S. James, a
short distance from the walls of the city. She made a vow to

him that she would wear, during a whole twelve-month, a sad-coloured frock, girt about her waist with a cord, such as is worn by the Friars Minor, the Order of which Blessed Bernardine was a member. This she vowed, in the hope that, through his intercession, she might at last be rid of the persecution of the Incubus. And accordingly, on the 28 September, the vigil of the Dedication of the Archangel S. Michael, and the festival of the Blessed Bernardine, she donned the votive habit. The next morning, which was Michaelmas Day, the afflicted woman repaired to the church of S. Michael, her own parish, already mentioned. It was now about ten o'clock, a time when crowds of people were going to mass. She had no sooner set foot on the threshold of the church, than her clothes and ornaments fell to the ground, and disappeared in a gust of wind, leaving her mother naked. There happened, fortunately, to be among the crowd two cavaliers of mature age, who, seeing what had taken place, very decently hastened to divest themselves of their cloaks with which they concealed, as well as they could, the woman's nudity, and having put her into a close coach, accompanied her home. The clothes and trinkets carried off by the Incubus were not restored by him before six months had elapsed.

I might not impertinently relate many other most amazing tricks and naughty japeries which that Incubus played on her, were it not wearisome. Suffice it to say that, for a number of years, he persevered in his temptation of her, but that, finding at last he was losing his pains, he desisted from his vexatious and wanton importunities.

29. In the above case, as well as in others that may be occasionally heard or read of, the Incubus attempts no act against Religion; he merely assails chastity. Consequently, consent is not a sin through ungodliness, but merely through incontinence.

30. Now, it is undoubted by Theologians and philosophers that carnal intercourse between mankind and the Demon sometimes gives birth to human beings; and that is how Antichrist is to be born, according to some Doctors, for example,

Bellarmine,[31] Suarez,[32] and Thomas Malvenda.[33] They further observe that, from a natural cause, the children thus begotten by Incubi are tall, very hardy and bloodily bold, arrogant beyond words, and desperately wicked. Thus writes Malvenda; as for the cause, he gives it from Franciscus Valesius:[34] "What Incubi introduce into the womb, is not any ordinary human semen in normal quantity, but abundant, very thick, very warm, rich in spirits and free from serosity. This, moreover, is an easy thing for them, since they merely have to choose ardent, robust men, whose semen is naturally very copious, and with whom the Succubus has connexion, and then women of a like constitution, with whom the Incubus copulates, taking care that both shall enjoy a more than normal orgasm, for the more abundant is the semen the greater the venereal excitement." Those are the words of Valesius, confirmed by Malvenda[35] who shows, from the testimony of various classical Authors, that such conjunctions gave birth to: Romulus and Remus,[36] according to *Livy* and *Plutarch;* Servius-Tullius, the sixth king of Rome, according to *Dionysius of Halicarnassus* and *Pliny the Elder;* Plato the Philosopher, according to *Diogenes Laertius* and *Saint Jerome;* Alexander the Great, according to *Plutarch* and *Quintus Curtius;* Seleucus, king of Syria, according to *Justin* and *Appian;* Scipio Africanus the Elder, according to *Livy;* the emperor Cæsar Augustus, according to *Suetonius;* Aristomenes the Messenian, an illustrious Greek commander, according to *Strabo* and *Pausanias;* as also Merlin[37] or Melchin the Englishman, born from an Incubus and a nun, the daughter of Charlemagne; Hauller, vol. II.; and, lastly, as shown by the writings of *Cochlæus* quoted by *Malvenda,* that damnable Heresiarch yclept Martin Luther.[38]

31. However, with due deference to so many and such erudite Doctors, who are assuredly well agreed upon this circumstance, I can hardly see how their opinion will bear examination. For, as Benedict Pereira,[39] the learned Jesuit, truly observes in his *Commentary on Genesis,* ch. 6, the whole strength and efficiency of the human sperm are contained in the spirits

which evaporate and evanish as soon as it issues from the genital vessels where it is warmly stored; all medical men are
unanimous as to this. It is consequently not posible that the
Demon should preserve in the state essential for generation
the sperm he has received; for it were necessary that whatever
vessel he endeavoured to keep it in should be equally warm as
the human genital organs, the warmth of which is nowhere to
be met with but in those organs themselves. Now, in a vessel
where that warmth is not intrinsical but extraneous, the spirits
are necessarily altered, and no generation can take place.
There is too this other objection, that generation is a vital act
by which man, begetting from his own substance, carries the
sperm through natural organs to the spot which is appropriate
to generation. On the contrary, in this particular case, the introduction of sperm cannot be a vital act of the man who begets, since it is not carried into the womb by his agency; and,
for the same cause, it cannot be said that the man, whose
sperm it once was, has begotten the fœtus which proceeds
from it. Nor can the Incubus be deemed its father, since the
sperm does not issue from his own substance. Consequentially,
a child would be born without a father, which is absurd. Third
objection: when the father begets in the course of nature, there
is a concurrence of two casualties: the one, material, for he
provides the sperm which is the matter of generation; the
other, efficient, for he is the principal agent of generation, as
all Philosophers maintain. But, in this case, the man who
only provided the sperm would contribute but a mere material,
without any action tending to generation; he could not therefore be regarded as the father of the child begotten under such
conditions; and this is clean opposed to the notion that the
child begotten by an Incubus is not his son, but the son of the
man whose sperm the Incubus has taken.

32. Besides, there is not a shadow of probability in what
was written by Valesius and quoted from him by us (*uide
supra No.* 30); and I am indeed surprised that any thing so ex-
travagantly absurd should have fallen from the pen of such a

learned man. Medical men are well aware that the size of the fœtus depends, not indeed on the quantity of matter, but on the quantity of virtue, that is to say of spirits held by the sperm; therein lies the whole secret of generation, as is well observed by Michael Ettmüller,[40] *Institutiones Medicæ Physiologæ:* "Generation," says he, "entirely depends upon the genital spirit contained within an envelope of thicker matter; that spermatic matter does not remain in the uterus, and has no share in the formation of the fœtus; it is but the genital spirit of the male, combined with the genital spirit of the female, that permeates the pores, or, less frequently, the tubes of the uterus, which it fecundates by that means." What bearing therefore can the quantity of sperm have on the size of the fœtus? Besides, it is not always a fact that men thus begotten by Incubi are remarkable for the huge proportions of their body: Alexander the Great, for instance, who is said to have been thus born, as we have mentioned, was very short; and the poet said of him:

Magnus Alexander[41] corpore paruus erat.

Besides, although it is generally a fact that those who are thus begotten excel other men, yet such superiority is not always shown by their vices, but sometimes by their bravery and even their virtues; Scipio Africanus, for instance, Cæsar Augustus, and Plato the Philosopher, as is recorded of each of them respectively by Livy, Suetonius, and Diogenes Laertius, were men of the highest morality. Whence it may be inferred that, if other individuals begotten in the same way have been wholly evil, it was not owing to the fact that they were born of an Incubus, but rather that they, of their own free will, chose to be bad.

We also read in the Bible, *Genesis*, ch. vi., v. 4, that giants were born when the sons of God went in to the daughters of men: this is the actual text. Now, those giants were men *of great stature*, says *Baruch*, ch. iii., v. 26, and far superior to other men. Not only were they distinguished by their huge size, but also by their physical powers, their rapine and their tyranny. Through their misdeeds the Giants, according to Cornelius à Lapide,[42] in his *Commentary on Genesis*, were the primary and principal cause of the Flood. Some contend that by Sons of God are meant the sons of Seth, and by daughters of men the daughters of Cain, because the former practised piety, religion and every other virtue, whilst the descendants of Cain were quite the reverse; but, with all due deference to S. John Chrysostom, S. Cyril, S. Theodore of Studium, Abbot Rupert of Deutz, S. Hilary and others who are of that opinion, it must be conceded that it hardly agrees with the obvious meaning of the text. Scripture says, in fact, that of the conjunction of the Sons of God and the daughters of men were born men of huge bodily size: consequently, those giants were not previously in existence, and if their birth was the result of that conjunction, it cannot be ascribed to the intercourse of the sons of Seth with the daughters of Cain, who being themselves of ordinary stature, could but procreate children of ordinary stature. Therefore, if the intercourse in question gave birth to beings of huge stature, the reason is that it was not the common connexion between man and woman, but the operation of Incubi who, from their nature, may very well be styled Sons of God. Such is the opinion of the Platonist Philosophers and of Francesco Giorgio the Venetian; nor is it discrepant from that of Josephus the Historian, Philo Judæus, S. Justin Martyr, Clement of Alexandria, Tertullian, and Hugh of S. Victor, who look upon Incubi as corporeal Angels who have fallen into the sin of lewdness with women. Indeed, as shall be shown hereafter, though seemingly distinct, those two opinions are but one and the same.

33. If therefore these Incubi, as is so commonly held, have begotten Giants by means of sperm taken from man, it is impossible, as aforesaid, that of that sperm should have been born any but men of approximately the same size as he from whom it came; for it would be in vain for the Demon, when acting the part of a Succubus, to draw from man an unwonted quantity

of prolific liquor in order to procreate therefrom children of higher stature; quantity is irrelevant, since all depends, as we have said, upon the vitality of that liquor, not upon its quantity. We are bound therefore to infer that Giants are born of another sperm than man's, and that, consequently, the Incubus, for the purpose of generation, uses a semen which is not man's. But what, then, are we to say with regard to this?

34. Subject to correction by our Holy Mother Church, and as a mere expression of private opinion, I say that the Incubus, when having intercourse with women, begets the human fœtus from his own seed.

35. To many that proposition will seem almost heterodox and hardly rational; but I beg of my readers not to condemn it precipitately; for if, as Celsus[43] says, it is improper to deliver judgement without having thoroughly inquired into the law, no less unfair is the rejection of an opinion, before the arguments upon which it rests have been weighed and confuted. I have therefore to prove the above conclusion, and must necessarily lay down certain premises.

36. Firstly, I premise, as an article of belief, that there are purely spiritual creatures, not in any way partaking of corporeal matter, as was ruled by the Lateran Council, during the pontificate of Innocent III.[44] (S. Firmilian of Cæsarea, S. Cyril, and other authorities confirm this.) Such are the blessed Angels, and the Demons condemned to everlasting fire. Some Doctors, as, for example, Domingo Bañez,[45] Sisto of Siena,[46] Giovanni Pico della Mirandola,[47] Luis de Molina,[48] Bartolomé Carranza,[49] have, it is true, professed, subsequently even to this Council, that the spirituality of Angels and Demons is not an article of belief. Other Doctors, as S. Bonaventura,[50] the Venerable Duns Scotus, Cajetan, Francesco Giorgio, have maintained that they are corporeal, whence Bonaventura Baron (*Scotus Defensus et amplificatus*) has drawn the conclusion that it is neither heretical nor erroneous to ascribe to Angels and Demons a twofold substance, corporeal and spiritual. Yet, the Council having formally declared it to be an article of belief

that God *is the maker of all things visible and invisible, spiritual and corporeal, Who has raised from nothing every creature spiritual or corporeal, Angelic or terrestrial,* I contend it is an article of belief that there are certain merely spiritual creatures, and that such are Angels; not all of them, truly, but a certain number.

37. Perhaps this may seem strange, yet it must be admitted not to be unlikely. If, in fact, Theologians concur in establishing amongst Angels a specific, and therefore essential, diversity, so considerable that, according to S. Thomas, there are not two Angels of the same species, but that each of them is a species by himself, why should not certain Angels be most pure spirits, and consequently of a very superior nature, and others corporeal, and therefore of a less perfect nature, differing thus from each other in their corporeal or incorporeal substance? This doctrine has the advantage of solving the otherwise insoluble contradiction between two Œcumenical Councils, namely the Seventh General Synod and the above-mentioned Council of Lateran. For, during the fifth sitting of that Synod, the Second of Nicea, a book was introduced written by John of Thessalonica against a pagan Philosopher, wherein occur the following propositions: *"Respecting Angels, Archangels and their powers, to which I also adjoin our own Souls, the Catholic Church is indeed of opinion that they are intelligences, but not entirely bodiless and senseless, as you Gentiles aver; she on the contrary ascribes to them a subtile body, aerial or igneous, according to what is written: He makes His Angels spirits, and His Ministers a burning fire."* And later: *"Although not corporeal in the same way as ourselves, made of the four elements, yet it is impossible to say that Angels, Demons, and Souls are incorporeal; for they have been seen many a time, wearing their own body, by those whose eyes the Lord had opened."* And after that book had been read through before all the Fathers in Council assembled, Tharasius, the Patriarch of Constantinople, submitted it to the approval of the Council, with these words: *"The Father showeth that Angels should be*

pictured, since their form can be defined, and they have been seen in the shape of men." Without a dissentient, the Synod answered: *"Yea, my Lord."*

38. That this approbation by a Council of the doctrine set forth at length in the book of John establishes an article of belief with regard to the corporeity of Angels, there is not a shadow of doubt: so Theologians toil and moil in order to remove the contradiction apparent between that decision and the definition, above quoted, by the Council of Lateran. One of them, Suarez, says that if the Fathers did not disprove such an assertion of the corporeity of Angels, it is because that was not the question. Another, Bañez, contends that the Synod certainly approves the conclusion, namely, that Angels might be pictured, but not necessarily the motive given, *their corporeity.* A third, Molina, observes that the definitions issued in Council by the Synod were thus issued only at the *seventh sitting,* whence he argues that those of the previous sittings are not definitions of belief. Others, again, such as Cardinal Cienfuegos[51] and Mirandola, write that neither the Council of Nicea nor that of Lateran intended defining a question of belief, the Council of Nicea having spoken according to the opinion of the Platonists, which describes Angels as corporeal beings, and which was then prevailing, whilst that of Lateran followed Aristotle, who, in his xiith book of *Metaphysics,* lays down the existence of incorporeal intelligences, a doctrine which has since been adopted by most Doctors in preference to that of the Platonists.

39. But any one can discern the invalidity of such answers, and Bonaventura Baron (*Scot. Defens.,* vol. 9) has no difficulty in showing clearly how unsatisfactory they are. In consequence, that we may make the two Councils agree, we must say that the Council of Nicea meant one species of Angels, and that of Lateran another: the former, corporeal, the latter on the contrary absolutely incorporeal; and thus are reconciled two otherwise seemingly irreconcilable Councils.

40. Secondly, I premise that the word Angel applies, not in-

deed to the kind, but to the office: the Holy Fathers are agreed thereupon (S. Ambrose, *On the Epistle to the Hebrews;* S. Hilary, *On the Trinity,* Book V.; S. Austin, *City of God;* St. Gregory, *Homily* 34 *on Scripture;* S. Isidore, *Supreme Goodness*). An Angel, says S. Ambrose most admirably, is thus styled, not because he is a spirit, but on account of his office: Ἄγγελος in Greek, *Nuntius* in Latin, that is to say *Messenger;* it follows that whoever is entrusted by God with a mission, be he spirit or man, may be called an Angel, and is indeed thus called in the Holy Scriptures, where the following words are applied to Priests, Preachers, and Doctors, who, as Messengers of God, explain to men the divine will (Malachias, ch. ii., v. 7). *"The lips of the priest shall keep knowledge, and they shall seek the law at his mouth, because he is the Angel of the Lord of Hosts."* The same prophet, ch. iii., v. 1, bestows the name of Angel on S. John the Baptist, when saying: *"Behold, I send my Angel and he shall prepare the way before my face."* That this prophecy literally applies to S. John the Baptist is testified by our Lord Jesus Christ, in the Gospel according to S. Matthew, ch. x., v. 10. Yea, more: God himself is called an Angel, because he has been sent by His Father to herald the law of grace. In proof of this we have the prophecy of Isaias, ch. ix., v. 6, according to the Septuagint: *"He shall be called an Angel of Wonderful Counsel."* And more plainly still in Malachias, ch. iii., v. 1: *"The Lord whom you seek and the Angel of the testament, whom you desire, shall come to his temple,"* a prophecy which literally applies to our Lord Jesus Christ. There is consequently nothing absurd in the contention that some Angels are corporeal, since men, who assuredly have a body, are called Angels.

41. Thirdly, I premise that neither the existence nor the nature of the natural things in this world have been sufficiently investigated to permit a fact to be denied, merely because it has never been previously spoken of or written about. In the course of time have not new lands been discovered which the Ancients knew not of? New animals, herbs, plants, fruits and

seeds, never seen elsewhere. And if that mysterious Austral land came at last to be explored, as has to this very day been vainly attempted by so many travellers, what unsuspected discoveries would be the result! Through the invention of the microscope and other instruments used by modern experimental Philosophy, combined with the more exact methods of investigation of Anatomists, have there not been, and are there not, every day, brought to light the existence, qualities and characteristics of a number of natural things unknown to ancient Philosophers, such as fulminating gold, phosphorus, and a hundred other chemical compounds, the circulation of the blood, the lacteal vessels, the lymph-ducts and other recent anatomical discoveries? To deride a doctrine because it does not happen to be mentioned in any ancient author would therefore be absurd, especially bearing in mind this axiom of Logic: *locus ab auctoritate negatiua non tenet.*

42. Fourthly, I premise that Holy Scripture and ecclesiastical tradition do not teach us any thing beyond what is requisite for the salvation of the soul, namely Faith, Hope, and Charity. Consequently, although a thing is not explicitly stated either by Scripture or tradition it must not be inferred that that thing has no existence. For instance, Faith teaches us that God, by His Word, made things visible, and invisible, and also that, through the merits of our Lord Jesus Christ, grace and glory are conferred on every rational creature. Now, that there be another World than the one we live in and that it be peopled by men not born of Adam but made by God, in some other way, as is implied by those who believe the moon to be inhabited; or further, that in the very World where we dwell, there be other rational creatures besides man and the Angelic Spirits, creatures generally invisible to us and whose being is disclosed but accidentally, through the instrumentality of their own power; all that has nothing to do with Faith, and the knowledge or ignorance thereof is no more necessary to the salvation of man than knowing the number or nature of all physical things.

43. Fifthly, I premise that neither Philosophy nor Theology is repugnant to the possible existence of rational creatures having spirit and body, and distinct from man. Such repugnance could be attributed only to God, and that is inadmissible, since He is almighty, or to the thing to be made, and that likewise cannot be justly attributed; for, as there are purely spiritual creatures, such as Angels; or merely material, such as the World; or lastly semi-spiritual and semi-corporeal, of an earthly and gross corporeity, such a man; so there may well be in existence a creature endowed with a rational spirit and a corporeity less gross, more subtile than man's. There is no doubt, moreover, but that after the Resurrection, the souls of the blessed will be united with a glorified and subtile body; from which it can be inferred that God may well have made a rational and corporeal creature whose body naturally enjoys the subtilty which will be conferred by grace on the glorified body.

44. But, the possible existence of such creatures will be still better set forth by answering the arguments which can be adduced against our conclusion, and replying to the questions it may raise.

45. First question: Should such creatures be styled rational animals? And if so, in what do they differ from man, with whom they would have that definition in common?

46. I reply: Yes, they would be rational animals, provided with senses and organs even as man; they would, however, differ from man not only in their more subtile nature, but also in the matter of their body. In fact, as is shown by Scripture (*Genesis*, II. 7), man has been made from the grossest of all elements, namely, slime, a gross mixture of water and earth: but those creatures would be made from the most subtile part of all elements, or of one or other of them; thus, some would proceed from earth, others from water, or air, or fire; and, in order that they should not be defined in the same terms as man, to the definition of the latter should be added the mention of the gross materiality of his body, wherein he would differ from the said animals.

47. Second question: At what period would those animals have been originated, and whence? From earth, like the beasts, or from water, like quadrupeds, and birds? Or, on the contrary, would they have been made, like man, by our Lord God?

48. I reply: It is an article of belief, expressly laid down by the Council of Lateran, that whatever is, in fact and at present, was made at the creation of the world. By His almighty power, God, at the beginning of time, raised together out of nothing both orders of creatures, spiritual and corporeal. Now, those animals also would be included in the totality of creatures. As to their formation, it might be said that God Himself, through the medium of Angels, made their body as He did man's body, to which an immortal spirit was to be united. That body being of a nobler nature than that of other animals, it was very meet it should be united to an incorporeal and most noble spirit.

49. Third question: Would those animals descend from one individual, as all men descend from Adam, or, on the contrary, would many have been made at the same time, as was the case with the other living things created from earth and water, wherein were males and females for the preservation of the kind by generation? Would there be amongst them a distinction between the sexes? Would they be subject to birth and death, to sense, passions, want of food, power of growth? If so, what are their provisions? Would they lead a social life, as men do? By what laws would they be ruled? Would they build up cities for their dwellings, cultivate the arts and sciences, possess property, and wage war between themselves, as men are wont to do?

50. I reply: It may be that all descend from one individual, as men descend from Adam; it may also be that a number of males and females were made in the beginning, who preserved their kind by generation. We will further admit that they are born and die; that they are divided into males and females, and are moved by the senses and passions, as men are; that they feed and grow according to the size of their body; their food, however, instead of being gross like that required by

the human body, must be delicate and ætherial, emanating through spiritual essences from whatever in the physical world abounds with highly volatile corpuscles, such as the flavour of meats, especially of roast, the bouquet of wine, the fragrancy of fruit, flowers, scents, which emit an abundance of those effluvia until all their subtile and volatile parts have completely evaporated. To their being able to lead a social life, with distinctions of rank and precedence; to their cultivating the arts and sciences, exercising functions, maintaining armies, building up cities, as it were; doing in short whatever is requisite for their preservation, I have in the main no objections to urge.

51. Fourth question: What would their figure be, human or otherwise? Would the ordering of the divers parts of their body be essential, as with other animals, or merely accidental, as with fluid substances, such as oil, water, clouds, smoke, etc.? Would those organic parts consist of various substances, as is the case with the organs of the human body, wherein are to be found very gross parts, such as the bones, others less gross, such as the cartilage, and others slender, such as the membranes?

52. I reply: As regards their figure, we neither can nor should make over definite assertions, since it escapes our senses, being too delicate for our sight or our touch. That we must leave to themselves, and to such as have the privilege of intuitive acquaintance with immaterial substances. But, so far as probability goes, I say that their figure tallies with the human body, save there be some distinctive peculiarity, should the very tenuity of their body not be deemed sufficient. I am led to that by this consideration, namely; Of all the works of God the human frame is the most perfect, and that whilst all other animals stoop to the ground, because their soul is mortal, God, as Ovid the poet, says, in his *Metamorphoses* (I. 85-6):

Os homini sublime dedit, cœlumque tueri
Iussit, et erectos ad sidera tollere uultus;

Gave man an erect figure, bidding him behold the heavens
And raise his face on high towards the stars,

man's soul having been made immortal for his heavenly home. Considering that the animals we are speaking of would be gifted with a spirit immaterial, rational, and immortal, capable therefore of salvation and damnation, it is proper to admit that the body to which that spirit is united may be like unto the most noble animal frame, that is to say, to the human frame. Whence it follows that in the divers parts of that body there must be an essential order; that the foot, for instance, cannot be an appendage to the head, nor the hand to the belly, but that each organ is in its right place, according to the functions it has to perform. As to the constituent parts of those organs, it is, in my opinion, obvious that there must be some more or less strong, others more or less slender, in order to meet the requirements of the working of the organism. Nor can this be fairly objected to on the ground of the slenderness of the bodies themselves; for the strength or thickness of the organic parts alluded to would not be absolute, but merely in comparison with the more slender ones. That, moreover, may be observed in all natural fluids, such as wine, oil, milk, etc.; however homogeneous and similar to each other their component parts may look, yet they are not so: for some are clayey, others aqueous; there are fixed salts, volatile salts, brimstone, all of which are demonstrated by a chemical analysis. So it would be in our case: for, supposing the bodies of those animals to be as subtile and slender as the natural fluids, air, water, etc., there would nevertheless be discrepancies in the quality of their constituent parts, some of which would be strong when compared with others more slender, although the whole body which they compose might be called slender.

53. It may be objected that this is repugnant to what was said above concerning the essential ordering of the parts among themselves; that it is seen that, in fluid and subtile bodies, one part is not essentially but only accidentally connected with

another; that a part of wine, for instance, just now contiguous with some other, soon comes in contact with a third, if the vessel be turned upside down or the wine shaken, and that all the parts together exchange positions at the same time, though it be still the same wine. Whence it should be inferred that the bodies of those animals would have no permanent figure, and would consequently not be purely organic.

54. I answer that I deny the assumption. In fact, if in fluid bodies the essential ordering of the parts is not apparent, it subsists none the less and causes a compound to preserve its own state. Wine, for instance, when pressed from the grape, seems a thoroughly homogeneous liquor, and yet is not so; for there are gross parts which, by the passage of time, subside in the casks; there are also slender parts which evaporate; fixed parts, such as tartar; volatile parts, such as brimstone and alcohol; others again, half volatile and half fixed, such as phlegm. Those several parts do not respectively maintain an essential order; for no sooner has the must been pressed from the grape, and been styled brimstone or volatile spirits, than it continues so closely involved with the particles of tartar, which is fixed, as not to be in any way able to escape.

55. That is the reason why must recently pressed from the grape is of no use for the distillation of the sulphurous spirits, commonly called *Brandy;* but, after forty days' fermentation, the particles of the wine change places: the spirits, no longer bound up with the tartaric particles which they kept in suspension through their own volatility, whilst they were, in return, kept down by them and prevented from escaping, sever from those particles, and continue confused with the phlegmatic parts from which they become easily released by the operation of fire, and evaporate: thus, by means of distillation, Brandy is made, which is nothing but the brimstone of wine volatilized by heat with the most slender part of phlegm. At the end of forty days another fermentation begins, which extends more or less, according as the maturity of the wine is more or less perfect, and the termination of which is dependent

on the greater or lesser abundance of sulphurous spirits. If abounding with brimstone, the wine sours and turns to vinegar; if, on the contrary, it holds but little brimstone, it ropes, and becomes what the Italians call *vino molle* or *vino guasto*. If the wine is at once ripe, as happens in other cases, it turns acid or ropes in less time, as is shown by every-day experience. Now, in this said fermentation the essential order of the parts of wine is altered, but not so its quantity nor its matter, which neither changes nor decreases: a bottle that had been filled with wine is, after a certain time, found to be filled with vinegar, without any alteration in its quantity of matter; the essential order of its parts has alone been modified: the brimstone, which, as we have said, was united to the phlegm and separated from the tartar, becomes again involved and fixed with the tartar; so that, on distilling the vinegar, there issues from it first an insipid phlegm, and then those spirits of vinegar, which are the brimstone of wine intermixed with particles of tartar that is less fixed. Now, the essential shifting of the aforesaid parts alters the substance of the juice of the grapes, as is clearly shown by the varied and contrary effects of must, wine, vinegar, and ropy or stummed wine; for which cause the two first are fit, but the two last unfit materials for consecration. We have borrowed the above exposition of the economy of wine from the able work of Nicolas Lémery,[52] chemist to the King of France, *Cours de Chimie*, p. 2, c. 9.

56. If now we apply that natural doctrine to our subject, I say that, being given the corporeity of the animals in question, subtile and slender like the substance of liquids; being given also their organization and figure, which demand an essential order of the various parts, an adverse hypothesis could raise no argument contrary to their existence; for, just as the jumbling together of the parts of wine and the diversity of their accidental dispositions do not alter their essential order, even so it would be with the slender frame of our animals.

57. Fifth question: Would those animals be subject to disease and other infirmities which afflict mankind, such as igno-

rance, fear, idleness, paralysis, etc.? Would they be wearied through labour, and require, for recruiting their strength, sleep, food, drink? And what food, what drink? Would they be fated to die, and might they be killed casually, or by the instrumentality of other animals?

58. I reply: Their bodies, though subtile, being material, they would of course be liable to decay: they might therefore suffer from adverse agencies, and consequently be diseased; that is, their organs might not perform, or painfully and imperfectly perform the office assigned to them, for therein consist all diseases of whatsoever kind with certain animals, as has been distinctly explained by the famous Michael Ettmüller, *Physiology*, ch. v. thesis 1. In sooth, their body being less gross than the human frame, comprising fewer elements mixed together, and being therefore less composite, they would not so easily suffer from adverse influences, and would therefore be less liable to disease than man; their life would also exceed his; for, the more perfect an animal, as a species, the longer its days; thus it is with mankind, whose existence extends beyond that of other animals. For I do not believe in the hundred years of crows, stags, ravens[53] and the like, of which Pliny tells his customary stories; and although his legends have been re-echoed by others without previous inquiry, it is no less clear that before writing thus, not one has faithfully noted either the birth or the death of those animals: they have been content to repeat these idle fables, as has been the case with the Phœnix, whose longevity is rejected as a myth by Tacitus,[54] *Annals*, Book vi. It were therefore to be inferred that the animals we are speaking of would live longer still than man; for, as shall be explained below they would be more noble than he; consequently also, they would be subject to the other bodily affections, and require rest and food, as mentioned (No. 50). Now, as rational beings and amenable to training, they might also continue ignorant, if their minds did not receive the culture and discipline of study and instruction, and some amongst them would be more or less versed in science, more or less

clever, according as their intelligence had been more or less educated. However, generally speaking, and considering the whole of the species, they would be more learned than men, not from the subtilty of their body, but probably because of the greater activity of their minds or the longer space of their life, which would enable them to learn more things than men: such are indeed the reasons assigned by S. Augustine[55] (*De diuinatione dæmonum*, ch. 3, and *De Spiritu et anima*, ch. 37), for the prescience of the future in Demons. They might indeed suffer from natural agencies; but they could hardly be killed, on account of the speed with which they could escape from danger; it is therefore most unlikely that they could, without the greatest difficulty, be put to death or mutilated by beast or by man, with natural or artificial weapons, so quick would they be to avoid the impending blow. Yet, they might be killed or mutilated in their sleep, or in a moment of inadvertence, by means of a solid body, such as a sword brandished by a man, or the fall of a heavy stone; for, although subtile, their body would be divisible, just like air which, though vaporous, is yet divided by a sword, a club, or any other solid body. Their spirit, however, would be indivisible, and like the human soul, entire in the whole and in each and every part of the body. Consequently, the division of their body by another body, as aforesaid, might occasion mutilation and even death, for the spirit, itself indivisible, could not animate both parts of a divided body. True, just as the parts of air, separated by the agency of a body, unite again as soon as that body is withdrawn, and constitute the same air as before, even so the parts of the body divided, as above mentioned, might unite and be revived by the same spirit. But in this case it must follow that those animals could not be slain by natural or artificial agencies: and it were more reasonable to maintain our first position; for, if they share matter with other creatures, it is natural that they should be liable to suffer through those creatures, according to the common rule, and even unto death.

59. Sixth question: Could their bodies penetrate other bod-

ies, such as walls, wood, metals, glass, etc.? Could many of them abide together on the same material spot, and to what space would their body extend or be restrained?

60. I answer: In all bodies, however compact, there are pores, as is apparent in metals where, more than in other bodies, it would seem there should be none; through a perfect and powerful microscope the pores of metals are discerned, with their different shapes. Now, those animals might, through the pores, creep into, and thus penetrate any other bodies, although such pores were impervious to other liquors or material spirits, wine, for example, salts of ammonia, or the like, because their bodies would be much more subtle than those liquors. However, notwithstanding many Angels may abide together on the same material spot, and even confine themselves in a lesser and lesser space, though not infinitely, as is shown by *Duns Scotus* (2 dist. quest. 6. Ad proposi. et quæst. 8), yet it were rash to ascribe the same power to those animals; for, their bodies are determined in substance and impervious to each other; and if two glorious bodies cannot abide together on the same spot, though a glorious and a non-glorious one may do so, as Godfrey of Fontaines[56] maintains (*Quolibet*, q. 5), and Duns Scotus agrees with him (2 distinct. 2, q. 8), much less would it be possible for the bodies of those animals, which are indeed subtile, yet do not attain to the subtility of the glorious body. As regards their power of extension or compression, we may instance the case of air, which, rarefied and condensed, occupies more or less room, and may even, by artificial means, be compressed into a narrower space than would be naturally due to its volume; as is seen with those large balls which, for amusement, one inflates by means of a blow-pipe or tube: air, being forced into them and compressed, is held in larger quantity than is warranted by the capacity of the ball. Similarly the bodies of the animals we are speaking of might, by their natural virtue, extend to a larger space, not exceeding however their own substance; they might also contract, but not beyond the determined space consistent with that same substance. And, con-

sidering that of their number, as with men, some would be tall and some short, it were proper that the tall should be able to extend more than the short, and the short to contract more than the tall.

61. Seventh question: Would those animals be born in original sin, and have been redeemed by our Lord Jesus Christ? Would grace have been conferred upon them and through what sacraments? Under what law would they live, and would they be capable of salvation and damnation?

62. I answer: It is an article of the Catholic faith that Christ has merited grace and glory for all rational creatures without exception. It is also an article of faith that glory is not conferred on a rational creature until such creature has been previously endowed with grace, which is the disposition to glory. According to a like article, glory is conferred but by merits. Now, those merits are grounded on the perfect observance of the commands of God, and this is accomplished through grace. The above questions are thus solved. Whether those creatures did or did not sin originally is uncertain. It is clear, however, that if their first Parent had sinned as Adam sinned, his descendants would be born in original sin, as men are born. And, as God never leaves a rational creature without a remedy, so long as it treads the way, if those creatures were infected with original or with actual sin, God would have provided them with a remedy; but whether such be the case, and of what kind is the remedy, is a secret between God and them. Assuredly, if they had Sacraments either identical with or different from those in use in the Church militant on earth, for the institution and efficacy of these they would be indebted to the merits of Jesus Christ, the Redeemer, who has made perfect Atonement and fullest satisfaction for all rational creatures. It would likewise be highly proper, nay necessary, that they should live under some law given them by God, through the observance of which they might merit salvation; but what would be that law, whether merely natural or written, Mosaic or of the Gospel, or different from all these and specially instituted by God, that

we are ignorant of, and know nothing. Yet, whatever it might be, there would follow no objection exclusive of the possible existence of such creatures.

63. The only argument, and that rather a lame one, which long meditation has suggested to me against the possibility of such creatures, is that, if they really existed in the World, we should find them mentioned somewhere by Philosophers, Holy Scripture, Ecclesiastical Tradition, or the Fathers: and since such is not the case, their utter impossibility should be inferred.

64. But that argument which, in fact, calls in question their existence rather than their possibility, is easily disposed of by our premises, Numbers 41 and 42; for no argument can stand by force of a negative authority. Besides, it is incorrect to assert that neither the Philosophers, nor the Scriptures, nor the Fathers have handed down any notion of them. Plato, as is reported by Apuleius (*The God of Socrates*) and Plutarch (*Isis and Osiris*), to whom Bonaventura Baron refers, declared that Demons were beings of the animal kind, passive souls, rational intelligences, aerial bodies, immortal; and he gave them the name of *Demons*, which of itself is nowise offensive, since it means *replete with wisdom;* so that, when authors allude to the Devil (or Evil Angel), they do not merely call him Demon, but *Cacodemon,* and say likewise *Eudemon,* when speaking of a good Angel. Those creatures are also mentioned in Scripture and by the Fathers, as we will show later.

65. Now that we have proved that those creatures are possible, let us go a step further, and show that they exist. Taking for granted the truth of the recitals concerning the intercourse of Incubi and Succubi with men and beasts, recitals so numerous that it would be sheer impudence to deny the fact, as is said by S. Augustine, whose testimony is given above (No. 10) (*City of God,* xv. 23), I argue: Where the peculiar passion of the sense is found, there also, of necessity, is the sense itself; for, according to the principles of philosophy, the peculiar passion flows from nature, that is to say that, where the acts and operations of the sense are found, there also is the sense, the

operations and acts being but its external form. Now, those Incubi and Succubi present acts, operations, peculiar passions, which spring from the senses; they are therefore endowed with senses. But senses cannot exist without concomitant component organs, without a combination of soul and body. Incubi and Succubi have therefore body and soul, and, consequentially, are animals; but their acts and operations are also those of a rational soul; their soul is therefore rational; and thus, from first to last, they are rational animals.

66. Our minor is easy of demonstration in each of its parts. And indeed, the appetitive desire of coition is a sensual desire; the grief, sadness, wrath, rage, occasioned by the denial of coition, are sensual passions, as is seen with all animals; generation through coition is evidently a sensual operation. Now, all that happens with Incubi, as has been shown above: they incite women, sometimes even men; if denied, they sadden and storm, like lovers: *amantes, amentes;* they practise perfect coition, and sometimes beget. It must therefore be inferred that they have senses, and consequently a body; consequently also, that they are perfect animals. More than that: in spite of closed doors and windows they enter wherever they please; their body is therefore slender: they foreknow and foretell the future, compose and divide, all which operations are proper to a rational soul; they therefore possess a rational soul and are, in fine, rational animals.

Doctors generally reply that it is the Evil Spirit that perpetrates those impure acts, simulates passions, love, grief at the denial of coition, in order to entice souls to sin and to undo them; and that, if he copulates and begets, it is with assumed sperm and a body not truly his own, as aforesaid (No. 24).

67. But then, there are Incubi that have connexion with horses, mares and other beasts, and, as shown by everyday experience, ill-treat them if they are averse to coition; yet, in those cases, it can no longer be adduced that the Demon simulates the appetite for coition in order to bring about the ruin of souls, since beasts are not capable of everlasting damnation.

Besides, love and wrath with them are productive of quite opposite effects. For, if the loved woman or beast humours
them, those Incubi behave very well; on the contrary, they use
them most savagely when irritated and enraged by a denial
of coition: this is amply proved by daily experience: those Incubi therefore have truly sexual passions and desires. Besides,
the Evil Spirits, the incorporeal Demons who copulate with
Sorceresses and Witches, constrain them to Demon worship,
to the abjuration of the Catholic Faith, to the commission of
enchantments, magic, and foul crimes, as preliminary conditions to the infamous intercourse, as has been above stated
(No. 11); now, Incubi endeavour nothing of the kind: they
are therefore not Evil spirits. Lastly, as Guazzo, who quotes
from Peltanus[57] and Thyræus,[58] tells us, at the mere utterance
of the Holy Names of Jesus or Mary, at the sign of the Cross,
the approach of Holy Relics or consecrated objects, at exorcisms, adjurations or priestly injunctions, the Evil Demon either shudders and takes to flight, or is agitated and howls, as is
daily seen with energumens and is shown by numerous nar-
ratives of Guazzo concerning the midnight sabbats of Witches,
where, at a sign of the Cross or the name of Jesus said by one
of the assistants, Devils and Witches all vanish together. Incubi, on the contrary, stand all those ordeals without taking
to flight or showing the least fear; sometimes even they laugh
at exorcisms, assault the Exorcists themselves, and rend the
sacred vestments. Now, if the evil Demons, subdued by our
Lord Jesus Christ, are stricken with fear by His Name, the
Cross and the holy things; if, on the other hand, the good
Angels rejoice at those same things, without however inciting
men to sin or offend God, whilst the Incubi, without having
any dread of the holy things, provoke to sin, it is clear that
they are neither evil Demons nor good Angels; but it is clear
also that they are not men, though endowed with reason. What
then should they be? Supposing them to have reached the goal,
and to be pure spirits, they would be damned or blessed, for
orthodox Theology does not admit of pure spirits on the way to

salvation. If damned, they would revere the Name and the Cross of Christ; if blessed, they would not incite men to sin; they would therefore be different from pure spirits, and thus, have a body and be on the way to salvation.

68. Besides, a material agent cannot act but on an equally passive material. It is indeed a trite philosophical axiom, that agent and patient must have a common subject: pure matter cannot act on any purely spiritual thing. Now, there are natural agents which act on those Incubi; they are therefore material or corporeal. Our minor is proved by the testimony of Dioscorides, Book II. ch. 168, and I. ch. 100; Pliny, xv. 4; Aristotle,[59] Problems, XXXIV.; and Apuleius, *De Uirtute Herbarum*, quoted by Guazzo, *Compendium Maleficarum*, Book III., ch. 13, fol. 316; it is confirmed by our knowledge of numerous herbs, stones and animal substances which have the virtue of driving away Demons, such as rue, St. John's wort, verbena, germander,[60] Palma Christi,[61] centaury, diamonds, coral, jet, jasper, the skin of the head of a wolf or an ass, women's menstrue, and a hundred other things: wherefore Guazzo tells us: *For such as are assaulted by the Demon it is lawful to employ stones or herbs, but without recourse to incantations.* It follows that, by their own native virtue, stones or herbs can bridle the Demon: else the above-mentioned Canon would not permit their use, but would on the contrary forbid it as superstitious. We have a striking instance thereof in Holy Scripture, where the Angel Raphael says to Tobias (vi. 8), speaking of the fish which he had drawn from the Tigris: *"If thou put a little piece of its heart upon coals, the smoke thereof driveth away all kinds of devils."* Experience demonstrated the truth of those words; for, no sooner was the liver of the fish set on the fire, than the Incubus who was in love with Sara was put to flight.

69. To this Theologians usually retort that such natural agents merely initiate the ejection of the Demon, and that the completive effect is due to the supernatural force of God or of the Angel; so that the supernatural force is the primary, direct,

and principal cause, the natural force being but secondary, indirect, and subordinate. Thus, in order to explain how the liver of the fish burnt by Tobias drove away the Demon, Valesius asserts that the smoke thereof had been endowed by God with the supernatural power of expelling the Incubus, in the same manner as the material fire of Hell has the virtue of tormenting Demons and the souls of the damned. Others, such as Nicolas of Lyra, Cornelius à Lapide, and Benedict Pereira, believe that the smoke of the heart of the fish initiated the ejection of the Demon by its own native virtue, but completed it by angelical and heavenly virtue: by native virtue, insomuch that it opposed a contrary action to that of the Demon; for the Evil Spirit applies native causes and humours, the native qualities of which are combated by the contrary qualities of natural things known to be capable of driving away Demons. This opinion is held by all those who treat of the art of exorcism.

70. But that explanation, however plausible the facts upon which it rests, can at most be received as regards the Evil Spirits which possess bodies or, through sheer malice, infect them with diseases and other infirmities; it does not at all meet the case of Incubi. For these neither possess bodies nor infect them with diseases; they, at most, annoy them by blows and ill-treatment. If they cause the mares to grow lean because of their not yielding to coition, it is merely by taking away their provender, in consequence of which they fall off and finally die. To that purpose the Incubus need not use a natural agent, as the Evil Spirit does when imparting a disease: it is enough that he should exert his own native organic force. Likewise, when the Evil Spirit possesses bodies and infects them with diseases, it is most frequently through signs agreed upon with himself, and arranged by a witch or a wizard, which signs are usually natural objects, indued with their own noxious virtue, and, of course, opposed by other equally natural objects endowed with a contrary virtue. But not so the Incubus: it is of his own accord, and without the co-operation of either witch or wizard, that he pursues his molestation. Besides, the natural

things which put the Incubi to flight exert their virtue and bring about a result without the intervention of any exorcism or blessing; it cannot therefore be said that the ejection of the Incubus is initiated by natural, and completed by divine virtue, since there is in this case no particular invocation of the divine Name, but the mere effect of a natural object, in which God co-operates only as the universal agent, the author of nature, the first of efficient causes.

71. To illustrate this important point, I will here relate two stories, the first of which I have from a good confessor of Nuns, a man of integrity and fair repute, and most worthy of credit; the second I was eye-witness to myself.

In a certain convent of holy Nuns there resided, as a boarder, a young maiden of noble family, who was tempted by an Incubus that appeared to her both by day and by night, and with the most earnest entreaties, the prayers of a passionate lover crazed for love, incessantly besought her to lie with him; but she, supported by the grace of God and the frequent use of the sacraments, stoutly resisted the temptation. Yet, notwithstanding all her devotions, fasts and vows, maugre the exorcisms, the blessings, the injunctions showered by exorcists on the Incubus that he should desist from molesting her; in spite of the vast number of Relics and other holy objects collected in the maiden's room, of the lighted candles kept burning there all night, the Incubus none the less persisted in appearing to her constantly, in the shape of an exceptionally handsome young man. At last, among other learned men, whose advice had been taken on the subject, was a very profound Theologian who, observing that the maiden was of a thoroughly phlegmatic temperament, surmised that that Incubus was an aqueous Demon (there are in fact, as is testified by Guazzo (*Compendium Maleficarum*, I. 19), igneous, aerial, phlegmatic, earthly, and subterranean demons who avoid the light of day), and so he prescribed a continual suffumigation in the room. A new vessel, made of earthenware and glass, was accordingly introduced, and filled with sweet calamus,[62] cubeb seed,[63] roots of both aristolochies,[64] great and small cardamom,[65] ginger, long-pepper,[66] caryophylleæ,[67] cinnamon, cloves, mace, nutmegs, calamite storax,[68] benzoin, aloes-wood and roots, one ounce of fragrant sandal, and three quarts of half brandy and water; the vessel was then set on hot ashes in order to force forth and upwards the fumigating vapour, and the cell was kept closed. As soon as the suffumigation was done, the Incubus came, but never dared enter the cell; only, if the maiden left it for a walk in the garden or the cloister, he appeared to her, though invisible to others, and throwing his arms round her neck, stole or rather snatched kisses from her, to her intense disgust. At last, after a new consultation, the Theologian prescribed that she should carry about her person pills and pomanders made of the most exquisite perfumes, such as musk, amber, civet, Peruvian balsam, and other essences. Thus furnished, she went for a walk in the garden, where the Incubus suddenly appeared to her with a threatening face, and in a black rage. He did not approach her, however, but, after biting his finger as if meditating revenge, suddenly disappeared and was never more seen by her.

72. Here is the other story. In the great Carthusian monastery[69] of Pavia there lived a Deacon, Augustine by name, who was subjected by a certain Demon to excessive, unheard-of, and scarcely credible vexations. Many exorcists made repeated endeavours to secure his riddance, yet all spiritual remedies had proved unavailing. I was consulted by the Vicar of the convent, who had the care of the unfortunate cleric. Seeing the inefficacy of all customary exorcisms, and remembering the above-related instance, I advised a suffumigation similar to the one that has been detailed, and prescribed that the young Deacon should carry about his person fragrant pills and comfits of the same kind; moreover, as he was in the habit of using snuff, and was very fond of brandy, I advised snuff and brandy perfumed with musk. The Demon appeared to him by day and by night, under various shapes, as a skeleton, a pig, an ass, an Angel, a bird; with the figure of one or other of the monks, once

even with that of his own Superior the Prior, exhorting him to keep his conscience clean, to trust in God, to confess frequently; he persuaded him to let him hear his sacramental confession, recited with him the psalms *Exsurgat Deus*[70] and *Qui habitat,* and the Gospel according to S. John: and when they came to the words *Uerbum caro factum est,* he genuflected devoutly, then donning a stole which was in the cell, and taking the aspergillum, he blessed with holy water the cell and the bed, and, as if he had really been the Prior, enjoined on the Demon not to venture in future to molest his subordinate; he next incontinently disappeared, thus betraying what he was, for otherwise the young Deacon would have taken him for his Prior. Now, notwithstanding the suffumigations and perfumes I had prescribed, the Demon did not desist from his wonted apparitions; more than that, assuming the features of his victim, he went to the Vicar's room, and asked for some snuff and brandy perfumed with musk, of which, he said, he was extremely fond. Having received both, he vanished in the twinkling of an eye, thus showing the Vicar that he had been mocked by the Demon; and this was amply confirmed by the Deacon, who affirmed upon his oath that he had not gone that day to the Vicar's cell. When these circumstances were told to me, I inferred that, far from being aqueous like the Incubus who was in love with the maiden above spoken of, this Demon was igneous, or, at the very least, aerial, since he delighted in hot substances such as warm vapours, perfumes, snuff and brandy. My surmises were greatly confirmed by the temperament of the young Deacon, which was choleric and sanguine, choler, however, somewhat predominating; for these Demons never approach any save those whose temperament tallies with their own. And this is another confirmation of my views regarding their corporeity. I therefore advised the Vicar to let the junior monk take herbs that are cold by nature, such as water-lily, agrimony,[71] spurge,[72] mandrake, house-leek, plantain, henbane, and others of a similar family, knit two little bundles of them and hang them up, one at his window, the other at the door of his cell, taking care to strow some also on the floor and on the bed. Marvellous to say! the Demon appeared again, but remained outside the room, which he would not enter; and, on the Deacon inquiring of him his motives for such unwonted reserve, he burst out into invectives against me for giving such advice, disappeared, and never returned thither again.

73. The two stories I have related make it clear that, by their native virtue alone, perfumes and herbs drove away Demons without the intervention of any supernatural force; Incubi are therefore subject to material conditions, and it must be inferred that they participate of the matter of the natural objects which have the power of putting them to flight, and consequently they have a body; which is what was required to be demonstrated.

74. But, the better to establish our conclusion, it behoves us to correct the mistake into which have fallen the Doctors quoted above, such as Valesius and Cornelius à Lapide, when they say that Sara was freed from the Incubus by the power of the Angel Raphael, and not by that of the fish callionymus[73] caught by Tobias on the banks of the Tigris. Indeed, saying the respect due to such great doctors, their construction manifestly clashes with the clear meaning of the Text, from which it is never justifiable to deviate, so long as it does not lead to absurd consequences. Here are the words spoken by the Angel to Tobias: *"If thou put a little piece of its heart on coals, the smoke thereof driveth away all kinds of devils, either from man or from woman, so that they come no more to them, and the gall is good for anointing the eyes in which there is a white speck, and they shall be cured"* (*Tobias*, ch. vi. vv. 8 and 9). We must notice that the Angel's assertion respecting the virtue of the heart, or liver, and gall of that fish is absolute, universal; for, he does not say: *"If thou puttest on coals little pieces of its heart, thou wilt put to flight all kinds of devils, and if thou anointest with its gall eyes in which there is a white speck, they shall be cured."* If he had thus spoken, I could agree with the construction that S. Raphael had brought about, by his

own supernatural power, the effects which the mere application of the smoke and the gall might not have been enough to produce: but he does not speak thus, nay, on the contrary, he says absolutely, that such is the virtue of the smoke and the gall.

75. It may be asked whether the Angel spoke the precise truth regarding the virtue of those things, or whether he might have lied; and likewise, whether the white speck was withdrawn from the eyes of the elder Tobias by the native force of the gall of the fish, or by the supernatural virtue of the Angel S. Raphael? To say that the Angel could have lied would be an heretical blasphemy; he therefore spoke the precise truth; but it would no longer be so if all kinds of Demons were not expelled by the smoke of the liver of the fish, unless aided by the supernatural force of the Angel, and especially, if such aid was the principal cause of the effect produced, as the Doctors assert in the present case. It would doubtless be a lie if a physician should say: such an herb radically cures pleurisy or epilepsy, and if it should only begin the cure, the completion of which required the addition of another herb to the one first used; in the same manner, S. Raphael would have lied when averring that the smoke of the liver expelled all kinds of devils, so that they should not return, if that result had been only begun by the smoke, and its completion had been principally due to the power of the Angel. Besides, that flight of the devil was either to take place universally, and by the act of any one whosoever might put the liver of the fish on the coals, or else it was only to occur in that particular case, when the younger Tobias put the liver on the coals. In the first hypothesis, any person making that smoke by burning the liver should be assisted by an Angel, who, through his supernatural virtue would expel the Devils miraculously and regularly at the same time; which is absurd; for, either words have no meaning, or a natural fact cannot be regularly followed by a miracle; and, if the Devil was not put to flight without the assistance of the Angel, S. Raphael would have lied when ascribing that virtue to

the liver. If, on the contrary, that effect was only to be brought about in that particular case, S. Raphael would again have lied when assigning to that fish, universally and absolutely, the virtue of expelling the Demon: now, to say that the Angel lied is not possible.

76. The white speck was withdrawn from the eyes of the elder Tobias, and his blindness healed, through the native virtue of the gall of that same fish, as many Doctors aver (Nicolas of Lyra, Dionysius, and the authorities quoted by Cornelius à Lapide in his glosses on *Tobias*, vi. 9). In fact, that the gall of the fish callionymous, which the Italians call *bocca in capo*, and of which Tobias made use, is a highly renowned remedy for removing whiteness from the eyes, all are agreed; Dioscorides, Galen, Pliny,[74] and Valesius. The Greek Text of *Tobias*, ch. xi, v. 13, says: *"He poured the gall on his father's eyes, saying: Have confidence, father; but there being erosion the old man rubbed his eyes, and the scales of the whiteness came out at the corners."* Now, since, according to the same text, the Angel had disclosed to Tobias the virtue of the liver and gall of the fish, and since, through its native virtue, the gall cured the elder Tobias's blindness, it must be inferred that it was likewise through its native force that the smoke of the liver put the Incubus to flight; which inference is conclusively confirmed by the Greek text, which, *Tobias*, ch. viii, v. 2, instead of the reading in the Vulgate: *"He laid a part of the liver on burning coals,"* (*Protulit de cassidili suo partem iecoris, posuitque eam super carbones uiuos*), says explicitly: *"He took the ashes of the perfumes, and put the heart and the liver of the fish thereupon, and made a smoke therewith; the which smell when the evil spirit had smelled, he fled."* The Hebrew text says: *"Asmodeus smelled the smell, and fled."* From all those texts it appears that the Devil took to flight on smelling a smoke which was prejudicial and hurtful to himself, and nowise did he flee from the supernatural power of the Angel. If, in ridding Sara from the assaults of the Incubus Asmodeus,[75] the operation of the smoke of the liver was followed by the

intervention of S. Raphael, it was in order to bind the Demon in the desert of Upper Egypt, as related, *Tobias*, ch. viii, v. 3; for, at such a distance, the smoke of the liver could neither operate on the Devil, nor bind him. And here we have the means of reconciling our opinion with that of the above-mentioned Doctors, who ascribe to S. Raphael's power Sara's complete riddance from the Devil: for, I say with them, that the cure of Sara was completed by the binding of the Devil in the wilderness, the deed of the Angel; which I concede; but I maintain that the deliverance properly called, that is to say, the ejection from Sara's bed-chamber, was the direct effect of the virtue of the liver of the fish.

77. A third principal proof of our conclusion regarding the existence of those animals, in other words, respecting the corporeity of Incubi, is adduced by the testimony of S. Jerome,[76] in his *Life of S. Paul, the first Hermit*. S. Antony, says he, set on a journey to visit S. Paul.[77] After travelling several days, he met a Centaur, of whom he inquired the hermit's abode; whereupon the Centaur, growling some uncouth and scarcely intelligible answer, pointed the direction with his out-stretched hand, and then fled with the utmost speed into a wood. The Holy Abbot kept on his way, and, in a dene, met a little man, almost a dwarf, with taloned hands, horned brow, and his lower extremities ending in the feet of a goat. At such a sight S. Antony[78] stood still, and fearing the arts of the Devil, comforted himself with a great sign of the Cross. But, far from running away, or even seeming frightened at it, the little fellow respectfully approached the old man, and tendered him, as it were a peace offering, dates as refreshment for his journey. The blessed S. Antony having then inquired who he was: "*I am a mortal,*" replied he, "*and one of the inhabitants of the Wilderness, whom the Pagans, in their many blind errors, worship under the names of Fauns, or Satyrs, or Incubi. I am on a mission from my people: we beg thee to pray for us unto the common God, whom we know to have come for the Salvation of the world, and whose Praises are sounded all over the earth.*"

Rejoicing exceedingly at the glory of Christ, S. Antony, turning his face towards Alexandria, and striking the ground with his staff, cried out: *"Woe be unto thee, thou harlot City, who worshipest animals as Gods!"* Such is the narrative of S. Jerome, who dwells at length on the fact, explaining its import in an ample discourse.

78. It were indeed rash to doubt the truth of the above recital, constantly referred to by the greatest of the Doctors of the Holy Church, S. Jerome, whose authority no Catholic will ever deny. Let us therefore investigate these circumstances which most clearly must confirm our opinion.

79. Firstly, we observe that if ever a Saint was assailed by the arts of the Demon, saw through his infernal devices, and carried off victories and trophies from the contest, that Saint was S. Antony, as is shown by his life written by S. Athanasius. Now, since in that little man S. Antony did not recognize a devil, but an animal, saying: *"Woe be unto thee, thou harlot City, who worshipest animals as Gods!"*, it is clear that it was no devil or pure spirit ejected from heaven and damned, but some kind of animal. Still more: S. Antony, when instructing his friars and cautioning them against the assaults of the Demon, said to them, as related in the Roman Breviary, 17 January (*Feast of S. Antony, Abbot, II Nocturn, lection vi.*): *"Believe me, my brethren, Satan dreads the vigils of pious men, their prayers, fasts, voluntary poverty, compassion and humility; but, above all, he dreads their burning love of our Lord Jesus Christ, at the mere sign of whose most Holy Cross he flies away disabled."* As the little man, against whom S. Antony guarded himself with a sign of the Cross, neither took fright nor fled, but approached the Saint confidently and humbly, offering him some dates, it is a sure sign that he was no Devil.

80. Secondly, we must observe that the little man said: *"I also am a mortal,"* whence it follows that he was an animal subject to death, and consequently called into being through generation; for, an immaterial spirit is immortal, because simple, and consequently is not called into being through generation

from pre-existent matter, but through creation, and, consequently also, cannot lose it through the corruption called death; its existence can only come to an end through annihilation. Therefore, when he said he was mortal, he professed himself an animal.

81. Thirdly, we must observe that he acknowledged he knew that the God of all had suffered in human flesh. Those words show him to have been a rational animal, for brutes know nothing but what is sensible and present, and can therefore have no knowledge of God. If that little man said that he and his fellows were aware that God had suffered in human flesh, it shows that, by means of some revelation, he must have acquired the knowledge of God, as we have ourselves the revealed Faith. That God assumed human flesh and suffered in it, is the essence of the two principal articles of our Faith: the existence of God one and threefold, His Incarnation, Passion and Resurrection. All that shows, as I said, that it was a rational animal, capable of the knowledge of God through revelation, like ourselves, and endowed with a rational, and consequently, immortal soul.

82. Fourthly, we must observe that, in the name of his whole race whose delegate he professed to be, he besought S. Antony to pray for them to the common God of all. Whence I infer that that little man was capable of salvation and damnation, and that he was not *in termino* but *in uia;* for, from his being, as has been shown above, rational and consequently endowed with an immortal soul, it follows that he was capable of salvation and damnation, the proper lot of every rational Creature, Angel or man. I likewise infer that he was on the way, *in uia,* that is, capable of merit and demerit; for, if he had been at the goal, *in termino,* he would have been either blessed or damned. Now, he could be neither the one nor the other; for, S. Antony's prayers, to which he commended himself, could have been of no assistance to him, if finally damned, and, if actually saved, he stood in no need of them. Since he commended himself to the Saint's prayers, it shows they could be of avail to him, and,

consequently, that he was on the way to salvation, *in statu uiæ et meriti.*

83. Fifthly, we must observe that the little man professed to be delegated by others of his kind, when saying: *"I am on a mission from my race,"* words from which many inferences may be deduced. One is, that the little man was not alone of his kind, an exceptional and solitary monster, but that there were many of the same species, since congregating they made up a race, and that he came in the name of all; which could not have been, had not the will of many been represented by, and centred in him. Another is, that those animals lead a social life, since one of them was sent in the name of many. Another again is, that, although living in the Wilderness, it is not assigned to them as a permanent abode; for S. Antony having never previously been in that desert, which was far distant from his hermitage, they could not have known who he was nor how great his degree of sanctity; it was therefore necessary that they should have become acquainted with him elsewhere, and, consequently, that they should have travelled beyond that wilderness.

84. Lastly, we must observe that the little man said he was one of those whom *the Pagans, blinded by error, call Fauns, or Satyrs, or Incubi:* and by these words is shown the truth of our principal proposition: that Incubi are rational animals, capable of salvation and damnation.

85. The apparition of such little men is of frequent occurrence in metallic mines, as is noted by George Agricola[79] in his book *De Animantibus subterraneis.* They suddenly appear to the miners, clothed like miners themselves, play and jump out together, laugh and titter, and flip little stones at them in joke: a sign, says the above-named Author, of excellent success, and of the finding of some branch or body of a mineral tree.

86. Peter Thyræus, of Neuss, in his book *De Terrificationibus nocturnis,* denies the existence of such little men, and supports his denial upon the following truly puerile arguments: given such little men, says he, how do they live, and where do

they dwell? How do they propagate their kind, through generation or otherwise? Are they born, do they die, upon what meat
do they feed? Are they capable of salvation and damnation,
and by what means do they procure their salvation? Such are
the arguments upon which Thyræus relies to support his denial of their existence.

87. But it really shows little judgement in a man to deny
that which has been written by grave and credible Authors,
and is confirmed by everyday experience. Thyræus's arguments are worthless and have been already refuted, Nos. 45
and following. The only question which remains to be answered
is this: Where do those little men, or Incubi, dwell? To that
I reply: As has been shown above (No. 71), according to
Guazzo, some are earthly, some aqueous, some aerial, some
igneous, that is to say, their bodies are made of the most subtle
part of one of the elements, or, if of the combination of many
elements, that yet there is one which predominates, either water or air, according to their nature. Their dwellings will consequently be found in that element which is preponderant in
their bodies: igneous Incubi, for instance, will only stay when
compelled, may be will not stay at all, in water or marshes,
which are adverse to them; and aqueous Incubi will not be
able to rise into the upper part of ether, the subtlety of which
region is repugnant to them. We see the like happen to men
who, accustomed to thicker air, cannot endure certain lofty
ridges of the Alps where the air is too subtle for their lungs.

88. Many testimonies of Holy Fathers, gathered by Molina,
in his *Commentary on St. Thomas*, would go to prove the corporeity of Demons; but, taking into account the above-quoted
decision of the Council of Lateran (No. 36), concerning the
incorporeity of Angels, we must understand that the Holy Fathers had in view those Incubi which are still on the way to
salvation, and not those demons that are damned. However, to
cut matters short, we merely give the authority of S. Augustine,[80] that eminent Doctor of the Church, and it will be clearly
seen how thoroughly his doctrine harmonizes with ours.

89. S. Augustine, then, in his *Commentary on Genesis*, Book II., ch. 17, writes as follows concerning Demons: *"They have the knowledge of some truths, partly through the more subtle acumen of their senses, partly through the greater subtilty of their bodies,"* and, Book III., ch. 1: *"Demons are aerial animals, because they partake of the nature of aerial bodies."* In his Epistle 115, to Hebridius, he affirms that they are *"aerial or ethereal animals, endowed with very acute intelligence."* In the *City of God,* Book XI., ch. 13, he says that *"even the worst Demon has an ethereal body."* Book XXI., ch. 10, he writes: *"The bodies of certain Demons, as has been believed by some learned men, are even made of the thick and damp air which we breathe."* Book XV., ch. 23: *"I dare not explicitly decide whether Angels, with an ethereal body, can feel the lust which would incite them to copulate with women."* In his Commentary on Psalm lxxxv., he says that *"the bodies of the blessed will, after resurrection, be like unto the bodies of Angels"*; on Psalm xiv., he observes that *"the body of Angels is inferior to the soul."* And, in his book *De Diuinatione Dæmonum,* he everywhere, and especially in ch. XXIII., teaches that *"Demons have very subtle bodies."*

90. Our view can also be confirmed by the testimony of the Holy Scriptures, which, however diversely construed by commentators, yet patently affirm our proposition. First, Psalm lxxvii., vv. 24 and 25, it is said: *"The Lord had given them the bread of heaven; Man ate the bread of angels."* David here alludes to manna, which fed the children of Israel during the whole time that they wandered in the wilderness. It will be asked in what sense it can be said of manna that it is the *Bread of Angels.* I am aware that most Doctors construe this passage in a mystical sense, saying that manna figures the Holy Eucharist, which is styled the *Bread of Angels,* because Angels enjoy the sight of God who, by concomitance, is found in the Eucharist.

91. A most proper construction assuredly, and it is adopted by the Church in the office of Corpus Christi; but it is in a

spiritual sense. Now what I seek is the literal sense; for in that Psalm David does not speak, as a prophet, of things to be, as he does in other places where a literal sense is not easily to be gathered; he speaks here as a historian, of things gone by. That Psalm, as is evident to any reader, is a plain epitome, or summing up of all the benefits conferred by God on the Hebrew People from the exodus out of Egypt to the days of David, and the manna of the Wilderness is spoken of in it; how, and in what sense is manna then styled the Bread of Angels? that is the question.

92. I am aware that many writers, for example, Nicolas of Lyra,[81] the Blessed Robert Bellarmine, Francis Titelmann,[82] Gilbert Genébrand,[83] and others, look upon the Bread of Angels as bread prepared by Angels, or sent down from Heaven by the ministry of Angels. But Cardinal Hugh of St.-Cher[84] explains that qualification by saying that this food partly produced the same effect upon the Jews, which the food of Angels produces upon the latter. Angels, in fact, are not liable to any infirmity; on the other hand Hebrew commentators, and Josephus himself, assert that whilst in the Wilderness, living upon manna, the Jews neither grew old, nor sickened, nor tired; so that manna was actually in its effects like unto the bread that Angels feed upon, for they know neither old age, nor disease, nor any weariness.

93. These interpretations should indeed be received with the respect due to the authority of such eminent Doctors. There is, however, one difficulty in this: namely that, by the ministry of Angels, the pillars of the cloud and fire, the quails, and the water from the rock were provided for the Hebrews, no less than the manna; and yet they were not styled the pillar, the water or the beverage of Angels. Why therefore should manna be called *Bread of Angels,* because provided by their ministry, when the qualification *Drink of Angels* is not given to the water drawn from the rock likewise by their ministry? Besides, in Holy Scripture, when it is said of bread that it is the *bread of somebody,* it is always the *bread of him* who feeds on it, not of

him who provides or makes it. Of this there are numberless instances: thus, *Exodus, xxiii.* 25: *"That I may bless your bread and your waters"; Kings*, book II., xii. 3: *"Eating of his bread"; Tobias, iv.* 17: *"Eat thy bread with the hungry,"* and v. 18: *"Lay out thy bread on the burial of a Just Man"; Ecclesiastes,* xi. 1: *"Cast thy bread upon the running waters"; Isaias,* lviii. 7: *"Deal thy bread to the hungry"; Jeremias,* xi. 19: *"Let us put wood on his bread"; S. Matthew,* xv. 26: *"It is not good to take the bread of the children"; S. Luke,* xi. 3: *"Our daily bread."* All those passages clearly show that, in Scripture, the bread of somebody is the bread of him who feeds upon it, not of him who makes, brings, or provides it. In the passage of the Psalm we have quoted, *Bread of Angels* may therefore easily be taken to mean the food of Angels, not incorporeal indeed, since these require no material food, but corporeal, that is to say of those rational animals we have described of, who live in the air, and, from the subtlety of their bodies and their rationality, approximate so closely to immaterial Angels as actually to fall under the same denomination.

94. I conclude then that, being animals, consequently reproducible through generation and liable to corruption, they require food for the restoration of their corporeal substance wasted by effluvia: for the life of every sensible being consists in nothing else but the motion of the corporeal elements which flow and ebb, are acquired, lost, and recruited by means of substances spirituous, yet material, assimilated by the living thing, either through the inhalation of air, or by the fermentation of food which spiritualizes its substance, as is shown by that great scholar Ettmüller (*Instit. Medic. Physiolog.,* ch. 2).

95. But, their body being subtile, equally subtile and delicate must be its food. And, just as perfumes and other vaporous and volatile substances, when adverse to their nature, offend and put them to flight, as testified by what we related above (Nos. 71 and 72), in the like manner, when agreeable, they delight in and feed upon them. Now, as is written by Cornelius à Lapide, *"Manna is nothing but an emanation of water and*

earth, refined and baked by the heat of the sun, and then co-agulated and condensed by the cold of the following night"; of course, I am speaking of the manna sent down from Heaven for the nourishment of the Israelites, and which wholly differs from our modern medicinal manna in use today; for this, in fact, according to Ettmüller (*Dilucid. Physiol.*, ch. 1), *"is merely the juice or transudation of certain trees which, during the night, gets mixed up with dew, and, the next morning, co-agulates and thickens in the heat of the sun."* The manna of the Israelites, on the contrary, derived from other principles, far from coagulating, liquefied in the heat of the sun, as is shown by Scripture, *Exodus*, xvi., 21: *"After the sun grew hot, it melted."* The manna of the Israelites was therefore undoubtedly of a most subtile substance, consisting as it did of emanations of earth and water, and being dissolved by the sun it disappeared: consequently, it may very well have been the food of the animals we are speaking of, and thus have been truly called by David *Bread of Angels*.

96. We have another authority in the Gospel according to S. John, x. 16, where it is said: *"And other sheep I have, that are not of this fold: them also I must bring, and they shall hear my voice, and there shall be one fold and one shepherd."* If we inquire what are those sheep that are not of this fold, and what is the fold of which Our Lord Jesus Christ speaketh, we are answered by all Commentators that the only fold of Christ is the Church to which the preaching of the Gospel was to bring the Gentiles, sheep of another fold than that of the Jews. They are, in fact, of opinion that the fold of Christ was the Synagogue, because David had said, Psalm xciv. 7: *"We are the people of his pasture, and the sheep of his hand"* and also because Abraham and David had been promised that the Messiah should be born of their race, because He was expected by the Jews, foretold by the Prophets who were Jews, and that His Advent, His acts, His Passion, Death and Resurrection were prefigured in the sacrifices, worship, and ceremonials of the Jewish law.

97. But, saving always the reverence due to the Holy Fathers and other Doctors, that explanation does not seem quite exhaustive. For it is an article of belief that the Church of the Faithful has been the only one in existence from the beginning of the world, and will thus endure to the end of time. The Head of that Church is Jesus Christ, the Mediator between God and men, by Whom all things were created and made. Indeed, faith in the Holy Trinity, though less explicitly, and the Incarnation of the Word were revealed to the first man, and by him taught his children, who, in their turn, taught them to their descendants. And thus, although most men had strayed into idolatry and deserted the true faith, many kept the faith they had received from their fathers, and observing the laws of nature, stayed in the true Church of the Faithful, as is noticed by Cardinal Francisco Toledo, S.J.,[85] in reference to Job, who was a saint among idolatrous Gentiles. And, although God had conferred especial favours upon the Jews, prescribed for them peculiar laws and ceremonials, and separated them from the Gentiles, yet those laws were not obligatory on the Gentiles, and the faithful Jews did not constitute a Church different from that of the Gentiles who professed their faith in one God, and looked for the coming of the Messiah.

98. And thus it came to pass that even among the Gentiles there were some who prophesied the advent of Christ and the other dogmas of the Christian faith, to wit *Balaam*,[86] *Mercurius Trismegistus*,[87] *Hydaspes*,[88] and the *Sibyls*[89] mentioned by Lactantius, Book I., ch. 6, as is remarked by the Venerable Cesare Baronius,[90] in his *Annals*, 18. That the Messiah was expected by the Gentiles is shown by many passages of Isaias, and plainly testified by the prophecy of Jacob, the Patriarch, thus worded, Genesis, xlix. 10: *"The sceptre shall not be taken away from Juda, nor a ruler from his thigh, till he come that is to be sent, and he shall be the expectation of nations."* Likewise in the prophecy of Aggeus ii. 8: *"I will move all Nations, and the Desired of all Nations shall come"*; which passage is thus commented upon by Cornelius à Lapide: *"The Gentiles before the*

advent of Christ, who believed in God and observed the nat-
ural law, expected and desired Christ equally with the Jews."
Christ Himself disclosed and manifested Himself to the Gentiles as well as to the Jews; for, at the same time as the Angel
announced His Nativity to the shepherds, by means of the
miraculous star He called the Magi to worship Him, and they,
being Gentiles, were the first among the Nations, as the shepherds among the Jews, to acknowledge and worship Christ
(*Uide* S. Fulgentius,[91] *Sermon* vi., *upon the Epiphany*). In like
manner, the advent of Christ was made known by preaching
(I am not speaking of the Apostles) to the Gentiles before it
was to the Jews. As is written by the Venerable Mother, Sister
Maria d'Agreda,[92] in her *Life of Jesus Christ and the Blessed*
Virgin Mary: "*When the Blessed Virgin Mary, fleeing with*
S. Joseph, from the persecution of Herod, carried the Infant
Jesus into Egypt, she tarried there seven years; and, during
that time the Blessed Virgin herself preached to the Egyptians
the faith of the true God and the advent of the Son of God in
human flesh." Besides, the Nativity of Christ was attended by
numerous prodigies, not only in Judæa, but also in Egypt,
where the idols tumbled down and the oracles were hushed;
in Rome, where a spring of oil gushed forth, a golden globe was
seen to descend from the skies on earth, three suns appeared,
and an extraordinary aureole, variegated like a rainbow, en-
circled the disc of the sun; in Greece, where the oracle of Del-
phi was struck dumb, and Apollo, asked the reason of his silence by Augustus, who was offering up a sacrifice in his own
palace where he had raised an altar to him, answered:

Me puer Hebræus, Diuos Deus ipse gubernans,
Cedere sede iubet, tristemque redire sub orcum;
Aris ergo dehinc tacitis abscedito nostris.
"A Hebrew child, who sways the Gods, and himself a God,
"Bids me quit my seat and return to the infernal regions;
"Depart therefore from our altars, henceforward mute."

So Nicephorus,[93] I. 17; Suidas,[94] and Cedrenus[95] in his *Com-*
pendium Historiæ relate.

There were many more prodigies warning the Gentiles of the advent of the Son of God: they have been collected from various Authors, by Baronius, and are to be found in his *Annals*, and by Cornelius à Lapide in his *Commentary upon Aggeus*.[96]

99. From all this it is clear that the Gentiles also belonged, as well as the Jews, to the fold of Christ, that is, to the same Church of the Faithful; it cannot therefore be correctly said that the words of Christ: *"Other sheep I have, which are not of this fold,"* are exclusively applicable to the Gentiles, who had, in common with the Jews, the faith in God, the hope, prophecy, expectation, predictive prodigies and preaching of the Messiah.

100. I therefore maintain that by the words *other sheep* may very well be understood those rational Creatures or animals of whom we have been treating hitherto. They are, as we have pointed out, capable of salvation and damnation, and Jesus Christ is the Mediator between God and man, wherefore every rational Creature (for rational creatures attain to salvation in consideration of the infinite merits of Christ, through the grace He confers upon them, without which salvation is impossible of attainment), every rational creature, I say, must have cherished, at the same time as the faith in one God, the hope of the advent of Christ, and have had the revelation of His Nativity in the flesh and of the principles of the law of grace. Those were therefore the sheep which were not *of that human fold,* and which Christ had to bring; the sheep which were to hear His voice, that is, the announcement of His advent and of the evangelical doctrine, either directly through Himself, or through the Apostles; the sheep which, partaking with men of heavenly bliss, were to realize *one fold and one shepherd.*

101. To this interpretation, which I hold to be in no way improper, force is added by what we related, according to S. Jerome, of that little man who requested S. Antony to *pray,* for him and his fellows, unto the common God, whom he knew to have suffered in human flesh. For, it implies that they were aware of the advent and of the death of Christ, whom, as

God, they were anxious to propitiate, since they sought, to that effect, the intercession of S. Antony.

102. Thereto tends also the fact mentioned by Cardinal Baronius (*Annals*, 129), quoting Eusebius of Cæsarea, *Præparatio Euangelica*, v. 9, and Plutarch *De Defectu Oraculorum*, as being one of the prodigies which took place at the time of the death of Christ. He relates that in the reign of the Emperor Tiberius, when Christ suffered, whilst mariners bound from Greece to Italy, were by night, and during a calm, in the vicinity of the Isles of the Echinades,[97] their ship hulled not far from shore. All the crew then heard a loud voice calling upon Tramnus, the master of the ship. When he had answered to his name, the voice replied: "What time thou art hard by such a marsh, announce that *the great Pan is dead.*" This Tramnus did, and there arose suddenly, as from a numberless multitude, groans and shrieks. Doubtless, they were Demons, or corporeal Angels, or rational animals living near the marsh on account of their aqueous nature, and who, hearing of the death of Christ, described by the name of Great Pan, burst into tears and wailed, like some of the Jews who, after witnessing the death of Christ, went home smiting their breasts (*S. Luke*, xxiii. 48). From all that has been concluded above, it is therefore clear that there are such Demons, Succubi and Incubi, endowed with senses and subject to the passions thereof, as has been shown; who are born through generation and die through corruption, who are capable of salvation and damnation, more noble than man, by reason of the greater subtilty of their bodies, and who, when having intercourse with humankind, male or female, fall into the same sin as man when copulating with a beast, which is inferior to him. Also, it not unfrequently occurs that those Demons slay the men, women, or mares with whom they have had long protracted intercourse; and the reason is that, being liable to sin whilst on the way to salvation, *in uia*, they must likewise be open to repentance; and, in the same manner as a man, who habitually sins with a beast, is enjoined by his confessor to destroy that beast, with a view to

suppressing the occasion of relapsing, it may likewise happen that the penitent Demon should slay the animal with which it sinned, whether man or beast; nor will death thus occasioned to a man be reckoned a sin to the Demon, any more than death inflicted on a beast is imputed as a sin to man; for, considering the essential difference between a Demon of that kind and man, the man will be the same thing to the Demon as the beast is to man.

103. I am aware that many, perhaps most of my readers, will say of me what the Epicureans and some Stoic Philosophers said of S. Paul (*Acts of the Apostles*, xvii. 18). *"He seemeth to be a setter forth of new gods,"* and will deride my doctrine. But they will none the less have to answer the foregoing arguments, to show what are those Incubi Demons, commonly called *Goblins*, who dread neither exorcisms, nor holy objects, nor the Cross of Christ, and they must explain the various effects and phenomena we have related when we were propounding that doctrine.

104. What we have hitherto concluded accordingly solves the question laid down Nos. 30 and 34, to wit: how a woman can be got with child by an Incubus Demon? In fact, it cannot be brought about by sperm assumed from a man, agreeably to the common opinion, which we confuted, Nos. 31 and 32; it follows, therefore, that she is directly impregnated by the sperm of the Incubus, who, being an animal and capable of breeding, has sperm of his own. And thus is fully explained the begetting of Giants from the intercourse of the Sons of God with the Daughters of men: for that intercourse gave birth to Giants who, although like to men, were of higher stature, and, though begotten by Demons, and consequently of great strength, yet equalled their sires neither in might nor in power. It is the same with mules, which are intermediate, as it were, between the kinds of animals from whose promiscuousness they are sprung, and which excel indeed the most imperfect, but never equal the most perfect: thus, the mule excels the ass, but does not attain the perfection of the mare, which has begotten it.

105. In confirmation of the above conclusion, we observe that animals sprung from the mixing of different kinds do not breed, but are barren, as is seen with mules. Now we do not read of Giants having been begotten by other Giants, but rather of their having been born of the Sons of God, that is Incubi, and the Daughters of men: so being thus begotten of the demoniac sperm mixed with the human sperm, and being, as it were, an intermediate species between the Demon and man, they had no generative power.

106. It may be objected that the sperm of Demons, which must, by nature, be most fluid, could not mix with the human sperm, which is thick, and that, consequently, no generation would ensue.

107. I reply that, as has been said above, No. 32, the generative power lies in the spirit that comes from the generator at the same time as the spumy and viscous matter; it follows that, although most liquid, the sperm of the Demon, being nevertheless material, can very well mix with the material spirit of the human sperm, and bring about generation.

108. It will be alleged in answer that, if the generation of Giants had really come from the combined sperms of Incubi and women, Giants would still be born in our time, since there is no lack of women who have intercourse with Incubi, as is shown by the Acts of S. Bernard[98] and S. Peter[99] of Alcantara, and by other examples related in various authors.

109. I reply that, as has been said above, No. 71, from Guazzo, some of those Demons are earthly, some aqueous, some aerial, some igneous, and they all dwell in their respective element. Now, it is well known that animals are of larger size, according to the element they live in; and it is the same with fishes, many of which are diminutive, it is true, as happens with animals that live on land; but, the element water being larger than the element earth, since the container is always larger than the contents, fishes as a species, surpass in size the animals that dwell on land, as shown by whales, tunnies, cachalots, saw-fish, sharks, and other cetaceous and viviparous fish which far sur-

pass in size all animals that live on land. Consequently, these Demons being animals, as has been shown, their size will be proportionate to the extent of the element they dwell in, according to their nature. And, air being more extensive than water, and fire than air, it follows that ethereal and igneous Demons will far surpass their earthly and aqueous fellows, both in stature and might. It would be to no purpose to instance, as an objection, birds which, although inhabitants of the air, a more extensive element than water, are smaller, as a species, than fishes and quadrupeds; for, if birds do indeed travel through the air by means of their wings, they no less belong to the element earth, where they rest; otherwise, some fishes that fly, such as the sea-swallow, would have to be classed among aerial animals, which is not the case.

110. Now, it must be observed that, after the Flood, the air which surrounds our earthy and aqueous globe, became, from the damp of the waters, thicker than it had been before; and, damp being the principle of corruption, that may be the reason why men do not live as long as they did before the Flood. It is also on account of that thickness of the air that ethereal and igneous Demons, who are more corpulent and gross than the others, can no longer dwell in that thick atmosphere, and if they must descend into it occasionally, do so only when obliged, much as divers descend into the depths of the sea.

111. Before the Flood, when the air was not yet so thick, Demons came upon earth and had intercourse with women, thus procreating Giants whose stature was nearly equal to that of the Demons, their fathers. But now it is not so: the Incubi who approach women are aqueous and of small stature; that is why they appear in the shape of little men, and, being aqueous, they are most lecherous. Lust and damp go together: Poets have depicted Venus as born of the sea,[100] in order to show, as is explained by Mythologists, that lust takes its source in damp. When, therefore, Demons of short stature impregnate women nowadays, the children that are born are not giants, but men of ordinary size. It should, moreover, be known that when De-

mons have carnal intercourse with women in their own natural body, without having recourse to any disguise or artifice, the women do not see them, or if they do, see but an almost doubtful, vague, barely sensible shadow, as was the case with the female we spoke of, No. 28, who, when embraced by an Incubus, scarcely felt his touch. But, when they want to be seen by their mistresses, and to taste to the full the joys of human copulation, they assume a visible disguise and a palpable body. By what means this is effected, is their secret, which our circumscribed Philosophy is unable to discover. The only thing we know is that such disguise or body could not consist merely in concrete air, since this must take place through condensation, and therefore by the influence of cold; a body thus formed would feel like ice, and in the venereal act could afford women no pleasure, but would give them pain; and it is the reverse that takes place.

112. The distinction being admitted between wholly spiritual Demons, who have intercourse with witches, and Incubi, who have to do with women that are nowise witches, we must now inquire into the heinousness of the crime in both cases.

113. The intercourse of witches with Demons, from its accompanying circumstances, apostasy from the Faith, the worship of the Devil, and so many other abominations as related above, Nos. 12 to 24, is the greatest of all sins which can be committed by man; and, considering the hideous enormity against Religion which is presupposed by coition with the Devil, Demoniality is assuredly the most grievous of all carnal offences. But, taking the sins of the flesh as such, exclusive of the sins against Religion, Demoniality should be reduced to simple pollution. The reason, a most convincing one, is that the Devil who swives a witch is a pure spirit, has reached the goal and is damned, as has been said above; if, therefore, he copulates with witches, it is in a body assumed or made by himself, according to the common opinion of Theologians. Though set in motion, that body is not a living one; and it follows that the human being, male or female, who has connexion with such

a body, is guilty of the same offence as if he copulated with an inanimate body or a corpse, which would be simple pollution, as we have shown elsewhere. It has, moreover, been truly observed by Cajetan, that such intercourse can very well carry with it the guilt of other crimes, according to the body assumed by the Devil, and the member used: thus, if he should assume the body of a kinswoman, or of a nun, such a crime would be incest or sacrilege; if coition took place in the shape of a beast, or *in uase præpostero*, it would be Bestiality or Sodomy.

114. As for intercourse with an Incubus, wherein is to be found no element, no, not even the least, of offence against Religion, it is hard to discover a reason why it should be more grievous than Bestiality and Sodomy. For, as we have said above, if Bestiality is more grievous than Sodomy, it is because man degrades the dignity of his kind by mixing with a beast, of a kind much inferior to his own. But, when copulating with an Incubus, it is quite the reverse: for the Incubus, by reason of his rational and immortal spirit, is equal to man; and, by reason of his body, more noble because more subtile, so he is more perfect and more dignified than man. Consequently, when having intercourse with an Incubus, man does not degrade, but rather dignifies, his nature; and, taking that into consideration, Demoniality cannot be more grievous than Bestiality.

115. It is, however, commonly held to be more grievous, and the reason I take to be this: that it is a sin against Religion to hold any communication with the Devil, either with or without a compact, for instance by habitually or familiarly companying with him, by asking his assistance, counsel or favour, or by seeking from him the revelation of things to be, the knowledge of the past, of absent things, or of circumstances otherwise hidden. Thus, men and women, by mixing with Incubi, whom they do not know to be animals but believe to be devils, sin through intention, *ex conscientia erronea*, and their sin is in intention the same, when having intercourse

with Incubi, as if such intercourse took place with devils; wherefore the guilt of their crime is exactly the same.

Note by Isidore Liseux

The manuscript of *Demoniality* breaks off with the conclusion just given. In a purely philosophical and theoretical acceptation, the work is complete: for it was enough that the author should define, in general terms, the grievousness of the crime, without concerning himself with the proceedings which were to make out the *proof*, or with the *penalty* to be inflicted. Both those questions, on the contrary, had, as a matter of course, a place assigned to them in the great work *De Delictis et Pœnis*, which is a veritable *Code for the Inquisitor;* and Father Sinistrari of Ameno could not fail to treat them there with all the care and conscientiousness he has so amply shown in the foregoing pages.

The reader will be happy to find here that practical conclusion to *Demoniality*.

Proof of demoniality

Summary

1. *Distinctions to be made in the proof of the crime of Demoniality.*

2. *Signs proving the intercourse of a Witch with the Devil.*

3. *The frank confession of the Sorcerer himself is requisite for a full conviction.*

4. *Tale of a Nun who copulated with an Incubus.*

5. *If the indictment is supported by the recitals of eyewitnesses, torture may be resorted to and employed.*

1. As regards the proof of that crime, a distinction must be made of the kind of Demoniality, to wit: whether it is that which is practised by Witches or Wizards with the Devil, or that which other persons perform with Incubi.

2. In the first case, the compact entered into with the Devil being proved, the evidence of *Demoniality* follows as a necessary consequence; for, the purpose, both of Witches and Wizards, in the midnight sabbats that take place, after feasting and dancing, is none other but that infamous intercourse; moreover there can be no witness of that crime, since the Devil, visible to the Witch, escapes the sight of all beside. Sometimes, it is true, women have been seen in the woods, in the fields, in groves and dingles, lying on their backs, naked to their very navels, in the posture of venery, all their limbs quivering with the orgastic spasm, as is noted by Guazzo, book I., chap. 12, v. *Sciendum est saepius*, fol. 65. In such a case there would be a very strong suspicion of this crime, particularly if supported by other signs; and I am inclined to believe that such a circumstance, sufficiently proved by good witnesses, would justify the Judge in resorting to torture in order to ascertain the truth; especially if, shortly after that action, a sort of black smoke had been seen to issue from the woman, and she had been noticed to rise, as is also noted by Guazzo; for it might be inferred that that smoke or shadow had been the Devil himself, fornicating with the woman. Likewise if, as has more than once happened, according to the same author, a woman had been seen to fornicate with a mysterious stranger who, when the action was over, suddenly disappeared.

3. Again, in order to prove conclusively that a person is a Wizard or a Witch, the actual confession of such person is requisite: for there can be no witnesses to the fact, unless perhaps other Sorcerers giving evidence at the trial against their accomplices; and from their being confederates in the crime, their statement is not conclusive and does not justify the recourse to torture, should not other indications be forthcoming, such as the seal of the Devil stamped on their body, as afore-

said, No. 23, or the finding in their dwelling, after a search, of signs and instruments of the diabolic art: for example, bones and, especially, a skull, hair artfully plaited, intricate knots[101] of feathers, wings, feet or skeletons of bats, toads,[102] or serpents, unfamiliar and, perhaps, noxious seeds, wax figures, vessels filled with unknown powder, oil or viscid ointments, etc., as are usually detected by Judges who, upon a charge being brought against Sorcerers, proceed to their apprehension and the search of their houses.

4. The proof of copulation with an Incubus offers the same difficulty; for, no less than other Demons, the Incubus is, at will, invisible to all but his mistress. Yet, it has not seldom happened that Incubi have allowed themselves to be surprised in the act of carnal intercourse with women, now in one shape, now in another.

In a certain Convent (I mention neither its name nor that of the town where it is situate, so as not to recall to memory a past scandal), there was a Nun, who, as is usual with women and especially with nuns, had quarrelled about some silly trifles with one of her sister-nuns, the occupant of the cell adjoining hers. Quick at observing all the doings of this religious with whom she was at loggerheads, our neighbour noticed that, several days in succession, instead of walking with her companions in the garden after dinner she retired to her cell, where she locked herself in with unwonted precautions. Curious to know what she could be doing there all that time, the inquisitive Nun betook herself to her own cell. Presently she heard a sound, as of two voices conversing in subdued tones (which she could easily do, since the two cells were divided but by a slight partition), then a certain noise,[103] the creaking of a bed, groans and sighs, as of two lovers in an orgasm of love. Her wonderment was now raised to the highest pitch, and she redoubled her attention in order to ascertain who was in the cell. But when, three times running, she had seen no other nun come out save her rival, she strongly suspected that a man had been secretly introduced and was kept hidden there. She went accordingly and reported the whole thing to the Abbess, who, after taking counsel with the Discreets,[104] resolved that she would herself listen to the sounds and observe the strange happenings which had been thus denounced to her, so as to avoid any hasty or inconsiderate act. In consequence, the Abbess and her confidents repaired to the cell of the informer, and thence heard the voices and other noises that had been described. Inquiry was made to ascertain whether any of the Nuns could be shut in with this other one; and when this was found not to be the case, the Abbess and her attendants went to the door of the closed cell, and knocked repeatedly, but to no purpose: the Nun neither answered, nor opened. The Abbess threatened to have the door broken in, and even ordered a lay-sister to force it with a crow-bar. The Nun then opened her door: a search was made and no one found. Being asked with whom she had been talking, and the why and wherefore of the bed creaking, of the long-drawn sighs, etc., she denied everything.

But, since matters went on just the same as before, the rival Nun, becoming slyer and more inquisitive than ever, contrived to bore a hole through the partition, so as to be able to discover exactly what was happening inside the cell; and what should she espy but a comely youth lying with the Nun, a sight she took good care to let the others enjoy by the same means. An accusation was soon laid before the Bishop: the guilty Nun still endeavoured to deny all; but at last, threatened with the torture, she confessed to having been long indecently intimate with an Incubus.

5. When, therefore, indications are forthcoming, such as those detailed above, a charge might be brought after a searching inquiry; yet, without the confession of the accused, the offence should not be regarded as fully proven, even if the intercourse were actually beheld by eye-witnesses; for it sometimes happens that, in order utterly to undo an innocent female, the Devil feigns such intercourse by means of some glamour or de-

lusion. In those cases, the Ecclesiastical Judge therefore must trust but to his own eyes alone.

Penalties

With regard to the penalties applicable to *Demoniality*, there is no law that I know of, either civil or canonical, which inflicts a punishment for a crime of that kind. Since, however, such a crime implies a compact and communion with the Devil, and apostasy from the faith, not to speak of the evil deeds, damage, and other almost numberless outrages perpetrated by Sorcerers, as a rule it is punished, out of Italy, by the gallows and the stake. But, in Italy, it is very seldom that offenders of this kind are delivered up by the Holy Inquisition to the secular power.

Notes

1. H. C. Lea, *Materials Toward a History of Witchcraft*, Thomas Yoseloff, New York, 1957 (3 vols.). All references to this work are to the Yoseloff edition, hereafter to be listed as *Materials*.

2. Lengthy and valuable discussions of Hebrew demonology and angelology are to be found in Lea's *Materials* and in Edward Langton's *Essentials of Demonology*, Epworth Press, London, 1949. While I have drawn upon many other sources, there is little of Hebrew demonology in this book that is not dealt with by one or both of those volumes.

3. Cf. L. W. de Laurence, *The Great Book of Magical Art, Hindu Magic and East Indian Occultism*, The de Laurence Co., Chicago, 1939.

4. Many writers give versions of this "confession," sometimes dated 1321, sometimes much earlier (when the story is credited to the Manichaeans). Lea, *Materials*, pp. 158, 159, has taken his account from Dollinger.

5. John Chrysostom (c. 345-407): Famed for his eloquence, hence his name, which means "golden-mouthed." Chrysostom served as archbishop of Constantinople and authored various Homilies, but late in life was banished to the shores of the Black Sea, where he died.

6. Justin Martyr (died c. 163-65): A Father of the Christian Church who supposedly died, as his name indicates, a martyr's death. As a Christian (he had earlier been a Platonist and a Stoic), he wrote two "Apologies" and another work called "A Dialogue With Trypho the Jew."

7. Justin Martyr is said to have told the emperor to his face that the pagan gods were all devils. Saint Paul declared: "But I say that the things which the Gentiles sacrifice they sacrifice to devils and not to God; and I would not that ye should have fellowship with devils." (I Corinthians, 10:20). Compare Psalms, 96:5: "For all of

the gods of the Gentiles are devils." Some later Christian translations of the Scriptures have emasculated the Old Testament declaration while leaving the New Testament one intact.

8. Sulpicius Severus (c. 360-425): Disciple and biographer of Saint Martin.

9. Clement of Alexandria (c. 160-215): A Father of the Church. Noted for his philosophical treatises, he was born in Athens but lived most of his life in Alexandria. A converted pagan, Clement was learned in Greek literature, philosophy, and religion.

10. Commodianus (c. 250): A Christian Latin poet whose works attacked heretics, pagans, and Jews, ridiculed the gods of mythology, and proclaimed the coming of the Anti-Christ and the end of the world. An African, he was converted rather late in life. His two extant works are the *Instructiones* and the *Carmen apologeticum*.

11. Tertullian (c. 160-220): Sometimes called the "Father of Ecclesiastical Latin," and a Father of the Church, he was a prolific writer, especially of polemics against heretics and pagans. He is probably best known for his "Credo quia absurdum est"—words which, in fact, he never wrote. Nonetheless, they do not distort his view that a faith based upon the authority of Christ is better than a faith based upon reason.

12. *De Haeresibus*, n. 108.

13. Paracelsus (c. 1493-1541): Physician, alchemist, magician, sometimes called the father of chemotherapy and the father of psychiatry. His ideas, which continue to have great influence among occultists, are well represented in A. E. Waite's *The Hermetic and Alchemical Writings of Paracelsus*, London, 1894 (2 vols.).

14. Pierre de Lancre (1553-1631): A witch trial judge who by his own boast burned more than six hundred persons. He authored several other works besides the *Tableau* (his most important) and enjoyed great renown as a magistrate. Robbins remarks that he bequeathed his library to his bastard son, a Jesuit.

15. Ernest Jones, *On the Nightmare*, Grove Press, New York, 1959, p. 85.

16. Johann Nider (1380-1438): A Dominican, he was papal inquisitor and rector of the University of Vienna. A Thomist, he was the author of the *Formicarius*, an encyclopaedic work much cited by demonologists. It was not published, however, until around 1500, more than half a century after his death.

17. Martin Del Rio (1551-1608): Jesuit scholar and author of the *Disquisitionum Magicarum*, along with many books of sermons and a scholarly edition of Seneca. Despite his scholarship, which was

in fact formidable, he was altogether credulous in the areas of witch-craft and demonology and was implacable in his hatred of witches and demands for their extermination. Beyond doubt he was respon-sible for many deaths.

CHAPTER 2

1. The word *succubus* means "lying under," and the word *incubus* has the meaning of "lying above." In the late Latin, *succubus* was an equivalent of "harlot" (prostitute). However, in common usage a succubus is a (usually sexless) evil spirit or demon in female form, and an incubus is a malign spirit in male form. The terms *incubus* and *succubus* are also used sometimes as equivalents for "lover," "paramour," "mistress," etc. For example: When her husband goes out the front door, her incubus comes in the back (meaning a human lover).

2. Saint Anthony (died c. 356): At the time of his death, Anthony was very old, perhaps more than one hundred years. His biography is often attributed to Athanasius. Born in Egypt, Anthony is re-garded as the founder of Christian monasticism. He went to live in the desert as a holy hermit when he was about thirty years of age. Around 305, he began to acquire disciples who came to visit him and then took up residence in huts nearby. The Devil sought endlessly to tempt him, sending demons disguised as beautiful harlots, etc. His imitators were similarly troubled, and the temptations of the hermit-saints are described over and over again by demonologists seeking thus to establish the reality of seductive and lascivious devils. The many remarkable paintings inspired by these incidents should not pass unnoticed.

3. Montague Summers, *The History of Witchcraft*, University Books, New York, 1956, p. 41.

4. Cf. Lea, *Materials*, p. 67.

5. Biographical material on Remy will be found in Summers' notes to Sinistrari's *Demoniality*, Appendix B of this volume.

6. Nicolas Remy, *Demonolatry*, John Rodker, London, 1930, p. 41.

7. Henri Boguet (c. 1550-1619): A most eminent attorney and author of a standard legal text in addition to his *Discours des sorciers*, a witch book so important as to rival in its influence the *Malleus Maleficarum*. As a judge and burner of witches, Boguet was especially noted for his cruelty, which included the torture and execution of prepubertal children.

8. Henri Boguet, *An Examen of Witches* (*Discours des sorciers*), John Rodker, London, 1929, p. 20.

9. The song is about a Negro trumpet player who has made the rounds of Pigalle bistros, become drunk, and fallen into a gutter where he lies. Drunken visions pass through his mind, and at intervals he repeats to himself the words: "God is black."

Where personal gods are not the color of their inventors, and are not similar to them in many other respects, they are inherited or imposed gods. As Xenophanes remarked in the sixth century B.C., "If oxen or lions had hands, and could paint with their hands, and produce works of art as men do, horses would paint the forms of the gods like horses, and oxen like oxen, and make their bodies in the image of their several kinds." Or in other words, and as an old saying has it, "Man creates God in his own image." However, when man creates a devil, he creates him in the image of his enemy (which is likely to include attributes antithetical to those given to the god). Thus, the white devil of the black man, and the black devil of the white man, are likely to testify to racial antagonisms. But as I have pointed out elsewhere, there are other reasons to be found to explain why the Christian Devil is represented as a black man (and why black is understood to be the color of evil). These reasons are not pertinent, however, to the white devil of the Negro, who is undoubtedly for the most part a product of racial hostility. (Today's red devil is a fatuous creation, his color being that of fire. In general it is to be expected that a red devil will be taken much less seriously than a black [or a white] one.)

10. Sylvester Prierias, whose book was first published at Rome, had first-hand experience of trying witches and so encountered a number of women who had given themselves to demons. He also believed in demonic rapes, and pointed out that virtuous (chaste) nuns are often so victimized. Prierias was the teacher of Bartolomeo Spina, O.P., who succeeded him (by appointment of Paul III) as Master of the Sacred Palace. Spina (b. Pisa, 1475; d. Rome, 1546) was the author of the *Quaestio de strigibus et lamiis*, published at Venice in 1523, two years after the appearance of Prierias' *De Strigimagis*.

11. Remy, *Demonolatry*, pp. 13, 14.

12. De Lancre, for one, mentions the testimony of a witch who described her demon as possessing testicles.

13. *An Examen of Witches*, p. 257.

14. *An Examen of Witches*, pp. 261, 262.

15. Cf. Lea, *Materials*, p. 299.

16. Remy, *Demonolatry*, p. 28.

17. Saint Hilarion (Saint Hilary), in his *Life* of Saint Jerome, says that naked women (succubi) formed a circle around that holy man whenever he lay down to try to get some rest. Saint Hippolytus was similarly tormented, and there is the story of an eremite seduced by a succubus whose debaucheries were so excessive as to cause him to perish within a month of his fall.

18. *An Examen of Witches*, p. 18.

19. Cf. *Materials*, p. 150.

20. Pico della Mirandola (1469-1533): A demonologist whose *Strix* was the first history of witchcraft to be published in Italian (as *La Strega*, 1524). Mirandola describes the intercourse with demons as yielding pleasures more intense than those to be obtained from intercourse with mortals, and such testimony seems to have been often forthcoming from Italian witches. A copy of *La Strega* is to be found in the Cornell University Library. Cf. Robbins, whose biographical sketches of the demonologists are much to be commended.

21. According to Mirandola, one gentleman attending La Signora's Sabbat actually mistook her for the Virgin. He then offered her a host which he happened to have with him, and everyone disappeared, leaving him alone on the mountaintop. He had to walk a hundred painful miles to get home, his horse having vanished with the rest. La Signora was said to wear an elegant dress, fashioned of gold, which sounds like inappropriate attire for the Virgin.

22. Richard Bovet, *Pandaemonium*. A 1951 edition is available from The Hand and Flower Press, Aldington, Kent. I have made use of that edition, which has an introduction and notes by Summers.

Bovet (born c. 1641, death date unknown) attended Wadham College, Oxford, and little else is known of his life. There are probably nine existing copies of the 1684 edition of *Pandaemonium*, two of which were to be found in 1930 at the Newbury Library (Chicago) and the Library of Harvard University. Of Bovet's poetic works, even more rare, Harvard and Yale have copies. Montague Summers has called *Pandaemonium* "without question one of the most extraordinary works in the immense library of occult research." That seems a gross overvaluation.

23. *Pandaemonium*, pp. 132, 133.

CHAPTER 3

1. Saint Basil (c. 329-379): A Father of the Church. Like some others of the early Christian leaders, he was a student of the (pagan) Greek philosophers. Basil practiced law for a time at Caesarea, his native city, and then founded the monastic (Basilian) society which perpetuated his name. He is often referred to as Basil the Great.

2. Jerome Cardan (c. 1501-1576): A scholar whose interests ranged far and wide, he was equally at home in the scientific and the occult realms. He is the source of a great number of anecdotes about the relations of humans with demons and about wonders generally. Cardan was born at Pavia and died at Rome.

3. Sprenger and Kramer, *Malleus Maleficarum,* Pushkin Press, London, 1951—a book so celebrated it were an impudence to offer a summary. All quotes from the *Malleus Maleficarum* are from the 1951 edition, hereafter referred to as *Malleus.* The translation is by Summers, who has also contributed an introduction, bibliography, and notes.

4. *Malleus,* p. 26.

5. See, for example, his discussion in *The History of Witchcraft,* pp. 95-98.

CHAPTER 4

1. Ulrich Molitor (died c. 1492): A doctor of Roman and Canon Law and professor of law at the University of Constance. He was one of the earliest writers on witchcraft. Though extremely superstitious and gullible, Molitor is regarded as a moderate by comparison to most demonologists.

2. *Malleus,* p. 27.

3. Boguet, *An Examen of Witches,* writes: "We know that there are many monsters born in the sea from the union of two fishes of different species; and that some are even found which resemble men, which are said by some naturalists and doctors to be procreated from the semen of a dead man . . ." Speaking specifically of the Merman, he adds (p. 38): "As for the Merman, it is difficult to believe that he is generated from the semen of a dead man, or that the corpse of a dead man is able to secrete semen competent for procreation. There can be no doubt that the Merman is generated

of two fishes, and that Nature, which delights in variety, gives him the form of a man in the upper parts: in the same way on land she has brought animals which resemble man, such as the monkey, and the Brazilian beast called the sloth, which is about the size of a fox, and is like a woman about the face and hair, except for its much misshapen muzzle."

4. Martin of Arles: Author of the *Tractatus de Superstitionibus* (1517). He was a professor of theology and canon of Pampeluna.

5. *Demonolatry*, p. 12.

6. *Demonolatry*, pp. 12, 13.

7. Allen Edwards, *The Jewel in the Lotus*, Julian Press, New York, 1959, p. 105.

8. For a very full biographical sketch of Sinistrari see the introduction to his *Demoniality* in this volume.

9. Ludovico Maria Sinistrari, *Demoniality*, Isidore Liseux, Paris, 1879, p. 211. All quotes in this book are from the Liseux edition just cited. This being the case, they may differ somewhat from the same passages found in the Summers translation of *Demoniality* reproduced in full in this volume (Appendix B).

I have chosen to reproduce the Summers "translation"—it might be more appropriately said that Summers has *edited* the translation by Liseux—for the reason that it is generally superior if not so in every detail. Also, Summers has added clarifying passages and data, and his introduction and notes are, as always, excellent.

Of my having chosen to include *Demoniality*, rather than some other demonological work, it will certainly be pointed out that the incubus as understood by Sinistrari is atypical, and that the Reverend Father of Ameno wobbles erratically between his own and the traditionalist views. There is no gainsaying these points, but it should be inquired whether equally strong objections might not be raised against any other works of suitable length that might have been chosen. Since mine is primarily a study of the sexual aspects of witchcraft, and still more particularly of the intercourse with demons, it seemed necessary to find a work relevant mainly to my subject. I am not displeased with the selection and believe that *Demoniality's* inclusion adds much to this volume.

10. *Demoniality*, p. 57.

11. *Ibid.*, p. 59.

12. *Ibid.*, p. 69.

13. Ludovico Maria Sinistrari, *Peccatum Mutum: The Secret Sin*, Collection Le Ballet de Muses, New York, 1958.

14. He writes (*Peccatum Mutum*, N. 19): "Thus some women,

who are provided with this kind of (enlarged) clitoris, run after other women, and especially girls. Plenty of them enter even into males, as Seneca says . . . I have it from the lips of a very trust-worthy Confessor, that while he was hearing, a case cropped up, in which a certain noble lady, being exceedingly fond of a lad, used to keep him at her house for going to bed with her, and she had carnal knowledge of him from behind and was violently in love with him."

It is worth noting that De Sade also spoke of this kind of buggery, while it was said to be common among the Romans.

Sinistrari advises that both participants in such a union should be burned. However, if the lad should be under eighteen years, it may suffice to confine him in a gaol, where he is to be scourged; "or he should be dragged for a few moments through a blazing fire."

CHAPTER 5

1. Cf. Dion Fortune, *Psychic Self-Defence*, Aquarian Press, London, 1957, p. 79: "At the moment of sexual union a psychic vortex is formed resembling a waterspout, a funnel-shaped swirling that towers up into other dimensions. As body after body engages, the vortex goes up the planes. In all cases the physical, etheric and astral bodies are involved; the vortex therefore always reaches as far as the astral plane; a soul upon the astral plane may be drawn into this vortex if it is ripe for incarnation, and thus enter the sphere of the parents. If the vortex extends higher than the astral plane, souls of a different type may enter this sphere, but such extension is rare, and therefore it is said that man is born of desire, for few are born of anything else."

2. Cf. *Materials*, p. 15. Also see Langton's discussion (*Essentials of Demonology*) of "Teaching of Jewish Apocryphal and Apocalyptic Literature."

3. Bellarmin, Suarez, Maluenda: See the biographical sketches in Summers' notes to *Demoniality* at the end of this volume (Appendix B).

4. Cf. *Encyclopaedia Britannica*: article on the Anti-Christ.

5. *Demoniality*, p. 55.

6. *Malleus*, p. 167.

7. The story may first have been told by Lycosthenes. Lea (*Materials*, pp. 632, 633) gives that version and notes that the young woman's mother was burnt after being strangled for her part in the deception, while the girl herself had her cheeks pierced with a hot

iron and was imprisoned for life. Among the physicians who examined Margaret and were deceived were the chief physician of Tuebingen and the personal physicians of Charles V and King Ferdinand.

8. He was branded a damnable sorcerer by later writers—probably because he opposed some of the more spectacular excesses of the witch-burners.

9. See Summers' note on Vallesius in the notes to Appendix B.

CHAPTER 6

1. William of Auvergne, also called William of Paris (died 1249): William was bishop of Paris and a famous theologian and philosopher. His works, however, were not published until long after his death (in Nuremberg, around 1500).

2. Boguet (*Examen of Witches*, p. 65) speculates about the view, often expressed, that devils are hair fetishists, or at least are much stimulated by long and/or beautiful feminine hair:

"But I have often marvelled at one thing which Satan does to witches when they assemble to produce hail:—he requires them to give him of their hair. I do not know whether he may be amorous of women's hair; but I may say that there are Theologians who have maintained that the bad angels are amorous of women's hair, and the Suffragan of Trèves even says that the Incubus devils attach themselves chiefly to women who have beautiful hair; and it is contended that St. Paul had this in mind when he wrote to the Corinthians that woman should go with her head covered because of the Angels."

3. Michael Psellus (c. 1018-1079): Professor of Philosophy at Constantinople and a prolific author on many subjects. He retired for a time to a monastery but found the life there distasteful and returned to the world. His character is described in very antagonistic terms by some writers.

4. *Demoniality*, p. 29.

5. *Ibid.*, pp. 31, 33. (Page 32 is Latin text facing English translation.)

6. *Demonolatry*, p. 11.

7. *Examen of Witches*, p. 40.

8. *Ibid.*, p. 29.

9. *Ibid.*, p. 30.

CHAPTER 7

1. *Malleus*, p. 113.

2. Giovanni Papini, *The Devil*, Eyre & Spottiswoode, London, 1955, p. 113. Papini gives an entertaining account of the writers, painters, and musicians who are particularly demonic, or who have been so regarded.

3. R. H. Robbins (*The Encyclopedia of Witchcraft and Demonology*, Crown, New York, 1959) reproduces (p. 464) the title page of Klein's dissertation, which dealt with the possibility of offspring resulting from the unions of witches with demons. A great many monstrous births are mentioned.

4. *Examen of Witches,* p. 156.

5. *Ibid.,* pp. 234, 235.

6. Demonologists were fond of the words of Seneca (*Hippolytus*): "The breed shows its descent; Degenerate blood reverts to its first type."

7. Guazzo: See Summers' biographical note at the end of this volume.

8. *Demonolatry,* p. 166.

9. Jean Bodin (1530-90): Celebrated jurisconsult and leading member of the Parlement de Paris, called by Montaigne the highest literary genius of his time. On the other hand, Bishop Francis Hutchinson called him "a pure sot." Despite these (possibly) conflicting estimates as to his worth, there is no doubt that Bodin was an impressively learned man. His *Demonomania* was only one of a dozen books authored by him and he was a professor of law at the University of Toulouse. Bodin was bloodthirsty even for a witch trial judge, scarcely allowed for the possibility that any accused person might be innocent, and did not hesitate to have children and invalids put to the torture. Robbins remarks that Bodin was one of the first to attempt a legal definition of a witch: "One who knowing God's law tries to bring about some act through an agreement with the Devil."

10. See Summers' biographical note at the end of this volume.

11. *Examen of Witches,* p. 57.

12. Catullus says: "Of son by mother is a witch conceived, If the foul Persian creed may be believed."

13. Jules Michelet, *Satanism and Witchcraft*, Walden, New York,

1939, gives a lengthy narration of the Gaufridi case. There are many other accounts readily available also.

14. Bernardo da Como (died 1510): Author of *De Strigiis* (written shortly before his death, published in 1566). In 1505 he was inquisitor of Como.

15. Paolo Mantegazza, *The Sexual Relations of Mankind*, Eugenics, New York, 1935, p. 96.

16. This quote is given by Gaston Dubois-Desaulle in his *Bestiality* (Panurge Press, New York, 1933, pp. 63, 64). There is more of it and it is surely worth reproducing in full. The women are described as "Dancing indecently, feasting ardently, coupling diabolically, sodomizing execrably, blaspheming scandalously, revenging insidiously, pursuing all horrible, filthy, and brutally unnatural desires, preciously guarding toads, vipers, lizards, and all sorts of poisons, loving a violently stinking goat, caressing him amorously, becoming intimate and coupling with him horribly and impudently: such were the infamies that they confessed."

17. *Demonolatry*, p. 72.

18. John Fian (burned at Edinburgh, 1591): His reputation as a wizard would seem to have been quite unearned. Linton described him as "a schoolmaster of Saltpans with no great idea to support him," and doubtless that was close to the mark.

Fian had the misfortune to be one of the seventy North Berwick witches. The trial was Scotland's most famous, and Fian was its star victim. The tortures to which he was subjected, and which are recited at length by Robbins, make chilling reading.

The whole case seems to have grown out of a baseless accusation by a malicious serving wench, Gilly Duncan, who gradually spun out a tale that included a plot against the life of the King. She named Fian as ringleader.

During the trial, and especially following his execution, fantastic stories were told about Fian's magical powers and deeds (and about the witchcraft of Agnes Sampson, another of those tried and executed). Many later writers accepted all of these phantasies and gossip as factual, or pretended to.

19. *Demoniality*, pp. 33, 35.

20. *Ibid.*, pp. 205, 207.

CHAPTER 8

1. *On the Nightmare,* p. 176.
2. Surely the idea that the Anti-Christ was to be born as the result of the union of a demon, or of the Devil, with a witch, carries with it the implication of diabolic fertility.

CHAPTER 9

1. Some writers say that *extispicium* requires the entrails of boys —that is, females and adult males will not do; but this seems a mere homosexual (Pedophilic) prejudice. There are numerous forms of divination requiring human sacrifice. Julian the Apostate is said to have employed a method requiring that the victim's throat be cut. This brings to mind the nuns of Cymbri, who slit the throats of human victims and then foretold the future by the dripping blood. Others made predictions from blood collected in cauldrons, and into which they peered as into magic mirrors. There is a kind of parthenomancy in which the womb of a freshly murdered virgin is torn out (while a more kindly parthenomancy calls only for probing the [erstwhile] virginal vagina with the turgid organ of some sorcerer). And one should not fail to recommend investigation of the methods of those celebrated monsters Gilles de Rais, Countess Elizabeth Báthory and Queen Zingua of Angola, whose divinations also called for bloody homicides.
2. *Malleus,* p. 66. Some demonological works have whole chapters on the crimes of midwives and how to prevent them.
3. *Demonolatry,* pp. 99, 100.

CHAPTER 10

1. Havelock Ellis, *Studies in the Psychology of Sex,* Random House, New York, 1936, Vol. II, Part II, p. 384.
2. *Examen of Witches,* p. 60.

CHAPTER 11

1. Emile Laurent and Paul Nagour, *Magica Sexualis,* Falstaff Press, New York, 1934, p. 43, quote this passage.
2. *Malleus,* p. 114.
3. For the doctorate *utriusque Juris.* The dissertation is titled *De Fallacibus Indiciis Magiae.*
4. Father Adam Tanner, S.J. The work was published at Cologne in 1629. Despite the skepticism of the view recorded in this paragraph, Tanner was a firm believer in witchcraft. As a means of combating its spread, he proposed that children receive sound training in their homes and that adults go to church and stop swearing, blaspheming, and telling dirty stories.

CHAPTER 12

1. Saint Hilary (c. 291-371): He was born at Tabatha and died on the island of Cyprus. Most of what is known of his life is recorded in the "Life of Saint Hilary" written by Saint Jerome.
2. Saint Gregory (c. 540-604): A Father of the Church who became Pope Gregory I. He is also called Gregory the Great. Born a Roman, he embarked upon a career as a public official but abandoned it to enter a monastery. He became pope in 590.
3. Boguet (p. 28) is voicing a common view when he suggests that such oracles were demons: "But it is far more difficult to believe that Satan can speak through the shameful parts of a woman, or when the person's mouth is shut, or when the tongue is thrust six inches out of the mouth; or that he can speak when he has no body at all, or one formed only of air. Yet this is known to happen; for we read that she who gave answer in the Delphic Oracle spoke through the lower and shameful parts, as did also a woman in Rhodige, an Italian town mentioned by Rhodiginus in his disquisitions." (See Summers' biographical note on Rhodiginus at the back of this volume.)
4. According to a frequently encountered estimate, there are 6,666 legions, each formed of 6,666 devils, for a total of 44,435,556. But added to this total, in addition to Satan (or Beelzebub), may be another 150 or so kings, dukes, counts, presidents, knights, etc. Some magicians hold that it is necessary to call every devil by name

if a magical operation is to be successful, which could account for the high rate of failures in magical operations.

5. It is, according to Robbins, the same printed by Maximilian van Eynatten in 1619.

6. *Magica Sexualis*, p. 82.

7. So, too, the nuns of the convent of Mont de Hesse in Germany. They complained of being possessed and assaulted by demons, but an investigator found dogs lolling wantonly on the beds of those who said they had been assailed, "shamelessly awaiting" the coming to bed of their human mistresses.

8. Chapman Cohen, *Religion and Sex*, Foulis, London, 1919, gives many such cases.

CHAPTER 13

1. Lea (*Materials*, p. 419), after Godelmann (*De Magis*), tells the story of a monk who approached Luther to ask him about some papal errors. Luther, however, recognized his caller as the Devil in disguise—a recognition requiring no supernatural powers of discernment, since the supposed monk's hands were like bird talons. The Devil, enraged at being caught in His deception, "departed muttering, letting a great fart which filled the room with stench for days and flinging the inkstand behind the stove." (This last part would seem to be the reverse of the famous incident of Luther's throwing an inkstand at the Devil.)

Jones (*On the Nightmare*, p. 176) has the fart at the other end: "Even many of the devices employed to ward off the Devil's assaults originate in infantile and sexual symbolism. A renowned one, often effective when all else failed, was to expose's one's buttocks and expel flatus at him; no less a person than Martin Luther had recourse to it." Jones has taken his version from Freimark (*Okkultismus und Sexualitaet*) and from J. G. Bourke (*Scatologic Rites of All Nations*), whose sources I have not checked.

It may be that we should think of Luther and the Devil as batting farts and inkstands back and forth like tennis balls.

2. *Magica Sexualis*, p. 39.

3. Saint Caesarius (c. 1170-1240): Often referred to as Caesar von Heisterbach. He was a monk of the Cistercian monastery of Heisterbach, near Bonn, and was prior of Heisterbach at his death. Caesarius authored the *Dialogus magnus visionum atque miraculorum*, which was Germany's "best-seller" of its time.

4. See the note on Saint Bernard in Notes to Appendix B.

5. Author of the *Bonum Universale*, c. 1258.

6. I am unable to locate my source for this story, but it seems to me that it appeared in the *Occult Review*, where Franz Hartmann published many such tales.

CHAPTER 14

1. It will be recalled that when Saint Jerome (c. 340-420) returned to the Holy Land in 385, after sojourning in Rome and Gaul, he was accompanied by the widow Paula and her daughter Eustochium. Jerome was the advisor of both, counseling Paula on the salvation of her soul, and Eustochium on the preservation of her virginity. Jerome seems to have been about as friendly to Eros as was Saint Paul.

2. *Demoniality*, p. 241.

3. Peter Binsfeld (c. 1540-1603): One of the more important writers on witchcraft. His *Tractatus de Confessionibus Maleficorum* was first published at Trèves in 1589 and went into many subsequent editions.

4. Daniel Defoe, *The Political History of the Devil*, London, Printed for T. Warner, at the *Black Boy* in *Pater-noster Row*, 1726, pp. 360, 361. The book does not have Defoe listed as author. On the title page is the following little poem, suggestive of the somewhat tongue-in-check attitude found throughout the book:

Bad as he is, the Devil may be abus'd,
Be falsly charg'd, and causelesly accus'd,
When Men, unwilling to be blam'd alone,
Shift off those Crimes on Him which are their Own.

CHAPTER 15

1. *Malleus*, p. 164.

2. De Lancre saw with his own eyes, while at Rome, a girl changed into a boy by the Devil.

3. In the eighteenth century the abbè Beccarelli, a false messiah who claimed to be able to command the services of the Holy Ghost, is said to have possessed such a drug and to have dispensed it to his followers. The drug was an aphrodisiac, and while physical

sex was not changed, men temporarily believed themselves transformed into women, and women thought themselves transformed into men. Their fornications occurred, as it were, in reverse. The reader will find some interesting data along these lines in my account of my own researches with mescaline, set forth at length in *Forbidden Sexual Behavior and Morality*, Julian Press, New York, 1962.

4. Saint Equitius was bishop of Matelica near the end of the fifth century.

5. *Malleus*, p. 93. There was also the case of Helias, a monk, who founded a monastery where he gave pious instruction to thirty women. Daily, the temptations of the flesh grew more severe, until at last he had to flee his own monastery and take refuge in a hermitage. There, he called upon God to either take his life or deliver him from his intolerable temptation.

That evening Helias had a dream. Three angels came to him and inquired if he would return to the monastery and the women if he were no longer tempted. Helias said that he would, and "They then exacted an oath to that effect from him, and made him an eunuch. For one seemed to hold his hands, another his feet, and the third to cut out his testicles with a knife; though this was not really so, but only seemed to be." (*Malleus*, p. 94).

This is a completely undisguised castration phantasy, lacking even the minimum of masking found in the previously mentioned ones, and is of a type encountered often enough among schizophrenics and some other psychotics and neurotics.

6. Cf. *Malleus*, p. 55.

7. The *Malleus*, Part I, Question IX, has a full discussion of disappearing penes.

8. *Demonolatry*, p. 112.

9. *Examen of Witches*, p. 90.

10. "City of the Lion," in the August, 1961, issue, p. 124.

CHAPTER 16

1. Manichees or Manichaeans: The Manichaean religion was founded by Mani in the third century and endured for more than one thousand years. From the tenth or eleventh century on there were many offshoot or derivative groups. Mani, a Persian, was crucified and his body flayed by Bahram I, King of Persia. Both the popes of Rome and the emperors of Constantinople savagely persecuted

the Manichaeans. Saint Augustine, who for a time embraced Mani's religion, went on to become its great antagonist in his time.

2. Cf. W. Sanger, *The History of Prostitution*, Eugenics, New York, 1937, p. 106.

3. The Cathars and the Waldenses both derived from the Manichaeans. Summers (*History of Witchcraft*, p. 17) writes: "Manichaeism further split up into an almost infinite number of sects and systems, prominent amongst which were the Cathari, the Aldonistae and Speronistae, the Concorrezenses of Lombardy, the Bagnolenses, the Albigenses, Pauliciani, Patarini, Bogomiles, the Waldenses, Tartarins, Beghards, Pauvres de Lyon."

The Cathars are still in existence today, and *Time* magazine recently reported (April 28, 1961) a resurgence of interest in the Cathar religion, especially in southern France.

4. *Satanism and Witchcraft*, pp. 341, 342.

5. E. and P. Kronhausen, *Pornography and the Law*, Ballantine, New York, 1959. See Part III: The Psychology of Pornography.

CHAPTER 17

1. Cf. *Magica Sexualis*, pp. 65, 66.

2. *On the Nightmare*, p. 207.

3. R. E. L. Masters, *Forbidden Sexual Behavior and Morality*, Julian Press, New York, 1962, pp. 328, 329 and pp. 349-351.

4. See *Magica Sexualis*, p. 69. Laurent and Nagour add: "Since the wife of the local executioner was suffering from frenzy and insomnia he had her rubbed with this green salve. She slept for thirty-six hours and would have continued sleeping for a much longer period if she had not been aroused by very drastic measures, cupping-glasses among them. She complained bitterly at awakening for she declared she had been torn away from the arms of a handsome young man."

5. A hazard faced by physicians and dentists is that of false but sincere accusations of rape made by patients emerging from anesthesia. Such rape phantasies are common enough with nitrous oxide that a dentist will usually not administer it unless he has an assistant standing by. The same phantasies sometimes occur with hypnotic subjects, and many hypnotists have been falsely accused of rape on that account.

6. *Satanism and Witchcraft*, p. 182.

7. *Forbidden Sexual Behavior and Morality*, pp. 327, 328.

8. Cf. *Satanism and Witchcraft*, p. 103: "At the . . . Witches' Sabbaths . . . the *Witches' herb*, infused in hydromel, beer, as well as in cider and perry, the strong drinks of the West, set the crowd dancing—but in wanton, luxurious measures, showing no trace of epileptic violence."

CHAPTER 18

1. Pierre Bayle (1647-1706): His discussions of witchcraft and sorcery are to be found in his *Réponse aux Questions d'un Provincial*, published in 1703.

2. Harold Palmer, *Psychopathic Personalities*, Philosophical Library, New York, 1957. His entire discussion of hysteria is well worth the reading.

3. *Demoniality*, pp. 231, 233.

4. *Magica Sexualis*, pp. 46, 47.

5. *Ibid.*, p. 45. The authors take note too of cases of spontaneous erotic sensation and orgasm in "nervous" women, and remark that "the feeling of coition is a frequent symptom of certain nervous diseases, especially incipient spinal diseases" (p. 44).

6. *On the Nightmare*, p. 87.

7. J. M. Bramwell, *Hypnotism*, Julian Press, New York, 1956, p. 297, says that Charcot "argued that hypnotism and hysteria were identical, because in both the urine presented similar characteristics." Moll is said to have responded that this was no wonder, seeing as how all of Charcot's hypnotic subjects were hysterics. The anecdote is an amusing one, but surely needs qualifying. And in any case, the point that many or all hypnotic phenomena may appear in hysteria cases should not be regarded as challenged.

8. Otto Snell (*Hexenprozess und Geistesstoerung*, Munich, 1891) mentions hysterical women who themselves stick needles into their breasts, genitals, and other body parts. He finds analgesia exceedingly commonplace in hysterics, and notes that even severe wounds may be inflicted with no pain being felt either at the time or subsequently. He gives a case reported by Jolly of an hysterical female who "in the excitement of an hallucination" opened an oven door, scooped out a handful of live coals, and applied them to her genitals. This terminated the hallucination, but she felt no pain either then or later. Lea, *Materials*, discusses Snell's book at the beginning of Vol. III.

9. Paramhansa Yogananda, who died in 1952, speaks (*Autobi-*

ography of a Yogi, Los Angeles, 1956) of first-hand experience of such phenomena. He tells of one Gandha Baba who produced for him upon request any scent Yogananda cared to name. Madame Blavatsky could produce not only the scents of flowers, but the flowers as well; but she was often caught *flagrante delicto* at sleight of hand and other skullduggery. Summers (*The History of Witchcraft*) discusses the odors associated with the various saints and advises that the very pus of Saint John of the Cross gave forth a strong scent of lilies. The "odour of sanctity," he remarks, "is more than a mere phrase." Some of these saints were also able to smell sinners, even when no one else could. Thus, "Saint Bridget of Sweden was wellnigh suffocated by the fetor of a notorious sinner who addressed her," and "Saint Lutgarde, a Cistercian nun, on meeting a vicious reprobate perceived a decaying smell of leprosy and disease" (p. 45). There are numerous examples.

10. Jean de Meung (c. 1240-1305): The famous poet who continued and completed the *Roman de la Rose* (begun by Guillaume de Lorris). De Meung's contribution satirizes monastic orders, celibacy, marriage, the wiles of women, etc.

CHAPTER 19

1. *Malleus*, p. 24.

2. *Ibid.*, p. 58. Apparently Kramer and Sprenger did not think much of mortal chances of resisting the urges of the secret parts, since those organs are described as a place where the fight is continuous and the victory rare.

NOTES TO APPENDIX B

Demoniality

1. JUAN CARAMUEL. Juan Caramuel y Lobkowitz, the famous Spanish theologian, was born at Madrid 23 May 1606; and died at Vigevano, 8 September, 1682. At an early age he joined the Cistercian Order, and having already been long famous for his learning, in 1638 he was created a Doctor of Theology by the University of Louvain. He filled in turn the dignities of Abbot of Melrose (Scotland), Abbot-Superior to the Benedictines of Vienna, and Grand-vicar to the Archbishop of Prague. He was elected Bishop of Konigratz, then Archbishop of Otranto, and at his death was Bishop of Vigevano.

His knowledge was encyclopaedic, and, according to Paquot

(*Memoires pour servir l'histoire litteraire des dix-sept provinces des pays-Bas*, Louvain, 1765-70, II., 175), he published no less than 262 works which seem to deal with all the arts and sciences. Especially celebrated in his *Theologia moralis ad prima atque clarissima principia reducta*, Louvain, 1643, a work which, although often spoken against and misunderstood, is of lasting value. S. Alphonsus Liguori has called Caramuel "the Prince of the Laxists."

2. CAJETAN. Tomaso de Vio Gaetani, Dominican Cardinal, philosopher, theologian, and exegete; was born 20 February, 1469, at Gaeta; and died 9 August, 1534, at Rome. His career was most notable, and he has been described as small in bodily stature but gigantic in intellect. It is said that he could quote from memory almost the entire Summa, and by Pope Clement VII. he was called "the Lamp of the Church." In Theology Cajetan is regarded as one of the foremost defenders and exponents of the Thomistic school. His commentaries on the *Summa Theologica*, the first in that extensive field, begun in 1507 and finished 1522, are his greatest work, and they were immediately recognised to be a classic in Scholastic literature. There are very many editions of the commentaries, sometimes including the text of the *Summa*, and sometimes without it. It is noteworthy, however, that Leo XIII. ordered these commentaries to be incorporated with the text of the *Summa* in the official Leonine edition of the works of S. Thomas, the first volume of which appeared at Rome in 1882.

3. SILVESTER. Francesco Silvester, a famous Dominican theologian, was born at Ferrara about 1474, and died at Rennes 19 September, 1526. He filled the highest offices in his order, being appointed Vicar-general by Clement VII., and on 3 June, 1525, in the general chapter held at Rome, he was elected Master-general. He wrote many theological works of great value, and he is especially praised for the clearness and elegance of his style.

4. BONACINA. Martino Bonacina, was an Oblate of S. Ambrose and S. Charles. He is regarded as one of the leading moral theologians of his age, and his works have several times been republished. He died suddenly in 1631, whilst on his way to fill the position of Nuncio of Urban VIII. at the court of the Emperor Ferdinand II. In Theology Bonacina is a Probabilist.

5. VINCENZO FILLIUCCI. Vincenzo Filliucci, S.J., was born at Siena in 1566, and died at Rome 5 April, 1622. He entered the Society of Jesus at the age of eighteen, and after a brilliant career he was summoned to Rome to fill the chair of Moral Theology in the Roman College, where he taught for ten years with great distinction. His

writings on moral theology have frequently been reprinted in various countries, and his authority is justly regarded as ranking very high. He was violently attacked by the Jansenists, and Pascal in his *Lettres Provinciales* makes great capital out of garbled quotations from the many works of this eminent author.

6. ALEXANDER VII. Twenty-eight propositions derived from the works of the most extreme Laxists were condemned by Alexander VII. 24 September, 1665. Of these the twenty-fourth proposition is as follows:—"Mollities, Sodomia, Bestialitas sunt peccata eiusdem speciei infimae; ideoque sufficit in confessione dicere se procurasse pollutionem." ("Masturbation, Sodomy, Bestiality, are sins of the same species; and therefore it is sufficient for a penitent to say in confession that he has committed self-abuse.") For these sins belong to separate species.

7. GABRIEL VASQUEZ. Gabriel Vasquez, S.J., the famous theologian, was born at Villaescusa de Haro, near Belmonte, Cuenca, in 1549 or 1551; and died at Alcala, 23 September, 1604. His career was most distinguished, and for six years he lectured on moral theology at Rome. Benedict XIV. calls him "the Luminary of Theology." His views on Grace and the Sacrifice of the Mass are famous. In particular he maintained very sound opinions on the Sacrament of Matrimony. Several of his discussions, however, have been disputed, and not without reason. Uir fuit acerrimo ingenio.

8. HENRIQUEZ. Enrique Henriquez, a noted Jesuit Theologian, born 1536; died 1608. His chief work is *Theologiae Moralis Summa*, published at Salamanca, 1591. S. Alphonsus highly esteems the authority of Henriquez on moral questions. The second work of Henriquez, *De Pontificis Romani Claue*, libri IV., Salamanca, 1593, is excesssively rare, as it was severely censured, and nearly all the copies burned.

9. MEDINA. Bartholomew Medina, a Dominican theologian, was born at Medina 1527, and died at Salamanca 1581. Practically his whole life was devoted to teaching theology at this latter town. He is usually called the "Father of Probabilism." But it seems more likely that he was merely formulating the teaching on this point when he wrote: "It seems to me that if an opinion is probable, it may be followed, even though the opposite opinion be more probable" (I-II., quest. 19, art. 6).

10. EPISCOPAL CAPITULARIES. The Capitularies or Capitula of Bishops were compilations of Ecclesiastical law, a summary of previous legislation epitomized for the clergy and people. Some capitularies were applicable to many dioceses, others seem to have been

intended for one diocese alone. Among the most famous Capitularies are the capitula of S. Martin, Metropolitan of Braga (571-80); the capitula of S. Boniface (died 754); the *Confessionale* and *Poenitentiale* of Ecgberht, Archbishop of York (735-51); for separate dioceses we have a very great number of capitularies, especially those of Hincmar, Archbishop of Reims (845-82). The capitularies enjoyed great authority throughout the earlier Middle Ages.

The Council of Ancyra was held in 314, and its Canons form a very important document in the early history of the Sacrament of Penance. They were adopted by many canonists and are maintained by Regino of Prüm. Pope S. Damasus I. reigned from 366 to 11 December, 384. Under him various Roman synods were held, and the papal decretals greatly increased in prestige.

11. LORINUS OF AVIGNON, S.J., born 1559, is famous for his vast commentaries upon the Bible.

12. FRANCESCO MARIA GUAZZO. Francesco Maria Guazzo, a member of the congregation of S. Ambrose ad Nemus, a local Milanese order, and a writer of extraordinary learning, published his encyclopaedic *Compendium Maleficarum* at Milan 1608, second edition 1626. The reader may refer to *The History of Witchcraft* (1926) by the present editor for an account of, and quotations from, Guazzo's work. He is certainly one of the most valuable of the earlier writers.

13. PAUL GRILLAND. The author of a valuable treatise, *De Sortilegiis*, published at Lyons in 1533.

14. NICOLAS REMY (Remigius). Born 1554, died at Nancy 1600. A magistrate of Lorraine, the "Torquemada lorrain," and Procureur-general under Duke Henri II. An all-important figure in the witch trials of that period. He is the author of a well-known work, *Daemonolatriae libri tres*, Lyons. 4to, 1595.

15. S. PETER DAMIAN. Cardinal-bishop of Ostia, Doctor of the Church, born 1007; died at Faenza 21 February, 1072.

16. ALFONSO À CASTRO. A Franciscan theologian, confessor to Charles V. and Phillip II; was born in 1495 at Zamora, Leon, Spain; and died at Brussels 11 February, 1558. Among his chief works are *Aduersus omnes haereses*, first edition Cologne, 1539; and *De Iusta Haereticorum punitione*, Salamanca 1547.

17. PIERRE CRESPET. A monk of the Celestine order, a mystical and ascetic writer, the author of *Deux livres da la haine de Satan et des malins esprits contre l'homme*, Paris, 1590.

18. BARTOLOMEO SPINA. A Dominican theologian, Master of the Sacred Palace under Paul III. He was born at Pisa about 1475, and died at Rome in 1546. Probably his most famous work is the *Tracta-*

tus de Strigibus et Lamiis, Venice, 1523, which has been often reprinted.

19. GIOVANNI LORENZO ANANIA. The author of *De Natura daemonum: libri iv.,* Venice, 1581. 8vo.

20. THE CROWN (Coroncina; chaplet). The rosary was delivered by Our Lady to S. Dominic, and is the great devotion of the Dominican order. See the Bull of S. Pius V., *Consueuerunt,* 17 September, 1569; also the *Vida di Santo Domingo* (Madrid, 1721) by Blessed Francisco de Possadas, O.P.

21. S. Francis girded himself with a rough rope in memory of the bonds wherewith Christ was bound during His passion, and a white girdle with three knots has since formed part of the Franciscan habit. Sixtus IV., by his Bull, *Exsupernae dispositionis,* erected the archconfraternity of the cord of S. Francis in the basilica of the Sacro Convento at Assisi, enriching it with many indulgences, favours which have been confirmed by pontiff after pontiff. Archconfraternities are erected not only in Franciscan, but in many other churches and aggregated to the centre at Assisi.

The Archconfraternity of Our Lady of Consolation, or of the Black Leathern Belt of S. Monica, S. Augustine and S. Nicolas of Tolentino, took its rise from a vision of S. Monica, who received a black leathern belt from Our Lady. S. Augustine, S. Ambrose, and S. Simplicianus all wore such a girdle, which forms a distinctive feature of the dress of Augustinian Eremites. After the canonization of S. Nicolas of Tolentino it came into general use as an article of devotion, and Eugenius IV., in 1439, erected the above Archconfraternity. A Bull of Gregory XIII., *Ad ea* (15 July, 1575) confirmed this and added various privileges and indulgences. The Archconfraternity is erected in Augustinian sanctuaries, from the General of which Order leave must be obtained for its extension to other churches.

The Scapular of Our Lady of Mount Carmel is the especial devotion of the Carmelite Order. The Blessed Virgin appeared to S. Simon Stock at Cambridge on Sunday, 16 July, 1251, and presenting him with the brown scapular, made him a particular promise, which is wont to be summed up in the words, "Whoever wears the scapular until death will be preserved from hell, and I will deliver him from Purgatory on the Saturday after his death." This promise was confirmed by the Bull *Sacratissimo uti Culmine* of John XXII., 3 March, 1322, which is known as the Sabbatine Privilege. There are many other scapulars, such as the scapular of the Most Blessed Trinity; of Our Lady of Ransom; of the Mother of Good Counsel; of the Immaculate Heart of Mary; the Black Servite scapular; the Black Passionist scapular; the Blue scapular; the Red scapular; the scapular of S. Joseph; the scapular of S. Michael; of S. Benedict, and very many more.

22. BLACK BOOK. These books or rolls were in charge of the chief officers of a district. They were guarded with the utmost care, since, as they contained the damning evidence of a full list of the witches belonging to any province, county, or district, their security was a matter of life or death. The signing of such a book is continually referred to in the New England Trials at the end of the seventeenth century. There is a somewhat vague story, no dates being given, that a Devil's book (a list of local witches) was carried off by a certain Mr. Williamson, who stole it whilst the witches were dancing on Minchmoore, Peebles. However, they at once gave chase to him and he was glad to abandon it and escape with his life.

This roll of witches must not be confused with books of charms and spells, nor with what we may term the Devil's Missal, which is used by Satanists in their blasphemous rites.

23. COELIUS RHODIGINUS. Lodovico Ricchieri, the famous Italian philologist, surnamed Rhodiginus from Rovigo (*Rhodigium*), where he was born about 1450, and where he died in 1525. His *Antiquarum lectionum, lib. xvi.*, was published at Venice, folio, 1516; Paris, folio, 1517. A more complete edition, comprising thirty books, was issued under the care of Camillo Ricchieri and Goretti at Bale, folio, 1550. I have used the folio Geneva edition of 1620, where the story to which Sinistrari refers will be found in column 1614. It arises from the discussion: *Quae sit adagii ratio, Serpentem foues, & te serpens. Inibi de lamiis mirum.* Menippus Lycius, a youth of twenty-five, dwelt at Corinth, in a suburb of which city the Lamia was supposed to reside.

The story is originally from Philostratus, *Uita Apollonii*, IV. Keats's exquisite poem *Lamia*, written in 1819, and published with *Isabella, The Eve of S. Agnes, and other Poems* in 1820, is founded upon this legend as related by Burton, *The Anatomy of Melancholy*, Part III., Sect. 2, Memb. 1, Sub-s. 1.

"Philostratus in his fourth book, *de vita Apollonii*, hath a memorable instance in this kind, which I may not omit, of one Menippus Lycius, a young man twenty-five years of age, that going between Cenchreas and Corinth, met such a phantasm in the habit of a fair gentelwoman, which taking him by the hand, carried him home to her house in the suburbs of Corinth, and told him she was a Phoenician by birth, and if he would tarry with her, 'he should hear her sing and play, and drink such wine as never any drank, and no man should molest him; but she being fair and lovely, would live and die with him, that was fair and lovely to behold.' The young man, a philosopher otherwise staid and discreet, able to moderate his passions, though not this of love, tarried with her awhile to his great content, and at last married her, to whose wedding, amongst other guests, came Apollonius, who, by some probable conjectures, found her out to be a serpent, a lamia, and that all her furniture was like Tantalus's gold described by Homer, no substance, but mere illusions. When she saw herself descried, she wept, and desired Apollonius to be silent, but he would not be moved, and thereupon she, plate, house, and all that was in it, vanished in an instant: many thousands took notice of this fact, for it was done in the midst of Greece."

24. HECTOR BOECE. Chronicler, and one of the founders of Aberdeen University, 1465-1536. The impetus he gave to historical studies at Aberdeen was of lasting effect. His works are highly esteemed.

25. *Scotorum Historiae*, VIII. I have used the first edition, 1526, where this story and other similar adventures may be read, folios cliv.-v. "In Gareotha regione, uico quatuordeum uix passuū millibus ab Aberdonia, adolescēs multa formositate, coram Aberdonēn antistite questus est palam, sese a demone Succuba (vt dicunt) gratissima omniū quę uidisset forma, multo antea menses infestatum eandē occlusis foribus noctu ad si ingredi blanditiis, in sui amplexus cōpellere. Dubia luce abiri sine strepitu poene, nullo se posse modo quū plures attentasset a tāta, actā turpi uesania liberari. Iubet cōtinus optimus episcopus adolescētē, alio se cōferre, & vt christiana religiōe magis laudatis, ieiuniis & oronibus plus solito accōmodaret uim: fore vt piis operibus incēto, uictus cacodemon tādē terga esset daturus. Euenit adolescēti salubre cōsiliū religiose exequuto, paucos post dies vti uenerādus antistes erat pfatus."

26. FOLLETTI. Cf. Burton, *Anatomy of Melancholy*, Part I., Sec. 2, Memb. 1, Sub-s. 2.—"Terrestrial devils are those Lares, Genii, Fauns, Satyrs, Wood-nymphs, Foliots, Fairies, Robin Goodfellows, Trulli &c., which as they are most conversant with men, so they do them most harm . . . some put our fairies into this rank, which have been in former times adored with much superstition, with sweeping their houses, and setting of a pail of clean water, good victuals, and the like, and then they should not be pinched, but find money in their shoes, and be fortunate in their enterprises."

27. PAVIA. The Largo di Santa Croce leads into the Piazza Castello.

28. San Michele, where the Kings were crowned, is one of the

most remarkable churches in North Italy, and it has been described as the most notable monument of Lombard Architecture.

29. PIUS V. Michele Ghisleri, O.P., 1504-1572; elected Pope 7 January, 1566. He was beatified by Clement X. in 1672, and canonised by Clement XI. in 1712. He is closely connected with Pavia, for he founded there the Collegio Ghisleri, in front of which stands his statue in bronze.

30. BLESSED BERNARDINE. Blessed Bernardine of Feltre, Friar minor, 1439-1494. He died at Pavia on 28 September. His body, which lies in the church of S. James, is much venerated. His feast (duplex minus) is kept by the Franciscans on 28 September.

31. BELLARMINE. Blessed Robert Francis Romolo Bellarmine, S.J., the famous theologian, writer and Cardinal, 1542-1621.

32. FRANCISCO SUAREZ. Doctor Eximius, 1548-1617. One of the greatest theologians of the Church.

33. THOMAS MALVENDA. O.P., 1566-1628. He was distinguished for the profundity of his theological and philosophical learning. One of his most famous works is the *De Antichristo*, libri XI., Rome, 1604. A truly profound and noble volume.

34. FRANCISCUS VALESIUS. Franciscus Valesius, a Spanish Doctor of Physic, flourished towards the end of the sixteenth century. He won a great reputation for his translations of, and commentaries upon, the older medical writers.

35. MALVENDA. I have used the first edition of the *De Antichristo*, folio, Rome, 1604. The passages quoted by Sinistrari are from Book II., c. IX. (pp. 77-9), whose rubric is: *Aliquot clarissimi uiri apud Gentiles, quos proditum est ex diis, hoc est ex incubis damoniis genitos.*

36. ROMULUS AND REMUS. Livy, I., 2, writes: "Ui compressa uestalis cum geminum partum edidisset, seu ita rata, seu quia deus auctor culpae honestior erat, Martem incertae stirpis patrem nuncupat."

37. MERLIN. Boece *Scotorum Historiae*, folio 1526, VIII., says: "Constans tum fama erat, Merlinũ incubi, ac nobilis Britãnici sanguinis foeminae cõcubitu, p̄gnatũ, magicis carminibus malos dęmones ad colloquia excire: & ex his quę futura essent cognoscere."

There is an old romance of Merlin: *Sensuyt le p̄mier volume de Merlin. Qui est le premier liure de la Table ronde. Avec plusiers choses moult recreatiue.* P. le Noir, Paris, 1528. Here the demons, alarmed at the number of men who have escaped them since the Birth of Our Lord, hold a council of war and resolve to send to the world one of their company to engender upon some virgin a child.

He shall be their vicegerent upon earth, and (*salua reuerentia*) according to their schemes endeavour to counteract the Redemption. The fiend deputed to this work obtains admittance into the house of a wealthy Briton, and true to his nature slays his host, seducing two of the three daughters. The youngest resists, but whilst in an enchanted sleep is swived by the devil. Witless of what has occurred she confesses to a holy hermit, Blaise, who protects her. She gives birth to Merlin, who is instantly baptized by Blaise, and thus the devil's designs are frustrated. Cf. James Huneker's tale *Antichrist; Visionaries*, 1905.

. One may compare Machiavelli's *Belphegor*, and the Oriental Saga of the angels Harut and Marut, in the commentators on (*Sura*, 11, 96) the Qu'ran. In the Chronicle of Philippe Moustres, Bishop of Tournai, a diabolical origin is attributed to Eleonora of Aquitaine, who espoused Louis-le-Jeune, King of France, and afterwards was wedded to Henry II. of England. J. Brompton (*Hist. Franc.*, XIII., 215) has preserved a similar legend, and in the *Livre de Badouin* (p. 13) Comtesse Jeanne de Flandre is supposed to be a daughter of the evil spirit. See Reiffenberg, Introduction to the *Chronicle of Philippe de Moustres*, p. lxviii.

With regard to Merlin one may consult *Die Sagen von Merlin* . . . by San Marte (A. Schulz), Halle, 8vo, 1853; and *Slavianskaia Skazania o Solomonye i kitrovrase i zapadnya legendy o Morolfe i Merline*. By A. Vesselovsky, S. Petersburg, 1872.

William Rowley's *The Birth of Merlin, or the Childe hath found his Father*, not printed until 1662, and once ascribed to Shakespeare, is a curious medley of farce and romance, awkward, but not wholly destitute of poetry. Herein the Devil appears as Merlin's father. He has got Joan Go-Too't, the Clown's sister, with child, and Merlin is born amid thunder and lightning. But Merlin, rebuking his father, who dubs him "Traitor to hell!" as

> an inferior lustful incubus,
Taking advantage of the wanton Flesh,

encloses him in a rock, and conveys his mother to a secure retreat.

Malvenda's authority is the *Chronica* of John Nauclerus, volumen secundum, generatio xv. "Inuentus est tum adolescens dictus Merlinus, cuius mater confessa est se a spiritu in hominis concepisse, hoc est, per incubum. hic Merlinus Ambrosius est dictus natus ex filia regis Demetae, quae monada erat." The marginal note has "Merlinus ab incubo daemone conceptus," p. 559, folio, Cologne, 1579.

38. MARTIN LUTHER. The story of Luther's alleged generation is

related by Malvenda in c. VI. of his *De Antichristo* with title, *Martinus Lutherus creditus a quibusdam uerus Antichristus.*

"Ex incubo daemonio genitum haud leuibus futilibusque coniecturis deprehensum est a plerisque, vt Coclaeus refert" (p. 71). See the *Historia Ioannis Cochlaei de Actis et Scriptis Martini Lutheri,* Paris, 1565.

Johann Cochlaeus, properly Dobeneck, and named Cochlaeus from his native place, Wendelstein, near Schwabach, was born 1479; and died 11 January, 1552, at Breslau. After a brilliant career as a student and professor of theology, he was ordained at Rome in 1518, and was shortly to make his mark as an active opponent of the Lutheran movement. With indomitable ardour he poured forth pamphlet after pamphlet, and although it is hardly to be expected that everything from his pen has the same value, the bulk of his work is an excellent refutation of the contemporary anarchy and looseness of thought. His editions of ecclesiastical writers, and such historical studies as *Historiae Hussitarum,* XII. *Libri* (1549), are of permanent value, as also is his sound criticism of Luther and the new tenets.

39. BENEDICT PEREIRA. Benedict Pereira, born about 1535 at Ruzafa, near Valencia; died 6 March, 1610, at Rome. He entered the Society of Jesus in 1552, and became famous in Rome for his lectures on scripture. His works are exceptionally lengthy and full. The main difficulties of Genesis are discussed and solved in his *Commentariorum et Disputationum in Genesim tomi quattuor,* Rome, 1591-99.

40. MICHAEL ETTMULLER. This famous German doctor was born at Leipzig, 10 May, 1644, and died 9 March, 1683. He was Professor of Botany, Surgery, and Anatomy at Leipzig, and won universal renown. A compendium of his many medical writings, *Opera omnia in compendium redacta,* was published at London, 8vo, in 1701. He left a son, Ernest Michael Ettmuller (ob. 1732), who although not so distinguished yet honourably carried on the family tradition.

41. MAGNUS ALEXANDER. This pretty pentameter, which is universally quoted as "an old saw" does not appear to have been traced to its original.

42. CORNELIUS À LAPIDE. Cornelis Cornelissen Van Der Steen (Cornelius Cornelii à Lapide), Flemish Jesuit and exegete, was born at Bocholt, 18 December, 1567; died at Rome 12 March, 1637. He wrote very ample commentaries upon Holy Scripture, with the exception of Job and the Psalms. His works have been reprinted again and again, translated into many languages, and are continually referred to by Biblical writers. I have used the Antwerp edition, folio, 1659, of the *Commentaria in Pentateuchum Mosis,* Cap. VI. (p.

107); upon the words *Gigantes autem erant* the gloss runs: "Burgensis putat gigantes fuisse daemones, humana specie indutos: Ualesius putat gigantes fuisse filios daemonum incuborum: Philo putat homines sceleratissimos uocari gigantes. Sed certum est gigantes fuisse homines monstruosa statura robore, latrociniis, & tyrannide insignes, vnde gigātes, per sua scelera, fuerunt maxima & potissima causa diluuii, vt patet Sap. 14, u. 6, Iob 26.5. Idem insinuat hic Moses: ea enim de causa descripturus diluuium, gigantes, quasi diluuii causam, praemittit, ita passim docent interpretes." *Wisdom,* XIV., 6: "And from the beginning also when the proud giants perished, the hope of the world fleeing to a vessel, which was governed by thy hand, left to the world seed of generation." *Job* xxvi., 5: "Behold the giants groan under the waters, and they that dwell with them."

43. CELSUS. Juventius Celsus, two Roman Jurists, father and son, both of whom are quoted in the *Digest*. Very little is known of the elder Celsus. The younger Celsus, who was the more celebrated, lived under Nerva and Trajan, by whom he was highly favoured. He wrote *Digesta* in thirty-nine books, *Epistolae, Quaestiones* and *Institutiones* in seven books. See Pliny, *Epistles*, VI., 5.

44. INNOCENT III. Born 1160 or 1161; died 1216. One of his greatest acts was the convocation of the Fourth Lateran Council, which he solemnly opened 15 November, 1215.

45. DOMINGO BAÑEZ. More properly Vañez. A famous Dominican theologian, born 1528, died 1604. He has been described as a figure of unprecedented distinction in scholastic Spain. Fidelity to S. Thomas was his strongest characteristic. "Never," he was wont to say, "never by so much as a finger-nail's breadth even in lesser things, have I ever departed from the teaching of S. Thomas."

46. SISTO OF SIENA. Dominican theologian and demonologist. His chief work is *Bibliotheca Sancta*, Libri V., Francofurti, folio, 1575 (secunda editio).

47. PICO DELLA MIRANDOLA. The famous Italian philosopher and scholar, 1463-1494.

48. MOLINA. Luis de Molina, S.J., one of the most learned and most renowned theologians of the Society of Jesus, was born at Cuenca 1535, and died at Madrid 1600. Professor of theology in the flourishing University of Evora, for twenty years he lectured upon the *Summa* of S. Thomas to thronging audiences. The results of this profound study of thirty years he published as *Concordia liberi arbitrii cum gratiae donis, diuina praescientia, prouidentia, praedestinatione et reprobatione*, Lisbon, 1588. The work, which is primarily

concerned with reconciling grace and free will, caused endless discussion and controversy. Molina's *Commentaria in primam partem D. Thomae* (2 vols.) was printed at Cuenca in 1592.

49. BARTOLOMÉ CARRANZA. Dominican Archbishop of Toledo, born 1503; died 1576. He was present at the council of Trent, but owing (it would seem) to malice and misrepresentation he fell under suspicion of unorthodoxy, and the Grand Inquisitor Valdes brought an action against him. The suit dragged on wearily and ended unsatisfactorily. The Archbishop was found not guilty of heresy, but he had rendered himself suspect of certain propositions tinged with Lutheranism.

50. BONAVENTURA BARON. A distinguished Irish Franciscan theologian, philosopher, and writer of Latin prose and verse, born at Clonmel, County Tipperary, 1610, and died at Rome 18 March, 1696. He especially devoted himself to a defence of the Scotist philosophy, and his *Scotus defensus et amplificatus* (3 vols.), Cologne, 1664, is a work of highest merit. He was appointed historiographer (1676) to Cosmo de'Medici, Grand-duke of Tuscany, and was elected a member of the Florentine Academy. His writings are both elegant, learned, and correct.

51. CIENFUEGOS. Cardinal Francisco Javier de Cienfuegos y Jovellanos, S.J., a famous theologian, is especially known for his writings on the Mass. He was given the Red Hat by Clement XI.

52. NICOLAS LÉMERY. The celebrated French chemist, was born at Rouen, 17 November, 1645, and died at Paris 19 June, 1715. He published his *Cours de Chimie, contenant la manière de faire les opérations qui sont en usage dans la médecine par une methode facile avec des raisonnements sur chaque opération, pour l'instruction de ceux qui veulent s'appliquer à cette science*, at Paris, 8vo, 1675. The work had an amazing success, and when Lémery was in England, 1683, he presented the fifth edition to King Charles II. It has been reissued no less than thirty-one times. The best edition is generally considered to be that of Baron, 4to, 1756.

53. CROWS, STAGS, RAVENS. *Pliny, Historia Naturalis*, VII., xlix., 48: "De spatio atque longinquitate uitae hominum, non locorum modo situs, uerum exempla, ac sua cuique sors nascendi incertum fecere. Hesiodus, qui primus aliqua de hoc prodidit, fabulose (ut reor) multa de hominum aeuo referens, cornici nouem nostras attribuit aetates, quadruplum eius ceruis, id triplicatum coruis. Et reliqua fabulosius in phoenice, ac Nymphis." Pliny often repeats these tales of the old age of these animals. Many authors write thus of the crow, *e.g.*, Lucretius, *De Natura Rerum*, V., 1083:

et partim mutant cum tempestatibus una
raucisonos cantus, cornicum ut saecla uetusta
coruorumque greges ubi aquam dicuntur et imbris
poscere et interdum uentos aurasque uocare.

Horace, *Carminum*, III., xvii., 13: aquae nisi fallit augur, Annosa cornix. Ovid, *Metamorphoseon*, VII., 274: Ora caputque nouem cornicis saecula passae. Aratus has: εννιάχηρα κορώνη. Cicero, *Tusculanarum*, III., xxviii., 69, writes: "Theophrastus autem moriens accusasse naturam dicitur, quod ceruis et cornicibus uitam diuturnam, quorum id nihil interesset; hominibus, quorum maxime interfuisset, tam exiguam uitam dedisset."

54. TACITUS. *Annals*, VI., 28: "Paullo Fabio L. Uitellio Coss. post longum saeculorum ambitum auis Phoenix in Ægyptum uenit. . . . De numero annorum uaria traduntur. Maxime uulgatum quingentorum spatium. Sunt qui adseuerent, mille quadringentos sexaginta unum interiici; proiresque alites Sesostride primum, post Amaside dominantibus, dein Ptolemaeo, qui ex Macedonibus tertius regnauit. . . . aduolauisse. Sed antiquitas quidem obscura. . . . Haec incerta et fabulosis aucta."

55. S. AUGUSTINE. *De Diuinatione daemonum*, written 406-411. Migne, XL., 581-592.

56. GODFREY OF FONTAINES. *Doctor Uenerandus*, born near Liège in the first half of the thirteenth century; a Canon of Liège, Paris, and Cologne. He was elected in 1300 to the see of Tournai, but refused the episcopate. During the last quarter of the century he taught theology at the University of Paris. He is the author of a most notable collection of disputations. *XIV. Quodlibeta.* A modern critical edition of these has been prepared by de Wulf.

57. PELTANUS. Theodore Peltanus, a Biblical scholar of note, who translated several commentaries from Greek into Latin. His glosses are valuable. His translation of the *Commentary on the Apocalypse* by Bishop Andrew of Caesarea was published 4to, 1584.

Andrew of Caesarea, Cappodocia, is assigned by Krumbacher to the first half of the sixth century, although by others he is variously placed from the fifth to the ninth century. His *Commentary on the Apocalypse* is important as the first exegesis of that book we know, the source whence most writers have largely drawn. The original has been printed by Migne, *Patres Graeci*, CVI., 215-458, 1387-94. See Krumbacher, *Gesch. der byzant. Lit.* (pp. 129-131), 2nd edition, Munich, 1897.

58. PETER THYRAEUS. Peter Thyraeus, S.J., Doctor of Theology,

the younger brother of the more famous Hermann Thyraeus, S.J., Jesuit provincial of the Rhine (born 1532; *ob.* 1591). Peter Thyraeus was born at Neuss on the Rhine, and owing to his learning occupied several important positions in that province. I have used the Rind edition of the *De Terrificationibus Nocturnis. Daemoniaci cum Locis Infestis et Terriculamentis Nocturnis*, auctore Petro Thyraeo Nouesiano, Societatis Iesu, Doctore Theologo. Coloniae Agrippinae, 8vo, 1604. Caput II. (p. 332), has as rubric: *Docetur Terrificationes, & dictos Tumultus non fieri ab Homuncionibus quibusdam: sed nec esse Tales, quales dicuntur, Homunciones.* The author decides that Spirits and Ghosts are the causes of these midnight noises and fears.

59. ARISTOTLE. The work known as the *Problems* is, of course, wrongly attributed to the great Greek philosopher. The earliest edition was printed in 1475 at Rome. There are translations into nearly all modern languages. In 1710 was published in London the twenty-fifth English edition. The book is frequently reprinted, and common even to-day.

The *De Uirtute Herbarum* is no longer considered to be the work of Apuleius.

60. GERMANDER. The name of the plants of the genus *Teuerium*. Harrison, *England*, II., xx., 1587 (ed. 1877; I., 326) has: "Our common germander or thistle benet is . . . of . . . great power in medicine." A. T. Thomson, *London Dispensary*, 1811 (ed. 1818; p. 398) writes: "Wall Germander [Teuerium Chamaedrys] has been accounted tonic, stomachic, [etc.]."

61. Palma Christi, the castor oil plant. *Ricinus communis.* Turner, *Names of Herbs*, 1548, notes: "Ricinus is called . . . in English Palma Christi." Even to-day almost miraculous effects are attributed to this plant by the native superstitions of the West Indies.

62. SWEET CALAMUS. *Calamus aromaticus*, an Eastern aromatic plant, said to be the sweet-scented Lemon Grass of Malabar, *Andropogon Schoenanthus*, Jeremias, vi., 20, the Vulgate has: Ut quid mihi thus de Saba affertis, et *calamum suaue olentem* de terra longinqua? The Douay Bible translates: "the sweet smelling cane"; Coverdale (1535): "Sweete smellinge Calamus." A.V.: "the sweet cane," so R.V. with marginal note "Or, *calamus.*" Some English herbalists have applied the name *calamus aromaticus* to the native Sweet Flag, or Sweet Rush (*Acorus calamus*).

63. Cubeb seed. The berry of a climbing shrub, *Piper Cubeba* or *Cubeba officinalis*, a native of Java and the adjacent isles. It re-

sembles a grain of pepper, and has a pungent spicy flavour. It is used in medicine and cookery.

64. *Aristolochies.* Aristolochia, a genus of shrubs, one of which, the Common Birthwort, is found in Britain. Topsell, *Fourfooted Beasts* (1607), speaks of: "Aristoloch, otherwise called Hartwort."

65. *Cardamon.* A spice used in medicine as a stomachic, and also for flavouring sauces and curries. The only kind in the British pharmacopoeia is the Malabar cardamom obtained from *E. Cardamomum.*

66. *Long-Pepper.* A condiment prepared from the immature fruit-spikes of the allied plants *Piper (Chavica) officinarum* and *Piper longum (C. Roxbrughii).* It was formerly supposed to be the flower of unripe fruit of *Piper nigrum.* Harley, *Materia Medica* (Sixth edition, 1876), p. 434, tells us: "Long Pepper has been employed by the Hindoos in medicine from the earliest times."

67. *Caryophylleae.* Greek, καρυόφυλλον = the clove pink.

68. *Calamite Storax.* Pechey, *Compleat Herbalist* (1694), 333, has: "The resin of storax, which is sold in the shops is two-fold, dry and liquid. The dry is called Storax Calamite . . . because it is put up in Reeds."

69. CARTHUSIAN FRIARY. The famous Certosa di Pavia, founded in 1396 by Gian Galeazzo Visconti.

70. EXSURGAT DEUS. Psalm lxvii. *Qui habitat,* Psalm xc.

71. AGRIMONY. *Agrimonia Eupatorica.* Or liver-wort, of the genus *hepatica,* applied to plants used in diseases of the liver, or having liver-shaped parts.

72. *Spurge.* One or other of several species of plants belonging to the very extensive genus *Euphorbia,* many of which are characterised by an acrid milky juice, possessing purgative and medicinal properties.

73. CALLIONYMUS. The Vulgate has: Ecce piscis immanis exiuit ad deuorandum eum [Tobiam]. *Liber Tobiae,* VI., 2. Callionymus = καλλιώνυμος, *i.e.,* with beautiful name, by which term Hipparchus mentions the fish *uranoscopus scaber.* Pliny, *Historia Naturalis,* XXXII., 7, writes: "Callionymi fel cicatrices sanat, et carnes oculorum superuacuas consumit. Nulli hoc piscium copiosius, ut existimauit Menander quoque in comoediis. Idem piscis et uranoscopos uocatur, ab oculo quem in capite habet." Gabriel Brotier in his notes upon Pliny, Barbou edition, Paris, 1779, tom. V., p. 467, translates callionymus by "le Tapeçon."

74. PLINY. *Historia Naturalis,* XXXII., 7: "Omnium piscium flu-

uiatilium marinorumque adeps liquefactus sole admixto melle, oculorum claritati plurimum confert: item castoreum cum melle. Callionymi fel cicatrices sanat, et carnes oculorum superuacuas consumit."

75. ASMODEUS. τὸ πονηρὸν δαιμόνιον. A demon identified by some rabbis with Samaël. He is also called Chammadaï and Sydonaï. A few commentators even hold that he is the same as Beelzebub or Apollyon (*Apocalypse*, ix. 2), an extremely unlikely view. Johan Weyer, however, in his *Pseudo-monarchia daemonum* appended to the 1577 edition of *De praestigiis daemonum*, gives some fantastic details concerning him. It has been suggested that Asmodeus is perhaps the Persian *Aëshma daêva*, who in the *Avesta* is next to Angromainyus, the chief of evil spirits. But the name Asmodeus may be Semitic. The Aramaic word 'áshmeday is cognate with the Hebrew hashmed, "destruction." Talmudic legend says that Asmodeus, or Asmodai, was implicated in the drunkenness of Noe, and has some truly extravagant tales concerning him and King Solomon. Moreover, Asmodeus is regarded as the counterpart of Lilith, and sometimes described as a jocular elf. (*Cf.* Le Sage's *Le Diable Boiteux*.) Wünsche; *Der bab. Talm.* II., 180-3. Asmodeus was one of the devils who possessed Madeleine Bavent of the convent of SS. Louis and Elizabeth at Louviers in 1642-43.

76. S. JEROME. The famous *Uita Pauli* was written 374-9. It may be found in Migne, XXIII., 17-28, and there is a separate edition by Tamietti, Turin, 1903.

77. S. PAUL. A.D. 341. S. Paul, who dwelt in the Lower Thebaid, died on 10 January, on which day he is commemorated in most ancient Martyrologies. But both Latins and Greeks have transferred his festival to 15 January so as to fall outside the closed Octave of the Epiphany. There are fine pictures of the meeting of S. Paul and S. Antony by Pinturicchio, Lucas van Leyden, Velasquez, and Guido. Brusasorci in a magnificent canvas shows us the Centaur and the Satyr, two diminutive figures in the background of the landscape where the solitaries are communing.

78. S. ANTONY. S. Antony the Great, father of monks, born about 251. His feast is celebrated in all kalendars, 17 January. The passage quoted by Sinistrari occurs in the Sixth Lection of the Second Nocturn at Matins.

79. GEORGE AGRICOLA. Georg Landmann, the celebrated German metallurgist, was born at Chemnitz, Saxony, 24 March, 1494, and died there in 1555. His chief work is the *De re Metallica*, Bâle, 4to, 1546. The *De Animantibus subterraneis* was published at Bâle, folio,

1657, with other of his treatises. The passage to which Sinistrari refers may be read upon p. 491: "Postremo in subterraneanī animantium, seu, quod placet theologis, substantianī numero haberi possunt daemones, qui in quibusdam uersantur fodinis. Eorum autem duplex est genus. Sunt enim truculenti & terribiles aspectu, qui plerunq; metallicis infesti atq; inimici sunt. . . . Sunt deinde mites, quos Germanorum alii, ut etiam Graeci, uocant Cobalos [Kobolts] quod hominum sunt imitatores. Nam quasi laetitia gestientes rident, & multa uidentur facere, quum prorsus nihil faciant. Alii nominant uirunculos montanos . . . uidentur autem esse seneciones & uestiti more metallicorum. . . . Quanquam uero interdum glareis lacessunt operarios, rarissime tamen eos laedunt. Nec laedunt unquam nisi prius ipsi cachinno fuerint, aut maledicto lacessiti. . . . Sed daemones montani potissimum laborant in his specubus e quibus metalla effodiuntur iam, uel ea effodi posse spes est. Quodcirca metallici non deterentur a laboribus, sed omnem inde capientes alacriori animo sunt & uehementius laborant."

80. S. AUGUSTINE. The *De Genesi* was written 401-15; Migne, xxxiv., 245-486. The *Enarrationes in Psalmos*, composed in 415, will be found apud Migne, xxxvi., 66-1906.

81. LYRA. Nicholas of Lyra, Doctor planus et utilis, Franciscan, 1270-1340. His greatest work is the monumental *Postillae perpetuae in uniuersam S. Scripturam*, which was the first commentary on the Bible actually to be printed.

82. Francis Titelmann, Capuchin, Professor of Exegesis in the University of Louvain, whence he retired in 1536 wholly to devote himself to the religious life. He won a European reputation by his controversy with Erasmus, and has written very profound commentaries on the Scriptures.

83. Gilbert Génebrand, O.S.B., exegete and Oriental scholar, Archbishop of Aix, 1535-97. He was one of the most learned professors of the day, and his works were regarded as authoritative throughout Europe. One of the best known of these is his *Psalmi Dauidis uulgata editione, calendario hebraeo, syro, graeco, latino, hymnis, argumentis, et commentariis, etc., instructi* (Paris, 1577).

84. HUGH OF ST-CHER, a Dominican Cardinal of the thirteenth century; born about 1200, died in 1263. He is the author of many works on Holy Scripture, and is justly regarded as the first compiler of a Biblical Concordance, the model for all subsequent publications of this kind.

85. FRANCISCO TOLEDO. Philosopher, theologian, and exegete, born at Cordova, 1532; died at Rome, 1596. He entered the Society

of Jesus, 1558, and was professor at Rome, 1564; 17 September, 1593, he was created a Cardinal by Pope Clement VIII. By many scholars his Scriptural Commentaries were considered the clearest and most concise of the day. He was a prolific writer, and his works have run into numerous editions. Gregory XIII. esteemed him as a pillar of learning, whilst Soto ranks him as a genius.

86. BALAAM. *Numbers*, xxiv., especially v. 17: Orietur Stella ex Iacob, et consurget Uirga de Israel.

87. MERCURIUS TRISMEGISTUS. Hermes Trismegistus, the supposed author of a large number of works, many of which are still extant. As early as the time of Plato the Greek god Hermes was identified with the Egyptian Thoth. The Neo-Platonists regarded an Egyptian Hermes as the source of all intellectual knowledge, in fact, the Logos incarnate. It was pretended that from him Pythagoras and Plato had derived their wisdom. A large number of mystical and occult works were ascribed to this Hermes. Most of these writings belong to the fourth century of our era. Lactantius *De Falsa Religione*, I., 7, writes: "Quid, quod Mercurius ille ter maximus; cujus supra mentionem feci; non modo ἀμήτωρα, ut Apollo, sed ἀπάτωρα, quoque appellat Deum; quod origo illi non sit aliunde? Nec enim potest ab ullo esse generatus, qui ipse uniuersa generauerit. Satis (ut opinor) & argumentis docui, et testibus confirmaui, quod per se satis clarum est, Unum esse regem mundi, unam patrem, unum Deum."

88. Hydaspes, or Hystaspes, is said to have been an ancient King of the Medes from whom is derived the name of the river Hydaspes. (*Medus Hydaspes*, Vergil, Georgics, IV., 211; *fabulosus Hydaspes*, Horace, Odes I., xxii., 7.) Clement of *Alexandria, Stromata*, VI., says: "Librosque Graecos sumite, agnoscite Sibyllam, quomodo unum Deum significet, et ea quae sunt futura, et Hystaspen sumite et legite, et inuenietis Dei filium multo clarius et apertius esse scriptum, et quemadmodum aduersus Christum multi reges instituent aciem, qui eum habent odio, et eos qui nomen eius gestant, et eius fideles, et eius tolerantiam et aduentem." Other authors who mention King Hydaspes are Agathias in Book II. of his *History;* Ammianus Marcellinus, Book XXIII.; S. Justin Martyr in his *Apology*, II.; and Theodore Canterus, c. 19. Lactantius, *De Uita Beata*, VII., 15, writes: "Hystaspes quoque, qui fuit Medorum rex antiquissimus, a quo amnis quoque nomen accepit, qui nunc Hydaspes dicitur, admirabile somnium, sub interpretatione uaticinantis pueri ad memoriam posteris tradidit, sublatum iri ex orbe imperium, nomenque Romanum; multo ante praefatus, quam illa Troiana gens conderetur."

89. THE SYBILS. Lactantius, Book I., *De Falsa Religione*, discusses

these prophetic women at great length, and in his *De Uera Sapientia*, IV., 6, he distinctly says, that Christ "summi Dei filium . . . non tantum congruentes in unum uoces prophetarum, sed etiam Trismegisti praedicatio, et Sibyllarum uaticinia demonstrant." He then discusses the oracle delivered by the Erythraean Sibyl.

90. BARONIUS. The Venerable Cesare Baronius, Oratorian, Cardinal, and ecclesiastical historian, 1538-1607. His *Annals*, the first volume of which appeared in 1588, have earned for him the title of Father of Ecclesiastical History.

91. FULGENTIUS. Saint Fabius Claudius Gordianus Fulgentius; born 468; died 533; Bishop of Ruspe, N. Africa, is eminent among the Fathers of the Church for his sanctity, eloquence, writings, and theological learning. His sermons, if few in number, are eloquent and full of fervour. His works may be found in Migne, *Patres Latini*, LXV.

92. MARIA DE AGREDA. Maria Coronel, or, as she is more commonly known, Maria de Agreda, from the little town in Old Castile where she was born in 1602, was a discalced Franciscan nun. She entered her convent in January, 1619, and when only twenty-five years old, by Papal dispensation, she was made Abbess. With the exception of an interval of three years she remained Superior until her death 24 May, 1665. The convent under her administration became one of the most fervent in Spain. She had the greatest influence over King Philip IV., whom she advised excellently and with complete common sense. Her letters to the King have been printed. She died with the reputation of a saint, and the cause of her canonization was introduced before the Congregation of Rites 21 June, 1672. She has become famous by her great work, *La mistica ciudad de Dios, historia divina de la Virgen, Madre de Dios*. It was printed in Madrid in 1670. *The Mystical City* is a series of most profound revelations concerning the life of Our Lady. It met with extraordinary opposition, and, upon false information, was even censured at Rome. This sublime work, however, is sanctioned and praised in a Bull of Benedict XIV., 16 January, 1748. *La Mistica Ciudad de Dios* has been translated into French, 2nd edition, 6 vols., 1862. Chapters XXII-XXX. contain an account of the flight into Egypt, of the sojourn of Our Lady there, the miracles She worked, and how She converted many of the Egyptians.

93. NICEPHORUS. Callistus Xanthopulus Nicephorus, the author of an Ecclesiastical History, was born in the latter part of the thirteenth century and died about 1350. His work has been edited by Duchène, Paris, 1630, 2 vols., folio.

94. SUIDAS, the Greek lexicographer, who probably lived in either the tenth or eleventh century. The lexicon is a dictionary of words arranged in alphabetical order, but it is not well conceived, since some articles are ample and others very scanty. There are several editions, especially those by Gaisford, Oxford, 1834; and by Bekker, 1854.

95. CEDRENUS. Georgius Cedrenus, a Byzantine writer, author of an historical work, which begins with the creation of the world and goes down to A.D. 1057. Edited by Bekker, Bonn, 1838-39.

96. COMMENTARY UPON AGGAEUS, II. 8. Et mouebo omnes Gentes. Cornelius à Lapide writes at great length upon this verse. "Primo per bella ciuilia, . . . Ita Mariana. Secundò, in censu quo omnes profecti ad suas ciuitates, cogebantur profiteri se Augusto esse subiectos. Tertio, per praedicationem and miracula Christi & Apostolorum, perque portenta edita in caelo & in terra, tam nascente, quam patiente Christo, quae iam recensui, commotae sunt Gentes ad poenitentiam, & ad fidem Christi capessendam." See Cornelius à Lapide, *Commentaria in Aggaeum Prophetam*, Cap. II. v. 8. apud *Commentaria in Duodecim Prophetas Minores*, Antwerp, folio, 1720, pp. 615-20.

97. ECHINADES. Small islands at the mouth of the river Achelous, the largest river in Greece, Aspro Potamo. This river rises in Mount Pindus and falls into the Ionian Sea. The largest island, Dulichium, is at present united to the mainland.

98. S. BERNARD. S. Bernard of Clairvaux, 1090-1153. There are three early lives of this Saint, and his acts have been fully treated by the Bollandists.

99. S. PETER OF ALCANTARA, Franciscan of the Strict Observance, 1499-1562. His Feast is celebrated 19 October. There are several lives of the Saint and in particular that by Paulo, *Uita S. Petri*, Rome, 1669, may be noticed. See also the *Acta Sanctorum*, October, VIII, 636, *sqq.*

100. VENUS AS BORN OF THE SEA. Aphrodite sprang from the foam of the sea into which was thrown the mutilated body of Uranus. See Hesiod, *Theogony*, 180-209, also Apollodorus the Grammarian, *Bibliotheca*, I., 1; Servius on the *Aeneid*, V., 801; and *Eclogues*, VI., 18. Also Tibullus, I., ii., 39-40:—

Nam fuerit quicunque loquax, is sanguine natam,
  Is Uenerem e rapido sentiet esse mari.

101. INTRICATE KNOTS. *La Ghirlanda delle Streghe*, a long cord tied in elaborate knots with the feathers of a black hen inserted in the strands. This is hidden away in some secret place with appro-

priate maledictions, and the person at whom the bane is launched will be consumed with a swift disease no doctor can cure. Strangely enough one of these enchanted ropes was in 1886 found in the belfry of an English country church. All were puzzled, for it was evidently twined and twisted for some specific purpose. An old woman in the village identified it as a "witch's ladder," but it was not until an engraving had been published in *The Folk Lore Journal* that full information was received and the purport of the mysterious charm completely understood.

102. TOADS. When the North Berwick coven of witches, 1590, attempted the life of King James, Agnes Sampson pressed the Devil to destroy His Highness without delay. "The Deuill ansuerit, he sould do quhat he could, bott it wald be lang to, because it wald be thoirterit [thwarted], and he promeist to hir and thame ane pictour of walx, and ordenit hir and thame to hing, roist, and drop one taid, and to lay the droppis of the toad [mixed with other foulness and venom] in his hienes way, quhair his Maiestic wald gang inowre or outowre, or in ony passage quhair itt mycht drop vpoun his heines heid or body, for his hienes distructioune, that ane vther mycht haif rewlit in his Maiesties place." The magic use of wax figures passed from ancient Egypt to Greece and Rome. About the end of the seventh century the life of King Duffus of Scotland was attempted in this way, see G. K. Sharp's *Witchcraft in Scotland*, 1884, p. 21. The wax image appears again and again in the witch-trials throughout the centuries. In 1664 the chief indictment against Christian Green and Margaret Agar of Brewham, Somerset, was that they had made "pictures" of wax into which they stuck thorns and needles, whereby those whose figures the models were languished and died. Glanvill, *Saducismus Triumphatus*, 1681, Part II, pp. 147-167. The "oil or viscid ointments" were "flying ointments" three formulae for which have been preserved. In 1324 Dame Alice Kyteler of Kilkenny and a whole coven of witches were indicted by the Bishop of Ossory upon multiplied charges of sorcery. "In rifling the closet of the ladie, they found a wafer of sacramental bread, having the divels name stamped thereon in steed of Jesus Christ, and a pipe of ointment, wherewith she greased a staffe, upon which she ambled and gallopped through thicke and thin, when and in what manner she would." See my *Geography of Witchcraft*, pp. 85-91. Lambert Daneau, *Les Sorciers*, 1574 (English translation by Z. Jones *A Dialogue of Witches*, 1575), speaking of witches going to the sabbat says: "He [the devil] promisett that himself will conuay them thither, that are so weak that they cannot trauaile of themselues: which many tymes

he doth by meanes of a staffe or rod, which he deliuereth vnto the, or promiseth to doo it by force of a certen oynment, which he will geue them; and sometimes he offreth them an horse to ride vpon." Boguet, also, describing the journey to the sabbat, notes that some of the witches "encor se frottent auparauant de certaine graisse, & oignement."

103. CERTAIN NOISE. Poppysma. Ut explicat Pierre-Emmanuel Pierruges, *Glossarium Eroticum*, Parisiis, 1826: "Oris pressi sonus, similis illi quo permulcentur equi et canes. Obscene uero de susurro cunni laborium, quum frictu madescunt." Uerbum est Graecum ποππύζειν. Auctor autem inuenit hoc uocabulum apud Martialem, VII., 18, *In Gallam*.

Quum tibi sit facies, de qua nec femina possit
   Dicere; quum corpus litura nulla notet;
Cur te tam rarus cupiat, repetatque fututor,
   Miraris? Uitium est non leue, Galla, tibi.
Accessi quoties ad opus, mixtisque mouemur
   Inguinibus; cunnus non tacet, ipsa taces.
Di facerent, ut tu loquereris, et ipse taceret!
   Offendor cunni garrulitate tui.
Pedere te mallem: namque hoc nec inutile dicit
   Symmachus, et risum res mouet ista simul.
Quis ridere potest fatui poppysmata cunni?
   Quum sonat hic, cui non mentula mensque cadit?
Dic aliquid saltem, clamosoque obstrepe cunno:
   Et si adeo muta es, disce uel inde loqui.

Politian in his *Liber Miscellaneorum*, c. xxxii., discusses the word *poppýsma*. A note upon this passage in Martial (ed Lemaire, Paris, 1825, II., p. 212) says: "Poppysmata. Uox fictitia, a sono quo equis necdum domitis blandimur." Beau in his commentary upon Martial notes: "Les médecins appellent ces poppysmata une sonoréité vaginale et disent que la Galla dont il est question dans cette épigramme de Martial, était atteinte de pneumatose."

104. THE DISCREETS. In a convent of Poor Clares the Superiors under the abbess are the Vicaress, Novice Mistress, two Porteresses, and eight Discreets forming the Council. The officers are elected by the sisters in Chapter.

Selected bibliography of English language works

Alexander, W., *Demonic Possession in the New Testament*, Edinburgh, 1902.

Aradi, Z., *The Book of Miracles*, New York, 1956.

Ashton, J., *The Devil in Britain and America*, London, 1896.

Bach, M., *Strange Sects and Curious Cults*, New York, 1961.

Ballou, R. (Ed.), *The Bible of the World*, New York, 1939.

Baring-Gould, S., *The Book of Werewolves*, London, 1865.

———, *Curious Myths of the Middle Ages*, Boston, 1882.

Barrett, F., *The Magus or Celestial Intelligencer*, London, 1801.

Beaumont, E. De, *The Sword and Womankind*, New York, 1930.

Bloch, I., *Strange Sexual Practices*, New York, 1933.

———, *Marquis de Sade*, New York, 1958.

———, *Sex Life in England*, New York, 1934.

Boguet, H., *An Examen of Witches*, London, 1929.

Bovet, R., *Pandaemonium*, Aldington, Kent, 1951.

Bramwell, J., *Hypnotism: Its History, Practice and Theory*, New York, 1956.

Bromage, B., *The Occult Arts of Ancient Egypt*, London, 1953.

Budge, W., *Egyptian Magic*, New York, Undated.

———, *Amulets and Superstitions*, London, 1930.

Burckhardt, J., *The Civilization of the Renaissance in Italy*, New York, 1958.

Burkitt, F., *The Religion of the Manichees*, Cambridge, 1925.

Burton, R., *The Anatomy of Melancholy*, New York, 1927.

Cardan, J., *The Book of My Life*, New York, 1930.

Caron, M., and Hutin, S., *The Alchemists*, New York, 1961.

Cohen, C., *Religion and Sex*, Edinburgh, 1919.

Crawley, E., *The Mystic Rose*, New York, 1960.

Crowley, A., *Magick in Theory and Practice*, New York, Undated.

Cutner, H., *A Short History of Sex Worship*, London, 1940.

Davies, T., *Magic, Divination and Demonology Among the Hebrews and Their Neighbors*, London, 1898.

Day, J., *Ghosts and Witches*, London, 1954.

Defoe, D., *The Political History of the Devil*, London, 1726.

De Laurence, L., *The Great Book of Magical Art*, Chicago, 1915.

Dubois-Desaulle, G., *Bestiality*, New York, 1933.

Dulaure, J. -A., *The Gods of Generation*, New York, 1934.

❦ Durant, W., *The Age of Faith*, New York, 1950.

❦ ———, *The Renaissance*, New York, 1953.

✷ ———, *The Reformation*, New York, 1957.

❦ Edwardes, A., *The Jewel in the Lotus*, New York, 1959.

Eisler, R., *Man Into Wolf*, London, 1951.

Ellis, A., and Abarbanel, A. (Eds.), *The Encyclopedia of Sexual Behavior*, New York, 1961.

Ellis, H., *Studies in the Psychology of Sex*, New York, 1936.

Elworthy, F., *The Evil Eye*, London, 1895.

Ennemoser, J., *The History of Magic*, London, 1854.

Ferguson, I., *The Philosophy of Witchcraft*, New York, 1925.

Fortune, D., *Psychic Self-Defence: A Study in Occult Pathology and Criminality*, London, 1957.

✷ Frazer, J., *The Golden Bough*, New York, 1940.

———, *Folklore in the Old Testament*, London, 1919.

Freud, S., *Totem and Taboo*, London, 1919.

✷ ———, *The Interpretation of Dreams*, New York, 1960.

———, *Collected Papers*, New York, 1959.

Gallonio, A., *Torture of the Christian Martyrs*, New York (?), 1959.

Garçon, M., and Vinchon, J., *The Devil*, London, 1929.

Gardner, G., *Witchcraft Today*, New York, 1955.

Gifford, E., *The Evil Eye*, New York, 1958.

Gill, M. and Brenman, M., *Hypnosis and Related States*, New York, 1959.

Gilly, W., *Narrative of Researches Among the Vaudois*, London, 1824.

Glanvill, J., *A Blow at Modern Sadducism*, London, 1668.

❦ Grillot De Givry, *Witchcraft, Magic and Alchemy*, London, 1931.

❦ Goldberg, B., *The Sacred Fire*, New York, 1958.

Graf, A., *The Story of the Devil*, London, 1931.

Groddeck, G., *The Book of the It*, New York, 1961.

Guazzo, F.-M., *Compendium Maleficarum*, London, 1929.

Hartmann, F., *Magic White and Black*, Chicago, 1910.

Harvey, G., *The Secret Lore of Witchcraft*, Girard, Kan., 1946.

Hesse, E., *Narcotics and Drug Addiction*, New York, 1946.

Hobley, C., *Bantu Beliefs and Magic*, London, 1922.

Hogg, G., *Cannibalism and Human Sacrifice*, London, 1958.

Hole, C., *Witchcraft in England*, London, 1945.
Holmes, E., *The Albigensian or Catharist Heresy*, London, 1925.
Houston, Z., *Voodoo Gods*, London, 1939.
Iamblichus, *The Egyptian Mysteries*, New York, 1909.
James, E., *The Ancient Gods*, New York, 1960.
✸ James, W., *The Varieties of Religious Experience*, New York, 1958.
Jastrow, M., *The Religion of Babylonia and Assyria*, Boston, 1898.
Jesus-Marie, B. De (Ed.), *Satan*, New York, 1952.
Jones, E., *On the Nightmare*, New York, 1959.
Kaigh, F., *Witchcraft and Magic of Africa*, London, 1947.
Kiefer, O., *Sexual Life in Ancient Rome*, New York, 1956.
King, J., *Babylonian Magic and Sorcery*, London, 1896.
King, W., *The Gnostics and Their Remains*, London, 1887.
Kittredge, G., *Witchcraft in Old and New England*, New York, 1956.
Knight, R., *A Discourse on the Worship of Priapus*, London, 1865.
Kronhausen, P. and E., *Pornography and the Law*, New York, 1959.
Langton, E., *Essentials of Demonology*, London, 1949.
Larousse Encyclopedia of Mythology, New York, 1960.
Laurent, E., and Nagour, P., *Magica Sexualis*, New York, 1934.
Lea, H., *Materials Toward a History of Witchcraft*, New York, 1957.
    (An indispensable work—R.E.L.M.)
———, *The Inquisition of the Middle Ages*, New York, 1961.
———, *A History of Sacerdotal Celibacy in the Christian Church*,
    London, 1907.
Lenormant, F., *Chaldean Magic*, London, 1877.
Leuba, J., *The Psychology of Religious Mysticism*, New York, 1925.
Lévi, E., *The History of Magic*, London, 1957.
Licht, H., *Sexual Life in Ancient Greece*, New York, 1953.
Malleus Maleficarum, London, 1951.
Manas, J., *Divination Ancient and Modern*, New York, 1947.
Mantegazza, P., *The Sexual Relations of Mankind*, New York, 1935.
Masters, R., *Forbidden Sexual Behavior and Morality*, New York,
    1962.
McCabe, J., *The History of Flagellation*, Girard, Kan., 1946.
———, *The History of Torture*, Girard, Kan., 1949.
———, *A History of Satanism*, Girard, Kan., 1948.
Meerloo, J., *The Rape of the Mind*, New York, 1956.
Metraux, A., *Voodoo in Haiti*, New York, 1959.
Meyer, J., *Sexual Life in Ancient India*, New York, 1953.
✦ Michelet, J., *Satanism and Witchcraft*, New York, 1939.
Murray, M., *The Witch Cult in Western Europe*, Oxford, 1921.
———, *The God of the Witches*, New York, 1960.

Nevius, J., *Demon Possession and Allied Themes*, New York, 1893.

Niemoller, A. (Ed.), *Magical Secrets for Love*, Girard, Kan., 1947.

——, *Aphrodisiacs and Anti-Aphrodisiacs*, Girard, Kan., Undated.

✹ Oesterreich, T., *Obsession and Possession by Spirits Both Good and Evil*, Chicago, 1935.

Olliver, C., *An Analysis of Magic and Witchcraft*, London, 1928.

Pachter, H., *Magic Into Science*, New York, 1951.

Palmer, H., *Psychopathic Personalities*, New York, 1957.

✯ Papini, G., *The Devil*, London, 1955.

Partridge, B., *A History of Orgies*, New York, 1960.

Peebles, J., *The Demonism of the Ages*, Battle Creek, Mich., 1904.

Pike, E., *Encyclopaedia of Religion and Religions*, New York, 1958.

Pitts, J., *Witchcraft and Devil Lore in the Channel Islands*, Guernsey, 1886.

Praz, M., *The Romantic Agony*, New York, 1956.

Radin, P., *Primitive Religion*, New York, 1957.

——, *Primitive Man as Philosopher*, New York, 1957.

Rawcliffe, D., *Illusions and Delusions of the Supernatural and the Occult*, New York, 1959.

Reik, T., *The Creation of Woman*, New York, 1960.

——, *The Compulsion to Confess*, New York, 1959.

Remy, N., *Demonolatry*, London, 1930.

Rhodes, H., *The Satanic Mass*, London, 1954.

Robbins, R., *Encyclopedia of Witchcraft and Demonology*, New York, 1959. (An excellent source—R.E.L.M.)

Rogge, O., *Why Men Confess*, New York, 1959.

Sanger, W., *History of Prostitution*, New York, 1937.

Schenk, G., *The Book of Poisons*, London, 1956.

Scot, R., *Discoverie of Witchcraft*, London, 1930.

Scott, G., *The History of Corporal Punishment*, London, 1954.

——, *The History of Torture Throughout the Ages*, London, 1954.

Seabrook, W., *The Magic Island*, New York, 1929.

——, *Adventures in Arabia*, New York, 1927.

——, *Witchcraft: Its Power in the World Today*, New York, 1940.

✹ Seligmann, K., *The History of Magic*, New York, 1948.

Sergeant, P., *Witches and Warlocks*, London, 1936.

Seymour, S., *Irish Witchcraft and Demonology*, Dublin, 1913.

Shah, S. I., *Oriental Magic*, New York, 1957.

——, *The Secret Lore of Magic*, London, 1957.

Shah, S. I. A., *Occultism*, New York, Undated.

Sinistrari, L., *Peccatum Mutum*, New York, 1958.

✯ ——, *Demoniality*, Paris, 1879.

Sitwell, S., *Poltergeists*, London, 1940.

Skeat, W., *Malay Magic*, London, 1900.

Smith, H., *Changing Concepts of Original Sin*, New York, 1955.

Spalding, T., *Elizabethan Demonology*, London, 1880.

Spence, L., *Encyclopaedia of Occultism*, New York, 1959.

Stekel, W., *Sadism and Masochism*, New York, 1953.

Summers, M., *The History of Witchcraft*, New York, 1956.

———, *The Werewolf*, London, 1933.

———, *The Vampire: His Kith and Kin*, New York, 1960.

———, *The Geography of Witchcraft*, New York, 1958.

———, *Witchcraft and Black Magic*, New York, 1946.

Taylor, G., *Sex in History*, New York, 1954.

Taylor, N., *Flight From Reality*, New York, 1949.

Thompson, R., *Devils and Evil Spirits of Babylonia*, London, 1903.

———, *Semitic Magic*, London, 1908.

Thorndike, L., *The Writings of Peter of Abano*, Baltimore, 1944.

Thouless, R., *The Psychology of Religion*, Cambridge, 1961.

Underhill, E., *Worship*, New York, 1957.

Vaughan, T., *Magical Writings of Thomas Vaughan*, London, 1888.

Waddell, H., *The Desert Fathers*, Ann Arbor, Mich., 1957.

Waite, A. E., *Book of Black Magic and of Pacts*, London, 1898.

Wedick, H., *Dictionary of Magic*, New York, 1956.

Weihofen, H., *The Urge to Punish*, London, 1957.

Williams, C., *Witchcraft*, London, 1941.

Willoughby-Meade, G., *Chinese Ghouls and Goblins*, London, 1928.

Woodward, L., *Sex and Hypnosis*, Derby, Conn., 1961.

Wright, D., *Vampires and Vampirism*, Philadelphia, 1915.

Index

incest, 71-72
incubi, 8, 9, 235-242, 245-249; *see also* angels; demons, devils, incubi, and succubi, witches
    as Angels of Light, 13
    corporeality of, 245-250
    monogamy of, 61
    usages of word, various, 11
infanticide and infantophagy, 88-91
Innocent III, 219
Inquisition, the, 46, 119, 142, 149, 156, 263-267
Institutiones Medicae Physiologae, 217
intercourse, human, with devils, demons, incubi, succubi, 8, 11, 14, 16-27, 39-40, 60, 114-116, 117-126, 129, 157-158, 260-263; *see also* devils, demons, incubi, succubi
    cruelties of, 99-104, 157-158, 159-160
    reasons for, 49-57
    thought of Church concerning, 49, 108, 111, 114-116, 117-126, 129, 157-158
Isheth Zemunin, 176-177
Ishtar, 179
Isidore, Saint, 222
Isis, 179
Isis and Osiris, 234
Ivo of Chartres, 129

Jacob, 254
Jacquier, 97
Jerome, Saint, 25, 65, 119, 215, 245, 246
Jewel in the Lotus, The, 37, 153
Johann of Prum, 26-27
John of Lycus, Abbott, 15
John of Thessalonica, 220
Jones, Ernest, 9, 85, 136, 151, 160, 164-165
Josephus the Historian, 218
Jugatinus, 180
Julius III, Pope, 152
Justin Martyr, 7, 218
Justinus (Justin), 43, 176, 215

Kauas, 180
Kiesewetter, 151
Klein, Johann, 63, 137
koru, 135
Krishna, 179
Kronhausen, E. and P., 147

Lactantius, 8, 254
Lancre, Pierre de, 9, 18, 23, 56, 68, 71, 77
Lapide, Cornelius à, 218, 238, 242, 244, 254, 256
Lateran, Council of, 220, 249
Latomia, Catharina, 70
Laurent, 159
Lea, H. C., 3, 6
Leçons cliniques sur l'Hysterie, 158
Lémery, Nicolas, 229
Leviathan, 175
Leviathan, 165
Liber, Libera, 180
Lilith, 5, 174, 175
Lindsay, Thomas, 21
Liseux, Isidore, 263-267
Livy, 43, 215
longevity, of crows, stags, ravens, 230
Lucifer, 176
lust, of demons, 49-57
Luther, Martin, 63
    called Anti-Christ, 43
    driving off Devil, 93, 111
    offspring of demon, 43, 44, 215
lycanthropes, 90-92
Lycius, Menippus, 208

Macarius the Younger, Saint, 15
Machalath, 174
MD, 134-135
magic, sexual, 126-136
Magica Sexualis, 108
Maillat, Loyse, 96
Malleus Maleficarum, 31, 35, 45, 60, 88, 102, 121, 128, 168, 175
Maluenda (Malvenda) Thomas, 42, 43, 215
Mammon, 175
man, permanent sense of sexual inferiority, 171-172
Manichaeans, 97, 141
Mantegazza, 77
Margaret of Cortona, 112
Margaret of Esslingen, 45-46
Maria d'Agreda, Sister, 255
Marie de Mangrane, 53
Mariolatry, 98
Martin, Saint, 72
Martin of Arles, 36
masochism, 148
May, Sinchen, 103
Mechtildis, Saint, 109
Medina, Bartholomew, 202
Medizinischer Daemonismus, 9
Meriweather, Joanna, 95

Printed in the USA
CPSIA information can be obtained
at www.ICGtesting.com
LVHW041448260923
759377LV00002B/7